JESUS

THE **WAY,**
THE **TRUTH,**
AND
THE **LIFE**

MARCELLINO D'AMBROSIO

ASCENSION

West Chester, Pennsylvania

Ascension
Post Office Box 1990
West Chester, PA 19380
1-800-376-0520
ascensionpress.com

Cover art: *You Are Not Alone,* used with permission by artist
Cristian Costras (Saint-Étienne, France)

Cover design by Rosemary Strohm

Printed in the United States of America

22 23 24 25 8 7 6

ISBN 978-1-950784-18-9

CONTENTS

PREFACE

For the first sixteen years of my life, I was a yawning Christian. It would never have occurred to me to stop believing in Christ, but to get excited about him would have never occurred to me either! At age sixteen, I was a budding professional rock musician. The stage got me excited. The promise of a record deal got me excited. Going to church, on the other hand, was an obligation, a weekly interruption of my ordinary, real life.

That state of affairs was interrupted by two friends of mine whose lives had been turned upside down by an encounter they claimed to have had with Jesus. Both had stopped using drugs. That impressed me. Both exuded a new excitement, a deep peace, and a quiet joy. That impressed me even more.

One of them was Catholic, like myself, and she introduced me to other Catholics who were experiencing the same sort of thing. As I met them and prayed with them, I met *him*. At least I met him in a new and more intimate way than I ever had before. It suddenly came clear to me what it was all about ... the Creed, the sacraments, the saints. Ultimately, it was all based on this person, and it all was supposed to lead back to this person. This person was so incredibly fascinating, so powerful, so real, so alive, that he began to bring me alive in ways I never dreamed possible, leading me to places I never thought I'd go.

Sometimes the journey has been harrowing. Other moments have been exhilarating. This adventure has been going on now for over forty years. The one thing I can honestly say is that it has never been boring.

My journey has led me through a PhD program in Catholic theology, years of full-time university teaching, public speaking, and appearances in secular and Catholic media. I've written books and given lectures on saints and sacraments, the Creed and the commandments, the vices and the virtues. But it is my conviction that what I need to do and we all need to do at this moment in history is to turn our attention back to the man who dared to call himself the Way, the Truth, and the Life (John 14:6).

It has been over two thousand years since the birth of Jesus of Nazareth. Since that time, countless books have been written about him. Why would we possibly need another one, especially in a time in the Western world when many people are losing interest in Christianity and are dismissing it as outdated, dull, even repressive?

Many of those who believe in Jesus and those who have no interest in him have this in common: they apparently have not really encountered him. The one thing that is clear from the Gospels is that those who actually met Jesus of Nazareth were either mesmerized or appalled. They found him either fascinating or offensive. The one thing they could not do in his presence was yawn.

Yet that is precisely what many—both believers and unbelievers— seem to do.

Hence the reason for this book. The story of Jesus needs to be retold in a fresh way for people of this era. It needs to be retold in a way that helps people actually come face-to-face with this central figure of human history, this person whose birth is the very basis of the way the world tells time.

In my research, I have tried to glean some of the insights of prominent authors who have written popular works on Jesus in recent years—Fulton Sheen, Romano Guardini, Frank Sheed, Peter Kreeft, St. John Paul II, Pope Benedict, and Pope Francis. I've drawn from the Fathers of the Church and the saints. And since I'm a scholar, I needed also to consult some of the better biblical scholars of the last few decades, Catholic and Protestant, Christian and non-Christian.

All these people are giants on whose shoulders I stand to catch new glimpses of the man I've been trying to follow all of these years. With their help, I've tried to paint a portrait of him that will help you, the reader, arrive at a new and vivid vision of who he really is. What you learn may unsettle you. Or it may energize you. But I guarantee it won't bore you.

The multitude of writings I've consulted will remain in the background. You don't need to have a theology degree to understand this book. And though I'm writing from within the Catholic tradition of Christianity, you don't have to be Catholic or Christian, either. I've done my best to present a portrait of Jesus that anyone can see and understand. But it is a portrait that will challenge and stimulate everyone, including those who have been studying the Bible for years.

This book is part of a more extensive exploration called *Jesus: The Way, the Truth, and the Life.* If you find this book life-giving, I encourage you to explore all the related resources. The videos filmed in the Holy Land as part of this project will make the pages of this book come to life in a very vivid way. The workbook that accompanies the videos will draw you deeper into the text of the Gospels and will highlight their connection with the entire biblical heritage of the people of Israel.

Finally, though this is a fresh look at Jesus, it is in no way the last word on him. He is the Word, the eternal Word. And that is exactly why one who follows him can never be bored. No matter how much you come to see, know, and experience, there is always so much more!

INTRODUCTION

JESUS IN THE GOSPELS AND IN HISTORY

If our quest is to get to know who Jesus really is, the obvious question is how do we do that, given that he was born over two thousand years ago? What can we really know about him and where do we look for information? Before we begin telling his story, we need to spend a few moments addressing these questions.

KNOWING FACTS VERSUS KNOWING A PERSON

First, we need to pause to examine the way we human beings usually proceed when we are trying to get to know someone.

In the English language, we use the word *know* to refer to quite different things. It can refer to knowing a bit of data, a random fact. But we also use the same word for becoming personally acquainted with someone, "getting to know" someone. These two forms of knowledge are quite different. They are so different that in many languages, like French, Spanish, and Italian, there are two completely different verbs for these two types of knowing—in Spanish, *saber* is to know a fact, *conocer* is to get to know a person.

When it comes to knowing persons, learning some facts about them is certainly important. As we get to know a person as a friend or perhaps as a potential spouse, we want and need to know more about his or her history, family, and education. However, you may have had the experience of reading facts about a person on a resume or in a dating profile and then being quite shocked by the impression made when you actually met the person for the first time. The factual sketch is not irrelevant. But neither is it adequate to convey who this person really is.

This leads to the issue of what we can know about Jesus and how we can know it.

CAN CRITICAL HISTORY HELP US?

History involves the written record of the past. From the sixteenth century to the beginning of the nineteenth century, the study of history underwent a significant upgrade in method. This was the age of Renaissance and Enlightenment. New tools for knowing the past were discovered and refined. Archaeology began to evolve as a distinct scientific discipline. People have always unearthed, often by accident, curious artifacts from the past. But during these centuries, new ways to classify, date, and interpret such objects began to develop.

Another important discipline evolved during the same time. *Philology* literally means "love of words." It is the study of language, particularly written documents. Its goal is to evaluate the authenticity of documents; determine how, when, and by whom they were composed; and understand their meaning for their authors and their original audience. New philological methods demonstrated that some famous documents were forgeries. They also showed that other documents, while authentic, had been interpolated. That means that long after the author had written the original work, someone had added to it, trying to pass off the additions as part of the original. Careful removal of later interpolations resulted in the restoration of important original texts.

These disciplines put extremely valuable new tools in the hands of historians—tools for assessing and restoring the integrity of sources and for uncovering new sources. This was clearly a good thing. The negative side of this new, critical history was that for many of its practitioners, critical meant skeptical. Scholars called into question ancient documents, especially those that had been considered authoritative. Moreover, Enlightenment scholars so prided themselves on being scientific that they considered faith in the supernatural to be prescientific and superstitious.

So the first scholars to apply critical historical method to the examination of the Gospels tended to minimize their value as historical documents and dismiss them as works of myth or fable. Literary analysis was also providing new insight into just how much the Gospel writers followed normal and very human approaches to the use of sources, editing and arranging them to suit their purposes. Many scholars from this period assumed that the humanity of the biblical texts disproved any supernatural or divine origin.

Fortunately, history as a critical discipline has come a long way since the heyday of the Enlightenment. First of all, it has become clear that to approach history with the prior conviction that there is no supernatural, that miracles simply cannot happen, is not scientific objectivity at all but just another form of prejudice. Second, two hundred years of progress in archaeology, philology, and other disciplines has yielded impressive confirmation of the historical value of the New Testament documents. It has also uncovered other important sources, such as the Dead Sea Scrolls, that help us understand Jesus and the Gospels better.

ARE THERE SECULAR SOURCES ON JESUS?

First we must ask, Are there any other secular sources, outside the New Testament writings, that substantiate the fact that Jesus even existed?

Yes, there are. First, there is a Jewish historian from Jerusalem by the name of Flavius Josephus. When the Jews rebelled against the Romans in AD 66, Josephus was sent by the new rebel government to serve as governor of Galilee. After being captured by the Romans, Josephus defected to the Roman side. He moved to Rome after the conflict, and between AD 75 and AD 93 he wrote

an account of the Jewish War plus an extensive history of the
Jewish people called *Jewish Antiquities*. In the latter work, there
is a passage about Jesus of Nazareth. The text was interpolated in
the second century by a Christian, but with the help of philology
and literary criticism, the interpolation has been removed. The
following text is most likely what Josephus actually wrote about
sixty years after the crucifixion of Jesus:

> At this time there appeared Jesus, a wise man. For he was a doer
> of startling deeds, a teacher of people who receive the truth with
> pleasure. And he gained a following both among many Jews and
> among many of Greek origin. And when Pilate, because of an
> accusation made by the leading men among us, condemned
> him to the cross, those who had loved him previously did not
> cease to do so. And up until this very day the tribe of Christians
> (named after him) has not died out.[1]

There is also a famous Roman historian, Tacitus, who confirms
the execution of Jesus in the context of the story of the great fire
of Rome in AD 64. The fire occurred during the reign of Nero, and
Nero attempted to blame it on the Christians:

> Nero fastened the guilt and inflicted the most exquisite tortures
> on a class hated for their abominations, called Christians by the
> populace. Christus, from whom the name had its origin, suffered
> the extreme penalty during the reign of Tiberius at the hands of
> one of our procurators, Pontius Pilatus, and a most mischievous
> superstition, thus checked for the moment, again broke out not
> only in Judea, the first source of the evil, but even in Rome.[2]

We don't know where Tacitus and Josephus got their information
on Christ, but most historians agree that these two non-Christian
writers provide independent confirmation not only of the
existence of Jesus of Nazareth but of his execution at the hands
of the Roman procurator Pontius Pilate.

THE GOSPELS AND CRITICAL HISTORY

From a purely rational, historical point of view, are the New
Testament writings valuable and reliable sources of factual
information on Jesus of Nazareth?

It would be useful to have autographed, original copies of any New Testament writings, but we don't. This is not unusual. We have no autographed copies of any other works of ancient writers either. All we have are copies of copies.[3]

There are no other documents from the ancient world, including the famous writings of Homer and Caesar, with a more extensive or well-established textual history than the Gospels. No ancient writings have as short a gap between date of composition and earliest surviving manuscript. If any texts from the ancient world should be considered reliable from a textual point of view, those texts are the four Gospels.[4]

But how much in the Gospels would historians agree is historical fact established beyond a reasonable doubt?

Over the years, historians have learned not to take any account simply at face value. Authors always have a particular point of view, sometimes even an agenda. Other times they are relying on sources that may be mistaken. Still other authors have a habit of seriously exaggerating numbers, for example.

So historians have identified some commonsense principles to assess the value of written reports of the past. One is called multiple attestation: When you have more than one independent source reporting the same thing, that makes it more likely to have happened. Another is the criterion of embarrassment—when an author records something that is embarrassing to the cause he or she supports, it is unlikely that he or she made it up; on the contrary, the natural tendency would be for an author to cover it up. Therefore, when an embarrassing fact is recorded, it is most likely accurate. The execution of Jesus on the Cross, the most shameful of all punishments, was a scandal. It was also scandalous that he was betrayed by one of his twelve disciples and denied by another. It is unthinkable that spokesmen of Jesus' own movement would make up such scandalous facts.

Another principle for assessing historical reports is the criterion of discontinuity—when an action or a teaching attributed to a figure in the past contrasts both with the status quo of his own time and the culture of the historian recording it, it is likely to be true. Parables like the Good Samaritan or the Prodigal Son are a method of teaching characteristic of Jesus. Neither Old Testament writers before him (with the sole exception of Nathan's parable in 2 Samuel 12:1-13) nor the New Testament writers after him (like Paul) taught in this way. So it is very unlikely that the Gospel writers would have invented such a literary form and attributed it to Jesus.

There are several other similar principles employed by historians to assess the reliability of ancient historical accounts, including the Gospels.[5]

Let's say you gather a Jewish, a Catholic, a Muslim, and an atheist historian together on a committee to work on a common project. First, you verify that they agree on the commonly accepted criteria for assessing historical accounts. Then you provide them with the historical sources on the life of Jesus. Next, you announce the task: They are to look at the sources and must come up with a basic consensus statement on what can be established as fact about Jesus of Nazareth beyond a reasonable doubt. The statement that would result would look something like this:

Sometime late in the reign of Herod the Great, Jesus was born. After living most of his life in Nazareth of Galilee, he was baptized by John in the Jordan River, probably in or around the year AD 28. Shortly thereafter, he gathered a band of disciples around him, with an inner circle of twelve. He was an itinerant preacher who used parables to expound his message of the arrival of the kingdom of God. He drew large crowds who were convinced that he performed marvelous works of healing. He himself claimed to have performed such works, and his enemies did not deny the fact of the marvels but instead attributed them to evil forces. He drew fire from Jewish religious leaders for failing to observe customs pertaining to Jewish purity laws and Sabbath observance. After considerable friction with the lay and priestly leadership of the Jewish people, he was taken prisoner at the time of the Jewish Passover, in either the year 30 or 33, after being betrayed by one of his inner circle and denied by another. He was condemned by Pontius Pilate, tortured, and crucified. After several days, his tomb was found to be empty, and several of his disciples claimed they saw him alive.

THE GOSPELS AS MORE THAN HISTORY

It is valuable to know that this bare-bones compilation of facts is not simply a matter of faith but can be established by critical history.

But to return to the question we began by asking—knowing these facts about Jesus does not really do much to reveal what he is really like.

And that's where the Gospels come in. They are solidly based on a real historical person and recount events that actually happened. But their authors, though they do aim to provide us with "an orderly account" (Luke 1:3) of the Jesus story, aim to do much more. They write that we "may know the truth" (Luke 1.4). Jesus himself, according to John's Gospel, is the Truth in person (John 14:6). And the knowledge they wish to convey to us is the intimate knowledge of personal acquaintance. Through their writings, they aim to help us encounter him, to experience him. They write the story in such a way that the living figure of Jesus of Nazareth, reaching beyond time and space, emerges from the pages of their works to touch and change the reader's life.

They are not interested in passing along much of the information that would naturally be of interest to many secular historians and their readers. About the thirty or so years Jesus lived with his family in Nazareth they tell us next to nothing. They don't give us details of his physical appearance. They don't even attempt to put the many sayings, parables, and miracles of his public ministry into chronological order. Sometimes they do preserve rather striking historical details regarding places in Jerusalem or Galilee, customs of the times, names, even specific Aramaic words that Jesus uttered. In fact, the New Testament writings are some of our most important historical sources for learning not only about Jesus but about Jewish life in first-century Palestine.

But providing this sort of information is not the main goal of the Gospel writers. The evangelists want us to know who Jesus is, what he is really like, what he did for our salvation, and what this means for us. The thing they really want to get across is the difference Jesus makes for our lives now and into the future.

THE INSPIRATION OF THE HOLY SPIRIT

It has been the conviction of the Church from the beginning that the four evangelists had special help in achieving their goal. For the Church teaches that these works were inspired by the Holy Spirit in such a way that God is their ultimate author. That does not mean that the human writers had some ecstatic experience and were hijacked by a supernatural force. The experience, which can be discerned by a careful study of the texts, was precisely the opposite. The Spirit of God, who is a Spirit of freedom, did not violate the freedom and humanity of these four unique individuals. Rather, the Spirit empowered these authors, while remaining fully themselves—indeed becoming more truly themselves—to teach truly, faithfully, and without error the truth that God wanted to communicate to us through their words for the sake of our own salvation and liberation.[6]

Each of the four retained his own vocabulary, kept his own typical mode of thinking and speech, and fully engaged his own creativity. He proceeded in a normal, human way of literary composition. Luke, for example, was not an eyewitness, as he hints in his prologue. But, like any good historian, he investigated all the sources available to him, consisting of oral and written reports of those who had told the story before him. The evangelists edited and re-edited, as most writers do, and this can be detected in a careful study of the four Gospels, most particularly John.

Yet, throughout, there was more than providential guidance; there was a synergy between the four evangelists and the gentle but powerful movement of the Holy Spirit, breathing life and truth into them and their words. The conviction of the early teachers known as the Fathers of the Church was that it was not only the writers that were inspired—the words that they left behind are themselves inspired and God-breathed; they are, as it were, a temple full of the Holy Spirit. When people approach these texts in faith and openness, the texts become a place of rendezvous, a place to encounter God, a medium not only of enlightenment but of nourishment and transformation. If this is true, as the Church teaches and as countless Christian lives testify, these very human words have a divine depth that makes them inexhaustible. The more water one draws from this well, the more water bubbles up, living water that heals and refreshes.

WERE THERE OTHER GOSPELS?

In the 1940s, a trove of ancient papyri was unearthed in the arid sands of Egypt. This library, found at Nag Hammadi, belonged to a long-extinct Gnostic sect. Among the documents recovered was something called the gospel of Thomas. It caused a sensation and raised a suspicion. Were there other gospels that had been hidden from us, kept back by repressive church authorities? In fact, remnants and traces of other so-called gospels have been found: the gospels of Judas, of Mary Magdalene, of Peter. Why were they not included in the New Testament?

These apocryphal gospels, unlike the four canonical Gospels, appear to date from the middle of the second century, a hundred or more years after the time of Jesus.[7] More importantly, a lot is missing from their content—most particularly, the Cross. In many of the apocryphal gospels, Jesus does not come to save us by giving his life for us. In fact, the gospel of Thomas is simply a collection of sayings. Jesus appears in it as a sort of esoteric guru who saves us by revealing secret and mysterious knowledge—the signature concept of Gnosticism, a second-century heresy. About half of the sayings come from the canonical Gospels. The rest seem to flow from Gnostic thinking, including this one, which is not very complimentary to women:

> Simon Peter said to him, "Let Mary leave us, for women are not worthy of life." Jesus said, "I myself shall lead her in order to make her male, so that she too may become a living spirit resembling you males. For every woman who will make herself male will enter the kingdom of heaven." [8]

Another second-century writing, called the infancy gospel of Thomas, presents us with a five-year-old Jesus who takes revenge on two playmates who bother him by striking them dead.[9]

It is not hard to figure out why these so-called gospels, and others like them, were rejected in the days of the early Church. By the mid-second century, the four canonical Gospels had been part of the worship experience and culture of the apostolic Churches for a few generations. When documents like the gospel of Thomas or the infancy gospel of Thomas showed up, they would have been immediately rejected just as foreign tissue is rejected by a human body. They presented a portrait of Jesus that was alien to the Jesus the Church knew, believed, and loved. None of the Churches founded by an apostle, like Corinth or Antioch or Rome, had ever heard of these "gospels" or could vouch for them. There was no need for the pope or an ecumenical council to tell second-century Christians that the documents were inauthentic.

WHY FOUR GOSPELS?

Some heretics in the second century believed that only one gospel could possibly be right.[10] This idea was refuted a few decades later by the great bishop Irenaeus, a Church Father who had been mentored by Polycarp, the martyred bishop of Smyrna. (Polycarp was reputed to have personally known the apostle and evangelist John, son of Zebedee.) Irenaeus is our earliest witness to the authors of the four Gospels and notes how fitting it is for the universal Church to have a fourfold Gospel foundation, since four symbolizes the four points of the compass and therefore the whole world. The gospel that is to be preached to the four corners of the earth comes to us in a fourfold form.[11]

From another, less symbolic point of view, I would put it this way: I am very grateful to have two eyes and not just one. Two eyes provide depth perception that a single eye does not. Similarly, in a live televised event such as a football game, usually four or five cameras record the event from different places around and above the action. The view on your screen constantly alternates between these cameras. That's because the only way to get a comprehensive perspective on what is happening is to see it from various angles.

That's why the Holy Spirit inspired four Gospel accounts and why the Church has treasured each equally through the ages. Each evangelist, though divinely inspired, is nonetheless human and limited. No one human perspective on Jesus of Nazareth could possibly provide the full picture that we hope for. And that is why, in this book, we make use of all the Gospels and shift constantly between the four. The figure of Jesus that emerges from this approach will be that much more three-dimensional, alive, and intriguing.

CHAPTER I
JESUS AND HIS WORLD

Skeptics often dismiss the story of Jesus as just another myth from ancient times, like the tale of the Egyptian god Osiris who was killed and then brought back to life.

It is true that the ancient Near Eastern world was full of mythology—Greek, Roman, Mesopotamian, Egyptian. These cultures all had stories of gods, goddesses, demigods, and superheroes whose marvelous tales of mighty deeds occur in the haze of some remote, indefinite past.

One of the most striking features of Israelite religion in general is that it is a historical, not a mythological, faith. It is the conviction of Israel that the eternal, transcendent God intervened in history. He acted concretely in the lives of real people, like Abraham, and accomplished specific acts of deliverance, like the Exodus from Egypt.

The gospel of Jesus has to be understood against the background of this unique faith of Israel. It did not occur in some shadowy dream time or, as Paul tells Festus, off in some remote corner (Acts 26:26). It took place on the main stage of human history.

The gospel story begins with the Word of God entering personally into history, into our world, to an extent unprecedented—"and the Word became flesh and dwelt among us" (John 1:14). He did so in a very specific time, place, and cultural context. If we fail to take the time to understand the world of Jesus, we will never adequately understand *him*.

THE ROMAN WORLD AND ROMAN WAY

Actually, Jesus was born into not one world, but two. Two worlds were intersecting in the same place; two cultures, two ways, were butting heads and trying to come to terms with each other. Jesus was born in Judea, in the land of Israel, which had come under the control of Rome about sixty years before. The area had been known to the world for over five hundred years as Palestine,[12] and the Romans at this time viewed it as part of their larger province of Syria, even though they put a vassal king of Judea, named Herod, on the throne.

Rome controlled the Mediterranean by the end of the first century BC. From a small village on the Palatine Hill in 743 BC, Rome had gradually become a force to be reckoned with in Italy and, as the years passed, the world. As it grew, Rome gobbled up its Italian neighbors, the maritime empire of Carthage, and the remnants of Alexander the Great's Hellenistic empire. Though it was for centuries a republic, under Julius Caesar (100–44 BC) it became a dictatorship. In the chaos and civil war that followed his assassination, his adopted son, Octavian (63 BC–AD 14), emerged triumphant.[13] He reorganized the government into an imperial system though he preferred for himself the title of prince, or first citizen. Octavian's complete control put an end to hostilities and disorder, and so a kind of peace ensued. It was a peace enforced by power, won by the sword and maintained by the sword. Yet it was ironically heralded as a new era for mankind, good news for all peoples of the empire.

Octavian arranged to have Julius Caesar "deified," which conveniently made Octavian the son of a god. He was given the title of Augustus, meaning great or majestic one, and as *princeps*, or prince, he was hailed as the bringer of peace, a savior—indeed, the "prince of peace." As emperor, he also assumed the role of chief priest of Rome, the *pontifex maximus*.

The common language of the empire was more Greek than Latin. Alexander the Great's conquests had made Greek the international language of learning and commerce. So the proclamation of the glad tidings of the peaceful new era of Augustus Caesar was called an *evangelion,* Greek for "gospel" or "good news."[14]

The military victories of Caesar provided him with an opportunity to reaffirm and celebrate his divine status. Pomp and splendor characterized these "triumphs," and arches were often built through which the divine ruler would process with his armies along with their captives and booty. Such triumphal arches can be seen not only in Rome but in many cities throughout the former Roman Empire.[15] The triumphal marches were not just simply patriotic parades; they were religious events complete with sacrifices. Burning a sacrifice of incense to the divine Caesar ultimately became a civic duty, a sort of loyalty test for subjects of the empire.

The values of the Roman world seem to have been well summed up in the first letter of John: "the lust of the flesh and the lust of the eyes and the pride of life" (1 John 2:16).

Rome's time had finally come in the person of Augustus. Just before the victory of Augustus over Mark Antony, making Augustus sole ruler of the empire, Virgil wrote his famous poems called the *Eclogues.* In the fourth eclogue, a mysterious prophecy can be found: A child shall come from high heaven whose birth will usher in the final age, the golden age for the entire world. Many people of the empire interpreted this child to be Augustus Caesar. Later, Christians reading this would see it as a prophecy of the birth of Jesus.

THE JEWISH WORLD AND JEWISH WAY

Although he lived under Roman rule, Jesus was a Jew. The Jews were a people, yes, but they were more than that—they were a family. Their story began when their ancestor, Abraham, a pagan from Mesopotamia, had a religious experience. A God whose name he didn't know ordered him to leave behind the land between the Tigris and Euphrates and march into the desert with all his belongings. The end point of the journey was not revealed to him. But he was given a promise of a countless progeny, as numerous as the sands of the seashore, and a land that would serve as the home and the inheritance of this vast array of descendants (Genesis 22:17). In some mysterious way, all nations of the earth were to find blessing through him and his family.

At some point, the Jews were enslaved in Egypt. After several centuries of misery, God showed his power and his love by liberating his people from the clutches of the mightiest power of the world, the pharaoh of Egypt. This great act of deliverance, the seminal event of their history, came to be known as the Exodus.

But the story of the Red Sea is incomplete without Sinai. For in an encounter at this mountain, the motley crew of Abraham's descendants were joined together by a new and deeper bond. God offered them the opportunity to become his special possession, his own chosen people. They no longer were to be just Abraham's family, but God's family. They willingly accepted this proposal.

God then confirmed this new family relationship with blood sacrifice and a sacrificial meal (Exodus 24:1-11) and gave them the Law, the Torah, which stamped his seal on every aspect of their lives—diet, sex, family, and work. No aspect was exempt from his mark of sovereignty (Exodus 20–23). They were to be a holy people, a priestly people consecrated exclusively to him (Exodus 19:5-6).

From that moment forward, God literally pitched his tent in their midst—the Tent of Meeting. Simply called the Tabernacle,[16] it held the Ark of the Covenant, which bore the stone tablets that Moses had brought down from the mountain. God's presence was experienced as a visible cloud of glory that settled over this place of encounter, this Tent of Meeting. He accompanied the Jews on their journey. When the cloud arose, they would break camp; when it settled, they rested (Numbers 14:14; Nehemiah 9:19).

From the desert, Joshua led them across the Jordan River into the Promised Land of Canaan. They asked for and received a king to help defend them against the land's hostile inhabitants. Their second king, David, made them proud. He smashed the Philistines, their greatest enemies, and turned this fledgling nation into a mighty kingdom. David then made a move that had a great impact on the spiritual life of God's people from that time forward (2 Samuel 5:6-9). He conquered a pagan town in an area belonging to none of the twelve tribes. That meant it had no specific tribal association. It was strategically located between the tribes of the south and the tribes of the north so that all the people from every tribe could regard it as their own. The city was Jerusalem. After conquering it, David brought the Ark of the Covenant into the city, making it not only the political capital but also Israel's religious center, the dwelling place not only of the monarchy but also of God's name and God's glory.

Over time, Jerusalem became the only place where sacrifice to God was permitted. So the Temple built by David's son, Solomon, replaced the Tent of Meeting and became the new, unrivaled meeting place between God and Israel, the symbol of God's presence, God-with-us. Here heaven and earth intersected. Here the glory of God settled. Here the people of Israel came as pilgrims three times a year, celebrating the great festivals of Passover, Pentecost, and Tabernacles,[17] all linked to special events in their history.

God promised David that his dynasty, his "house," would endure forever (2 Samuel 7). But his son Solomon allowed wealth and foreign women to seduce him; he burdened the people with heavy taxation and labor. Solomon's son, Rehoboam, was even more abusive, provoking a rebellion. There was a split—the ten northern tribes seceded and declared their own kingdom, independent of the king of David's line reigning in Jerusalem. The Lord sent great prophets both to the North, like Elijah, and to the South, like Jeremiah. They called both Judah and Israel back to fidelity to the covenant. But such prophets were mostly ignored or, worse, persecuted.

Catastrophe ensued—the Northern Kingdom was conquered by the pagan Assyrians. The best and brightest of the Israelites were taken into exile, scattered, and resettled far and wide, destroying their unity and national identity. To further compromise Israelite identity, the best and brightest from other conquered provinces were resettled in the former Northern Kingdom of Israel. The people of this region of mixed ancestry gradually came to be known as the Samaritans, and a centuries-long cold war with their Judean cousins to the south began.

A century and a half later, the kingdom of Judah suffered a similar catastrophe. God, through Jeremiah, had warned the people not to resist the Babylonians. Instead, they rebelled, provoking the pagans to destroy the holy city of Jerusalem, burn down the Temple, and take their nobility and professional class as captives to Babylon. The glory of God departed from the ruined Temple, and the family tree of King David was cut to the ground. The last thing seen by the last Davidic king of Judah, Zedekiah, was the execution of all his sons. He was then blinded and taken in chains with the others to Babylon.

But the crucible of the Babylonian exile led this Judean remnant to repent, turn back to the Lord, and strengthen their distinct identity as the people of God. Allowed to return home seventy years later, the descendants of the exiles rebuilt Jerusalem and its Temple. Yet this second Temple was a mere shadow of the first one, the one erected by Solomon. The Ark of the Covenant had been lost, the glory had departed, and the Holy of Holies was empty. The returning Israelites had no son of David to take the throne. Instead, they were ruled by governors appointed by their Persian overlord. Soon after their return from exile, the people noticed that there were no longer any new prophets ... the Spirit of God had been quenched. Heaven was closed.

CULTURES COLLIDE

Alexander the Great soon conquered Palestine along with much of the rest of the known world. Thus began a period where people arrived speaking Greek, worshipping Greek gods, living according to Greek customs. They built Hellenistic cities in the Holy Land right alongside communities of observant Jews.

In 167 BC, the Greek overlord of the area, who resided in Syria, decided that he needed to unify his realm. He therefore required everyone to follow the same Greek customs and worship the same Greek gods. Some Jews accommodated. But a zealous priest named Mattathias began a rebellion. His son, known to history as Judas Maccabeus ("the hammer"), led the armies of zealous Jews against the professionally trained hosts of the king and won battle after battle. The king had desecrated the Jewish sanctuary, but on December 25, 164 BC, the Temple was cleansed and rededicated, initiating the feast we now know as Hanukkah, the Hebrew word for "dedication" (2 Maccabees 10).

This whole affair made the Jews of Palestine that much more determined to emphasize their distinct way of life and resist assimilation to the pagan ways of their neighbors. Though Judas Maccabeus was killed in a subsequent battle, the Jews were eventually victorious and declared their independence from the pagan king.

The priestly family of Judas Maccabeus, known as the Hasmoneans, then did something unheard of. They were not of the proper lineage to make one of their own the high priest. Neither were they of the line of David so as to crown one of their own a Davidic king. Moreover, the role of priest and king had always been distinct and separate in the history of Israel. Nonetheless, the Hasmonean leader Jonathan usurped the high priesthood and also declared himself king. So a former liberator became an illegitimate high priest and an illegitimate king. The heroes became the new oppressors.

A century later, to make matters even worse, two Hasmonean brothers got into a violent struggle over who would be the high priest and king. Civil strife ensued. One of the brothers called upon the Romans for help to secure his claim. The Romans were only too happy to get involved; after putting Jerusalem under siege and storming the Temple, they took control of it for themselves in 63 BC.

Ultimately, the Romans were wise enough to recognize that they did not have the experience to govern such a peculiar and unruly people. So they put a shrewd and ruthless local on the throne, Herod. He was a cousin of the Jews, a descendant of Esau, whose Edomite family had nominally converted to Judaism. Herod was crowned in Rome and soon earned the respect of his overlords by fighting off Rome's enemies and ruling his subjects with an iron fist. As long as Herod was in control, the Romans knew they would have no trouble in Palestine.

Herod aimed to ingratiate himself with the Jews by rebuilding the Temple in splendid style. At the same time, he tried to impress Caesar by building an innovative port on the Mediterranean, complete with a Roman theater, a hippodrome or horse-racing track, and even a temple dedicated not to the God of Israel but to the gods of Rome. He did not name the city after a prophet or holy man of Israel; he named it Caesarea in honor of his pagan patron. For the rest of his life, Herod played to both audiences, straddling two worlds.

JEWISH HOPE

The Jews of Palestine were beaten down. The Temple was being restored, true, but by a king who was not of David's stock and not even an ethnic Jew.[18] As magnificent as Herod's design was, the new Temple remained empty, the glory gone and the Spirit quenched.

But each time they traveled to Jerusalem for a festival, Jews were reminded of the drubbing given to Pharaoh by Moses, to the Philistines by David, and to the Greeks by Judas the Hammer. They were reminded that they had been in dire straits before, and God had always come through. They were reminded of the promises to the patriarchs and the promises to David. They recalled the oracles of the prophets about the Day of the Lord, when God would act decisively and usher in a new age. At each festival, their hope was revived.

What kind of hero would God use to do this?

For people who have some familiarity with the Christian story, the word "messiah" immediately calls to mind a spiritual figure who will save us from our sins so that we can go to heaven. That is not what people of Jesus' day thought about when they longed for God to send a messiah. Messiah means "anointed." In the Old Testament times, priests and kings were anointed, and at least one famous prophet, Elisha, was as well.

From what we can piece together from the evidence, it seems like a variety of "messiahs" were hoped for by people of this time. Most Jews had rather practical and worldly goals. They hoped for a son of David, a new Davidic king, who would do what David did—make the pagans pay dearly for their audacity and drive them out of God's land. What they had in mind was a new version of the story of Judas Maccabeus. True, he wasn't of David's family, but at least he did what a messiah ought to do—liberate the land and rededicate the Temple. A true successor of David could be expected to do even more.

But then again, hadn't Malachi said something about Elijah coming back before the Day of the Lord? (Malachi 4:5). And Moses too had promised that "the LORD your God will raise up for you a prophet like me from among you, from your brethren—him you shall heed" (Deuteronomy 18:15). Now, Moses had liberated them from Egypt and fed them with bread from heaven. That was a prophet they could get excited about. After nearly two hundred years of corrupt, illegitimate high priests, some were also looking for a truly holy priest who would lead Israel back into righteousness.

The wise men of the day speculated that God would act through one or more of these anointed ones—there does not seem to have been a clear consensus on which figure should be expected. But what is clear is that during the lifetime of Jesus, expectations were running high that God was about to act and about to act big. Soon and very soon "the day of the Lord" would dawn; a decisive move of God would take place that would usher in the final age. That meant victory for Israel and death to the pagans.

TWO WAYS AND THE WAY

So Palestine in the time of Jesus was a tinderbox. Two worlds, two ways of living, confronted each other and were set on a collision course, one people convinced its time had already come and another people convinced its time was about to come at any moment.

And into these colliding worlds is born one who says his kingdom is not from this world at all (John 18:36), who proclaims to both ways that HE is the Way (John 14:6), who is "gentle and lowly in heart" (Matthew 11:29) yet is perceived as such a threat that both worlds conspire to eliminate him.

CHAPTER 2

BETHLEHEM

True to the famous Christmas carol, Bethlehem during the reign of Herod was a little village of a few hundred families. Small though it was, this hill town in the Judean mountains had a big place in history. The famous biblical story of Ruth, the devoted daughter-in-law of Naomi, concludes in Bethlehem (ca. 1100 BC). There Ruth had a son by the name of Obed, who became the grandfather of David, the shepherd boy who slew Goliath and became the greatest king in Israel's history.

CITY OF DAVID

So Bethlehem became famous as David's town. But since David conquered Jerusalem and moved his royal court there, Jerusalem also became the City of David. From that point on, the princes who were to succeed their fathers as anointed kings were born in Jerusalem.

Yet after several hundred years of Jerusalem-born kings, this prophetic oracle was uttered:

> But you, O Bethlehem Ephrathah, who are little to be among the clans of Judah, from you shall come forth for me one who is to be ruler in Israel, whose origin is from of old, from ancient days. (Micah 5:2)

A future ruler, born like David in Bethlehem, "whose origin is from of old, from ancient days." The origin of any baby, even a prince, is when he is conceived. What could this ancient origin mean?

"ORIGIN FROM OF OLD"

By the time of Herod, the people of Israel were disillusioned with their leadership, to say the least. Other than Moses, Joshua, and David, not many of their shepherds had even come close to living up to their responsibilities. Most were negligent. Many were predatory. The prophets made clear that it wasn't only the people who were disgusted with the situation; God himself was fed up.

There are passages in the Old Testament where God speaks as if he is done waiting for the shepherds to do right by his flock, as if he has determined somehow to come himself and straighten things out. Especially notable is this oracle from Ezekiel:

> The shepherds have fed themselves, and have not fed my sheep; therefore, you shepherds, hear the word of the Lord: Thus says the Lord GOD, Behold, I am against the shepherds; and I will require my sheep at their hand, and put a stop to their feeding the sheep; no longer shall the shepherds feed themselves. I will rescue my sheep from their mouths, that they may not be food for them.
>
> For thus says the Lord GOD: Behold, I, I myself will search for my sheep, and will seek them out. As a shepherd seeks out his flock when some of his sheep have been scattered abroad, so will I seek out my sheep; and I will rescue them from all places where they have been scattered. (Ezekiel 34:8-12)

This determination on God's part was an answer to his people's pleas, like this one voiced by Isaiah: "O that you would tear the heavens and come down!" (Isaiah 64:1).

During his public ministry as recorded in the Gospel of John, Jesus speaks as if his birth was not the beginning of his story. He tells the Pharisees, "Before Abraham was, I am" (John 8:58). He speaks of himself as being "from above," as being "bread which came down from heaven" (John 8:23; 6:41).

In his prologue, John tells us that the Word of God, somehow "with God" and at the same time God, existing from the beginning, enters our world and is "made flesh." In other words, the Divine Word, through which heaven and earth were made, becomes a human being in the person of Jesus (John 1:1-14).

DIVINE DESCENT

The entering of the divine Word into human life, with all its limitations, all its tragedy, is a plunge from the heights of immortal glory into the depths of human vulnerability. The apostle Paul emphasizes it as an act of extreme humility: Jesus, "though he was in the form of God, did not count equality with God a thing to be grasped, but emptied himself, taking the form of a servant, being born in the likeness of men" (Philippians 2:6). The Divine One stoops to our level. He fully shares in our human experience yet somehow loses nothing of his divinity.

The Word Made Flesh

John's Gospel begins this way: "In the beginning was the Word" (John 1:1). This harkens back to the first few lines of the Hebrew Bible. In the first chapter of Genesis, God speaks and things happen. The heavens and the earth come into existence in response to his Word.

Yet in several places in the Old Testament, God's Word seems to be somehow distinct from God. For example, the decisive action of wresting Israel from the clutches of Pharaoh is described as an action of God's Word. The Word is omnipotent and appears to have agency:

> For while gentle silence enveloped all things, and night in its swift course was now half gone, your all-powerful word leaped from heaven, from the royal throne, into the midst of the land. (Wisdom 18:14-15)

In a similar way, the Old Testament also speaks of Wisdom as if it were a person standing at God's side from before the world was created. This Wisdom served as God's instrument in the creation of all things. In this verse from Proverbs, Wisdom is speaking: "Then I was beside him, like a master workman; and I was daily his delight, rejoicing before him always" (Proverbs 8:30).

We need to interpret what John writes at the beginning of his Gospel in light of this background: "In the beginning was the Word, and the Word was with God, and the Word was God. He was in the beginning with God; all things were made through him, and without him was not anything made that was made" (John 1:1-3).

The Word described here is clearly distinct from God the Father ("the Word was with God") but is no less divine ("the

Word was God"). Like Wisdom in Proverbs, the Word, for John, is the means by which God created the world.

There is one final observation to be made. "Word," in Greek, is *logos*, from which comes our word "logic." In the philosophy called Stoicism, which was very popular in the first-century Roman world, the *logos* is a divine, creative principle. For the Stoics, *logos* is the inner logic of the universe, the rational principle holding all things together and making the world the intelligible, orderly cosmos that it is.[19] This and more seems to be included in John's teaching on the Word.

A few lines later in his prologue, John makes a striking affirmation: In Jesus, this divine Word through which the world was made, the Word and the divine Wisdom responsible for holding all things together "became flesh and dwelt among us" (John 1:14). The Greek word translated here as "dwelt" literally means "pitched his tent" among us, like Yahweh, who pitched the Tent of Meeting in the desert (Exodus 33:7 11) and who dwelt among the people in the Jerusalem Temple.

What the Gospels tell us is that, in Jesus, this is exactly what God did. He heard his people's cry and fulfilled his promise in a way beyond all expectation, in a way no one anticipated.

God, in other words, becomes human. This is Immanuel, God-with-us (Isaiah 7:14), in a sense that quite frankly boggles the mind.

So the gospel story begins with a free decision on the part of heaven, a remarkable gift of selfless love for us and total obedience to God. Jesus comes into the world declaring, "Behold, I have come to do your will, O God" (Hebrews 10:5-7).

THE STORY FROM MARY'S PERSPECTIVE

Nazareth is in Galilee, about a hundred-mile walk from Bethlehem. But Mary and Joseph find themselves having to make that arduous journey at the most inconvenient of times—when Mary is nine months pregnant. For Joseph is of the family of David and needs to return to his ancestral town to register for a census (Luke 2:1-5).

The journey is preceded by some unusual happenings. Luke tells the story from Mary's perspective. She is most likely between thirteen and fifteen years of age, the common time for betrothal in those days. She is engaged and therefore legally bound to Joseph, but they are not yet living together.

During this time, she is visited by the angel Gabriel and told that she will have a son. He will inherit the throne of his ancestor David and will be the final King, the one who will rule forever (2 Samuel 7:16). When she asks how this is to be since she is still a virgin, the angel explains that she will conceive not by Joseph, but by the power of the Holy Spirit. Davidic kings had been called "son of God" in an honorary sort of way in the Old Testament (see Psalm 2:7). But given this child's extraordinary conception, he will be called Son of God in a new and unique way, says Gabriel. "For," he tells her, "with God nothing will be impossible" (Luke 1:26-38).

Mary's response helps us understand what the Bible means by faith. Does Mary believe that God can do anything? Yes, and this sort of intellectual conviction is a necessary dimension of faith. Yet it is not enough. The real question is, Will she accept God's invitation to surrender to this plan though she can't quite see how it will all play out? How will she possibly convince Joseph that her pregnancy results from fidelity to God, not infidelity to him? She could be accused of adultery and stoned to death. Can she entrust herself to God when his will leads her into such a precarious situation? She risks Joseph's love and at the same time risks her life.

Her response, called her *fiat* in Latin, is brief: "I am the handmaid of the Lord; let it be to me according to your word" (Luke 1:38).

In Luke's Gospel, there are a series of sayings, called beatitudes, that are much like the more famous Beatitudes of Matthew's Gospel (see Luke 6 and Matthew 5). In the beatitudes of both Gospels, Jesus praises people who possess certain qualities that lead to blessedness and happiness. The surprising thing is that the first beatitude in Luke is uttered by Elizabeth and is addressed to Mary: "Blessed is she who believed that there would be a fulfilment of what was spoken to her from the Lord" (Luke 1:45). For Luke, Mary is the model of Christian faith.[20]

THE STORY FROM JOSEPH'S PERSPECTIVE

Matthew tells the same story from Joseph's perspective. Mary at least knows for certain that her pregnancy is not a result of infidelity. Joseph, on the other hand, has to take Mary's word for it. He is troubled by the news, as would be expected. Matthew describes him as a righteous or just man, and that is shown by the fact that he does not respond vengefully or expose Mary to shame and capital punishment. Instead, he considers divorcing her quietly.

At this juncture, Joseph has a visit from an angel in a dream confirming that the child in Mary's womb is "of the Holy Spirit." He is told that the son to be born should be called Jesus, our English form for the Hebrew name Yeshua. The reason for this is because the name means "Yahweh [God] is salvation." The angel tells him that indeed this child "will save his people from their sins" (Matthew 1:18-19).

So Joseph, in an act of faith that matches that of his betrothed, abandons his divorce plan and accepts the responsibility of caring for Mary and her unborn child. Then comes a rather unpleasant surprise—the census is announced, requiring that he walk about one hundred miles to his ancestral town with a pregnant wife. On top of that, when they arrive, there is no room for them in the inn. The only place they can find to stay is a stable with a manger, a feeding trough for animals, as the newborn's crib.

THE MANGER

The details of Luke's account of the Nativity are all meaningful, but the manger in particular is referred to as a "sign" and so is especially important. It points us back to a passage in the very first chapter of Isaiah: "An ox knows its owner, and an ass, its master's manger; But Israel does not know, my people has not understood" (Isaiah 1:3 NAB).

Most people in the Western world are familiar with the traditional nativity scene featured in many Christmas displays. Neither Luke's nor Matthew's account specifically mentions the presence of an ox and a donkey; the reason they appear in nativity scenes is because of that verse from Isaiah. The message of Isaiah's prophecy is that even animals are smart enough to know where their food comes from, but Israel does not know the hand that feeds it and does not recognize the food provided.

In Hebrew, the name Bethlehem means "house of bread." Jesus is bread from heaven sent by God, placed in a feeding trough for the life of the world, yet he is not welcomed by his own people. They fail to recognize God's gift. John notes this at the beginning of his Gospel: "He came to his own home, and his own people received him not" (John 1:11).

SHEPHERDS AND ANGELS

The traditional nativity scene also features shepherds and angels, who appear together in Luke's account. Bethlehem is only about five miles south of Jerusalem, home of the chief priests and the Jewish aristocracy. But it is not to them that angelic messengers are sent. Neither are angels sent to any respectable and prominent people who might reside in Bethlehem. They appear instead to shepherds, people on the margins of Jewish society.

True, the great King David had been a shepherd. But even in the story of David, his role as a shepherd was a sign of his lowliness. His older brothers got to go off to war and he, the youngest, was stuck pasturing the sheep. The shepherds of the gospel story are living in the open field a mile or so outside Bethlehem, on the edge of the desert. They are night watchmen and are just about at the bottom of the social ladder, classed with tax collectors.[21] It is to these despised ones that the angels announce the *evangelion*, the gospel or good news—the birth of a King who will be much more a savior than Augustus Caesar. These simple men receive the news with joy and respond in haste.

Matthew mentions visitors of a very different kind. Alongside the shepherds in the traditional nativity scene, we also find the three kings. If you read Matthew's account closely, the exact number of visitors is actually not mentioned—it is only the gifts that are three in number. And the visitors are called Magi or wise men, not kings.

The Magi are pagan wise men from Persia, the priestly, learned class of the land. Somehow, through their sincere pursuit of wisdom and truth, they recognize a sign in the heavens that they believe is associated with the birth of a Jewish King. Apparently, they realize that this Jewish King is important not only for Jews but for the rest of the world. They therefore make the difficult journey from the east all the way to Jerusalem to ask Herod where to find the newborn King

Herod discerns a threat to his power. He consults priests and sages, who refer him to the passage in Micah quoted earlier. Armed with this information, Herod tells the Magi that Bethlehem is the place. Herod asks the Magi to return and tell him the exact location of the child so that he too can offer him homage. In reality, he has quite different plans.

In Matthew's story, Herod and all Jerusalem are troubled, not gladdened, by the news brought by the Magi. No one hastens to Bethlehem to honor the child. Ironically, it is the pagan Magi who are overjoyed to see him and offer him gifts—of gold, frankincense, and myrrh (Matthew 2:1-12).

So why are the Magi depicted as kings riding camels? Because two of their gifts call to mind a prophecy from Isaiah which their journey to Bethlehem fulfilled:

> Nations shall walk by your light, and kings in the brightness of your rising. … Camels shall cover you, the young camels of Midian and Ephah; all those from Sheba shall come. They shall bring gold and frankincense, and shall proclaim the praise of the LORD. (Isaiah 60:3, 60:6)[22]

From the two very different groups of visitors reported by Luke and Matthew we learn this: From the beginning of Jesus' life, it is the least likely who welcome him—pagan Gentiles and marginalized Jews. The very wise and the very humble are the ones who recognize and accept him. Those who are neither wise nor humble totally miss him or are threatened by him.

THE LAW AND THE PROPHETS

Luke records two notable events in the days following the child's birth. The first is that Mary's baby is circumcised on the eighth day after his birth. We may think of this as rather routine. But circumcision indelibly marks a man as belonging to the covenant people of Israel. It is a prescription of the Law that will, when the child is thirteen, bind him to keep the Law in its fullness. Luke wants us to know that Jesus, Joseph, and Mary are observant, devout Jews. The uniqueness of this child does not prevent them from submitting to the Law of Moses in every respect.

The second event also shows their obedience to God through submission to the Torah. According to the Law of Moses, the flow of blood from the birth of a son renders a woman ritually impure and unable to enter the inner court of the Temple. On the fortieth day after childbirth, she is to be purified. She does this by coming to the Temple and offering a lamb and a dove or, if she can't afford a lamb, two doves (Leviticus 12). The fact that Mary offers two doves underscores that Joseph and Mary are humble, simple people of modest means.

There is yet another duty imposed upon them by the Law. Because God spared the firstborn sons of Israel on the night of the first Passover in Egypt, every firstborn son belongs to the Lord in a special way and needs to be "redeemed" (Exodus 13:11-16), which literally means "bought back." This is done when the father pays a priest some silver coins. This need not be done in the Temple.

But Luke 2 tells us that Mary, newly purified and able to enter the Temple's Court of the Women, chooses to bring her baby into the house of God to present him to the Lord. This harkens back to the Old Testament—the child Samuel is brought by his mother, Hannah, to the sanctuary not long after birth and dedicated to the Lord's service (1 Samuel 1:22-28). Jesus, like Samuel, is to remain consecrated to God for life. Rather than "buying him back" from God, the couple present him in the Temple, acknowledging that their son will always belong to God in a special and exclusive way.

In the Temple there is an unexpected meeting. Simeon is apparently a simple and devout layman who longs for the deliverance of Israel. He receives an inspiration from the Holy Spirit to come to the Temple just as Joseph, Mary, and the baby are in the Temple precincts. He recognizes the child, takes him in his arms, and proclaims a prophetic blessing.

His brief utterance makes several important affirmations. This child will bring glory to the people of Israel but will also be a light of revelation to the nations. Simeon ironically makes this statement in an area of the Temple that is off-limits to Gentiles under pain of death. He then goes on to predict that the salvation brought by this child will be costly; it will cause some to rise but others to fall. The child will be opposed and contradicted, and a sword will one day pierce Mary's soul (Luke 2:29-35).

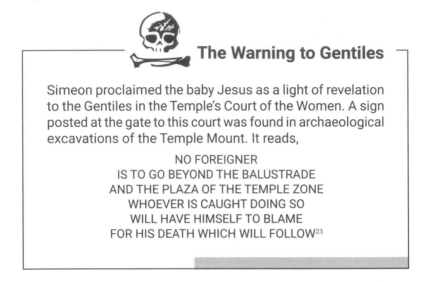

The Warning to Gentiles

Simeon proclaimed the baby Jesus as a light of revelation to the Gentiles in the Temple's Court of the Women. A sign posted at the gate to this court was found in archaeological excavations of the Temple Mount. It reads,

NO FOREIGNER
IS TO GO BEYOND THE BALUSTRADE
AND THE PLAZA OF THE TEMPLE ZONE
WHOEVER IS CAUGHT DOING SO
WILL HAVE HIMSELF TO BLAME
FOR HIS DEATH WHICH WILL FOLLOW[23]

This private celebration is joined by yet another person. A pious widow named Anna, who is described as a prophetess, is always in the Temple, praying. She rejoices to happen upon this intimate gathering and begins talking about the child to everyone. Just as the angels evangelized the shepherds, so Anna evangelizes the visitors to the Temple.

Like Mary and Joseph and the shepherds who visit the baby, Simeon and Anna are representatives of the best of their nation, the humble and righteous Israel that longs for God and watches for him. The entire infancy narratives could be seen as an illustration of Matthew's first Beatitude: "Blessed are the poor in spirit, for theirs is the kingdom of heaven" (Matthew 5:3).

It is notable that the scribes, the chief priests, and the aristocrats are noticeably absent. Even when the child is brought right into the Temple precincts, they fail to recognize him.

HEROD AND THE FLIGHT TO EGYPT

The scene of the Presentation in the Temple closes Luke's account of Jesus' infancy. But Matthew has yet another story to tell. The Magi are warned that Herod has designs on the child's life, and so they depart without reporting back to Herod. Enraged, Herod decides to stamp out the threat of a rival to his throne. He orders his soldiers to pay a visit to Bethlehem and massacre all boys under the age of two.

Some have wondered if Herod could possibly have been ruthless enough to have done such a thing. Here are a few facts about Herod: Concerned that they might be plotting against him, Herod killed one of his own wives (he had several) along with his three oldest sons. Paranoid as he was, he had not one but multiple well-garrisoned fortresses. The most famous of these was Masada. But the largest of these was the Herodium, built on top of a high mountain overlooking Bethlehem. During that era of the imperial splendor of Rome, this Herodian palace was among the largest in the entire world. The distance from the Herodium to Bethlehem is only three miles. Soldiers at this fortress receiving Herod's order could have executed it immediately.

Matthew's story of the massacre of innocent children fits right in with Herod's typical way of doing business. When he was on his deathbed, he gave orders that several of the leading men of Jerusalem be put to death as soon as he himself died. Otherwise, he feared, the days following his death would be a time of rejoicing, not mourning.

 **The Herods**

Anyone interested in exploring the family tree of the rulers referred to in the New Testament as "Herod" should prepare for a headache.

Originally, the family came from Idumaea, an area in the south of the Holy Land that included Hebron and the Negev desert. Since the Babylonian captivity, it had been occupied by Edomites (hence the name "Idumaea"), the Gentile descendants of Esau. After the stunning military success of the Maccabees in the 160s BC, one of the Hasmonean kings (descendants of the Maccabees) decided to reconquer this territory and impose the Jewish religion, including circumcision, on the pagan inhabitants.

The Hasmonean high priest or king who invited the Romans into Palestine, Hyrcanus II, chose an Idumaean named Antipater as his chief advisor. Antipater, like Hyrcanus II, cultivated close bonds with his Roman patrons.

The man who appears in the Christmas story as Herod, commonly called "the Great," was the son of Antipater. His mother was a pagan, an Arab princess. From the Jewish point of view, the Idumaeans were not true Jews in the first place. So the offspring of an Idumaean and a Gentile would be, at best, a half-pseudo-Jew.

But what Herod the Great lacked in pedigree he made up for in energy, ambition, and shrewdness. In response to political strife in the Holy Land, he fled to Rome, where he managed to get himself crowned king of the Jews. He then returned to Palestine and fought for recognition of his title, which he successfully achieved. He then imposed his authority with an iron fist.

Now the confusion begins. Herod the Great had five wives. Two of them had the same first name, Mariamne, and both happened to be descendants of high priests. These five women bore Herod eleven children. Two of them, sons of different mothers, had the same first name, Philip. The daughter of one of these Philips, Salome, married the other Philip, her half-uncle. Another of Herod the Great's granddaughters, Herodias (who, to add to the confusion, was also Salome's mother), divorced one half-uncle, Herod Philip, to marry another half-uncle, Herod Antipas. It was the denunciation of this incestuous union that cost John the Baptist his head. The dancer who asked for his head was Salome. The one who put her up to it was her mother, Herodias.

When Herod the Great died in 4 BC and his will was opened, it was discovered that he had bestowed the double portion of his realm, Judea and Samaria, upon his son Archelaus. The remaining half of his realm he split. A fourth was bequeathed to Archelaus' full brother, Herod Antipas, and the other fourth to their half brother Philip, Salome's husband. The title bestowed on these lesser rulers was *tetrarch*, derived from the Greek word for "a quarter." Herod Antipas ruled Galilee and Perea while Philip ruled what is now the Golan Heights (then called Gaulinitis) and the far north territory at the foot of Mount Hermon, called Paneas. There Philip founded a city that he named in honor of both Caesar and himself: Caesarea Philippi.

So what became of Archelaus, mentioned in Matthew 2:22? He was so hated from the beginning that a delegation of Jews from Judea went to Rome to beg Augustus to sack him and give them a Roman governor instead. Augustus wanted to give Archelaus a chance, out of respect for the will of his old friend Herod. But Archelaus' rule was so brutal and inept that in AD 6, after ten years of misery, both the Jews and the emperor had had enough. Archelaus was exiled to Gaul (modern France), and at last the Jews were given what they asked for—a Roman governor. Pontius Pilate was the fifth such governor, coming to power in AD 26 or 27. He lasted until AD 36 or 37, when he was removed by the new emperor, Caligula. Herod Antipas met the same fate around the same time.

So who is the King Herod who appears in the Acts of the Apostles (12:1-23), the one responsible for executing the

(continued)

apostle James and putting Peter in prison? This is Herod Agrippa I, grandson of Herod the Great. Herod Agrippa ruled with the title of king from AD 41 till his sudden death, described in Acts 12, in AD 44. The last in the Herodian line was his son, Herod Agrippa II, who appears to have been moved by Paul's preaching in Caesarea Maritima in Acts 26. Paul's appeal to Agrippa to accept the gospel was respectful and compelling. But apparently, to accept it would have cost Agrippa much; at his side sat his sister Bernice, with whom he was living in an openly incestuous union.

Herod Agrippa II was still on the throne when the revolt of the Jews against Rome broke out in AD 66. He and Bernice remained loyal to Rome.

JOSEPH: WALKING BY FAITH

As Herod hatches his murderous scheme to eliminate the newborn King, Joseph has another dream. He is warned of the brewing storm and told to flee the country and seek refuge in Egypt. Yet another leap of faith is demanded. Yet another long and arduous journey.

Back in Nazareth, it must have been hard enough for Joseph to have trusted his first dream and believed Mary's story of her virginal conception. But then follow hardship after hardship. If this child is so special, why does everything seem to keep going wrong? About a hundred-mile journey to Bethlehem. No room in the inn. And now this—a horde of soldiers coming for the child and the only path to safety a few-hundred-mile walk to Egypt, where they must hide among the Gentiles like refugees.

We don't know if Joseph was tempted to second-guess his dreams. I know I would have. Yet the remarkable thing about Joseph is that, in response to these trials, he is recorded as saying not one single word. The only thing recorded is his obedience and his walking. The two are actually related. Abraham, the model of faith in the Old Testament, was told by God to leave everything and march into the desert. Genesis 12:4 records his response: "So Abram went." Paul speaks of faith not so much as a feeling but as the obedient action of putting one foot in front of another: "We walk by faith, not by sight" (2 Corinthians 5:7).

Over a hundred miles to Bethlehem. Two hundred and fifty miles to Egypt. Another three hundred miles back to Nazareth.[24] Joseph kept on believing and kept on walking. Even in the dark.

A STORY OF OBEDIENCE

As Luke puts Mary forward as a model of faith, so Matthew puts forth Joseph. The irony is that they both, in their obedience, do no more than follow in the footsteps of the divine Word, whose obedience precedes and empowers their own. This bread from heaven, born as their child, becomes subject to them as his parents. In a paradox of mind-boggling proportions, creatures now become mentors to the Creator.

CHAPTER 3

NAZARETH

THE TOWN AND ITS NAME

Unlike Bethlehem, Nazareth had little to brag about before Jesus made it famous. It was a relatively recent settlement dating back only about two hundred years before the time of Christ.

The Northern Kingdom had been devastated by the Assyrian conquest in the eighth century BC. Between the horrible slaughter that came with war and the subsequent exile of the surviving leadership, the area had been depopulated. Around 200 BC, Jews from Judea came to Galilee to recolonize the ancient tribal lands of Zebulun and Naphtali. This might be the origin of the name Nazareth, derived from the Hebrew word *netser*, "offshoot," like a colony or settlement.

But since its planting, this tiny colony had not grown very much by the time Joseph and Mary returned there with their son. First-century Nazareth covered only about four acres. It consisted of about fifty houses of extended families, maybe three hundred to five hundred people. It really wasn't much more than a backwater agricultural hamlet. That's why it is never mentioned in the Old Testament and why Nathanael, on hearing that Jesus of Nazareth was the messiah, remarks flippantly to Philip, "Can anything good come out of Nazareth?" (John 1:46).

Matthew sees significance in the fact that Nazareth is Jesus' hometown: "And he went and dwelt in a city called Nazareth, that what was spoken by the prophets might be fulfilled. 'He shall be called a Nazarene' " (Matthew 2:23). Here Matthew seems to be broadly alluding to a few Scripture passages rather than directly quoting a particular text. Since *Nazarene* can mean offshoot, it harkens back to an ancient prophecy regarding the Davidic dynasty, whose trunk had been cut down to the roots: "There shall come forth a shoot from the stump of Jesse" (Isaiah 11:1).

But *Nazarene* can also be read to suggest *Nazirite*, someone set apart and consecrated to God by a special vow, like Samson (Judges 13:4-5) or Samuel (1 Samuel 1:11). Although there is no evidence that Jesus was a Nazirite, his presentation in the Temple was a spiritual consecration, fulfilling the angel's announcement to Mary that "the child to be born will be called holy" (Luke 1:35).[25]

FAMILY

People have often lamented that we know so little about Jesus' thirty or so years in Nazareth. But we actually know much more than is commonly thought. We know enough about everyday life in a Jewish town in this era to paint a helpful picture of these years, what part they play in the work Jesus came to do, and what significance they hold for us.

First, we have to adjust our view of the Holy Family. The artistic renderings of the Holy Family feature just Jesus, Mary, and Joseph. Yet, except for their stays in Bethlehem and in Egypt, Jesus, Mary, and Joseph were seldom alone.

The first-century homes that have been excavated in Nazareth are what archaeologists call courtyard homes. Picture a rectangular wall surrounding a compound. As you walk through the entryway, there is an open courtyard. Built against the inside of the walls enclosing the compound are several one-story structures of one or two rooms each. Some are storage rooms; others are living quarters. Still others are for the few animals the residents own.

People cook and congregate during most of the year outside in the courtyard. Grandparents reside in one structure, a brother with his wife and children in another structure, another brother with his family in another. Sabbath meals are eaten together. The people in the compounds next door are also relatives with whom you attend synagogue on the Sabbath and travel to Jerusalem for the great feasts. Just about everybody in Nazareth seems to be related to you in some way.

We don't know whether Jesus' grandparents were alive when he was growing up or whether, if alive, they lived in the same courtyard house as Jesus. This would have been quite normal.[26] We do know the names of some of the kin he grew up with: "Is not this the carpenter, the son of Mary and brother of James and Joses and Judas and Simon?" (Mark 6:3).

Though in Greek, the language of the New Testament, there is a distinct word for "cousin," in Aramaic, the everyday language of Jesus' world, there is not. The generic word for "brothers and sisters" refers to both siblings and cousins. The fact that cousins often were raised together in the same courtyard house makes this lack of precision a little more understandable.

The Christian community, from at least the second century, expressed their belief that Jesus was the only son of Mary. This has been taught authoritatively through the centuries by the Catholic and Orthodox Churches. The interpretation of "brothers of the Lord" to mean his kinsmen is supported by an often-missed biblical fact. In Matthew 27:55-56 and Mark 15:40, another Mary is mentioned at the foot of Jesus' cross, and she is identified as the mother of James[27] and Joses (or Joseph), two of those identified as Jesus' "brothers" in Mark. John mentions that Jesus' mother was at the foot of the Cross along with one of her sisters (John 19:25). John does not mention the name of this aunt of Jesus, but it may correspond to the Mary mentioned in Matthew and Mark who is the mother of James and Joses. This would confirm that these two men were Jesus' cousins.

THE PILGRIMAGE FEASTS

Understanding the rhythm of the great feasts of Israel is critical to helping us appreciate how Jesus experienced life both in Nazareth and later during the public ministry. There were three ancient pilgrimage feasts that all male Israelites thirteen and older attended: Passover and the Feast of Unleavened Bread in the spring; Pentecost, the Feast of Weeks, about fifty days later; and Sukkot, the Feast of Booths or Tabernacles,[28] in the fall (Exodus 23:14-17; Leviticus 23:4-44). Each feast lasted a week, and men traveled to Jerusalem for the celebration, often with their families. From Nazareth to Jerusalem is about a hundred miles, about five days of walking. Thus, the feast, including travel time, took nearly three weeks. If pilgrims were ritually impure through contact with Gentiles or with a corpse, they had to arrive in Jerusalem a week early to purify themselves before the feast. That made the feast experience last nearly a month.

Women and small children were not obligated to attend, but Luke tells us that it was the custom of Jesus, Mary, and Joseph to go to Jerusalem together for Passover (Luke 2:41); he does not mention how they observed the other feasts. Particularly devout Jews would bring the whole family whenever possible and would also try to attend the more recent (and therefore not obligatory) feast of Hanukkah in December. This joyous feast, celebrating the rededication of the Temple under Judas Maccabeus, had many of the same features as the Feast of Booths, including processing with palm and willow branches and joyfully shouting "Hosanna."

People traveled to these feasts in large groups of family and townspeople forming caravans. The whole journey had a festive air. People would tell stories at campfires each night along the way and meet up with friends and family from far and wide who were also coming to Jerusalem for the feast. As they streamed toward the Temple and ascended the southern steps, they would sing pilgrimage psalms together.[29] Passing through the Huldah gates, they entered the Temple plaza, which was already crowded with excited throngs of pilgrims.

On the first night of the Festival, the Temple courts would be thronged with thousands of people watching the righteous men of the assembly dancing before the Lord with torches in their hands. It was said that he who has not experienced the festivities of the Feast of Booths "has never seen rejoicing in his life."[30]

Such shared experiences tightly bonded people together and united them around Jerusalem and the Temple. Each feast was something to look forward to amid the hard work of everyday life.

THE FINDING OF JESUS IN THE TEMPLE

When you understand the extended-family, caravan dynamic of these journeys, you can see how Jesus could have been left behind in Jerusalem when the group left to return to Nazareth after the conclusion of Passover festivities. With the caravan strung out in a long line on the road, Mary thought Jesus was with Joseph. Joseph thought he was with his cousins and uncles. It was only at the first caravan stop when everyone finally gathered together that they discovered he was missing.

The story of the losing and finding of Jesus in the Temple illustrates not only how human the Holy Family was but also how extraordinary Jesus is. When Mary and Joseph finally find him among the teachers, listening and asking the sages questions, Mary is understandably upset and asks a different sort of question: "Son, why have you treated us so? Behold, your father and I have been looking for you anxiously." To this Jesus replies, "Did you not know that I must be in my Father's house?" (Luke 2:48-49).

Mary says "your father" referring to Joseph. Jesus speaks of "my Father" referring to God. To call God one's Father was not normal in Israel, as we will discuss further in chapter 8. Jesus had remained behind because he had an intense hunger for God. If the Temple was God's dwelling place on earth, why would

Jesus ever want to leave it? And having a fully human intellect, he yearned to learn more about his Father as well—there was nothing more important for him to learn than the ways of God. Even at age twelve, he was conscious of his unique Sonship, his special bond with the one he called his Father.

Following this exchange, Luke writes, "He went down with them and came to Nazareth, and was obedient to them" (Luke 2:51).

JOSEPH AS MENTOR

"And Jesus increased in wisdom and in stature, and in favor with God and man" (Luke 2:52).

This comment is important for two reasons: It points back to the story of the prophet Samuel, who is described the same way (1 Samuel 2:26). And it also makes plain that Jesus, despite his origins "from above," despite his absolutely unique Sonship, must still grow and develop intellectually and spiritually.

As fascinating as the sages were at the Temple, Jesus' most important teacher and mentor in things human and spiritual is Joseph.

Clearly, Joseph is not the biological father of Jesus. In Christian tradition, he is commonly referred to as Jesus' foster father. But today, at least in America, a foster father does not necessarily accept his foster child as his own, take full financial and legal responsibility for the child, give the child his own name, and make him his legal heir. This is what an adoptive father does. And it is precisely what Joseph does for Jesus. Jesus' Davidic lineage is established by the ancestry of his legal father, who is of the tribe of Judah.[31]

It is important to remember that genes are not all that parents pass on to their children. We now know just how profoundly a child's emotional health, self-concept, and personality are shaped in the first few years of life by his or her parents.

In Jesus' time, mothers would spend the most time with both sons and daughters when they were infants and toddlers. But fathers and other adult relatives would increasingly take the lead in the formation of sons as they moved into boyhood and approached adolescence. Adult men would involve their sons in both prayer and work as soon as the boys were able to talk and do simple chores.

The amount of time children spent with their parents, uncles, and grandparents was much greater at that time than is typical now in the West. The influence of the father and other male relatives on a boy's formation was thus much greater than it commonly is today. Fathers didn't "go to work" for most of the day and then see their sons only when they came home. Nor did children typically spend most of the day at school, away from their parents. In Jesus' day, men often worked at or near home and brought their sons with them to work.

Much more is transmitted by this kind of constant contact than just ideas or the skills of a trade. A whole way of looking at the world—attitudes, patterns of thinking and speaking, gestures, and habits—are imparted by one generation to another. Jesus had to learn to be a man; this he learned largely from Joseph, with strong assistance from his uncles and perhaps grandfathers.[32]

SPIRITUAL MENTORSHIP

To this day in Orthodox Jewish circles, men and women usually pray separately. If you go to the Western Wall of Jerusalem, you will see that it is divided into two sections, with two separate entrances, one for men, the other for women. A low wall separates the two.

This was very much the case, perhaps more so, in first-century Palestine. The Temple itself had a Court of the Women where ritually pure Israelite men and women could pray. Closer to the altar and the sanctuary there was the Court of Israel, where only ritually pure Israelite men could pray.

There were traditional daily prayers obligatory for men; women's prayer requirements were somewhat different. Men were obliged to fulfill all the prescriptions of the Law, including the three pilgrimage feasts. Women were not.[33] Men could read the Torah aloud as lectors in the synagogue; women could not.[34]

This meant that fathers were the overall spiritual leaders of their families. Fathers took the lead in teaching prayer, Torah, and religious duties to their sons.

DAILY PRAYER

For Jesus and all Jews, the most important commandment is this:

> Hear, O Israel: The LORD our God is one LORD; and you shall love the LORD your God with all your heart, and with all your soul, and with all your might. And these words which I command you this day shall be upon your heart; and you shall teach them diligently to your children, and shall talk of them when you sit in your house, and when you walk by the way, and when you lie down, and when you rise. (Deuteronomy 6:4-7)

The first part of this passage became the *Shema*, the great creed of Israel—that God is one. The command to love God with all of one's being, which follows the creed, is the Great Commandment. The call to keep these words on one's heart means that the creed and the commandment were recited often. This was not done in Aramaic, the everyday language of the people at that time, but in Hebrew, the ancient language of the Torah. Most likely the Hebrew words of the *Shema* were the first thing whispered into the ear of a newborn and the last words of a dying Jew.[35]

How often was the *Shema* to be recited? Because of the command in the text to "talk of them … when you lie down, and when you rise," the sages of Israel agreed on a bare minimum of twice a day—early in the morning soon after rising and at night before going to sleep.

There is no doubt that Mary recited the *Shema* often. There is a beautiful statue in Jerusalem in the Church of St. Anne, Mary's mother, of Mary as a young girl learning the *Shema* at her mother's feet. Undoubtedly, she whispered this prayer into the ear of her newborn son.

Yet the obligation to recite the *Shema* at least twice a day was for men only. So it was the duty of a father to teach the *Shema* to his son and to pray it with him daily. And since Jews would never think of praying without thanking and blessing God, a beautiful series of blessings developed to be recited before and after the *Shema*. The prayer before the *Shema* was known as the *Birkat Yotser*, a "doorway of praise."[36] It was also said in Hebrew. Since it was recited at both dawn and dusk, it extolled the Lord as the creator of sun and stars. And since the holy angels never cease praising the Lord, it joined the angelic chorus in singing, "Holy, holy, holy is the LORD of hosts; the whole earth is full of his glory" (Isaiah 6:3).[37] The inclusion of this Sanctus in the Eucharistic liturgy of the early Church is a testimony of the profound continuity between Jewish and Christian liturgies.

An additional custom of daily prayer was well established by the time of Jesus. We see it attested in the book of Daniel, written about two hundred years before. Daniel's enemies wanted to get him condemned by the king. So they induced King Darius to issue a decree that no one was to pray to any god but Darius for the next thirty days. They knew that Daniel faithfully prayed three times a day to his God and would not heed this idolatrous decree. Therefore, all they needed to do was to go to his home during his set hours of prayer. They were certain they would find him praying on his knees in front of an open window facing Jerusalem. And this is how they got him thrown into the lion's den (Daniel 6:10-17).

This thrice-daily prayer came to be known simply as "the prayer," or the *Tefilluh*. It was prayed in the morning at the time of the morning sacrifice in the Temple; again at 3:00 PM, the hour of the evening sacrifice; and finally at sundown, when the Temple gates were closed. It was not considered an absolute obligation for first-century Jews, but to pray the *Tefillah* in this way was a sign of special piety and so was standard for Pharisees and other devout Jews, including women.[38]

The afternoon hour of prayer was heralded by a loud trumpet blast from the pinnacle of the Jerusalem Temple. In this way people outside the Temple courts could join in the prayer as the sacrifice was being offered on the altar. Jesus' words about hypocrites who loved to pray on street corners probably refer to this. Some people appear to have conveniently arranged to be in a public place at 3:00 PM so that they could show everyone how pious they were (see Matthew 6:5).

The earliest written text we have for the *Tefillah* comes from a few hundred years after Jesus' time, but scholars have identified the parts of that prayer that were most likely prayed in the first century. Some of the distinct and characteristic phrases of this prayer are echoed in several sayings of Jesus in the Gospels, so there is little doubt that this prayer was an integral part of his prayer life.

The *Tefillah* was ingrained in the consciousness of every devout Israelite. Two notable petitions of this prayer praise God as the one who heals the sick and who raises the dead. This helps us appreciate what pious Jews must have thought when they heard reports of Jesus of Nazareth doing these very things.[39]

OBSERVING THE SABBATH AND READING TORAH

As pious Jews, Jesus and his family would have observed the Sabbath. That meant rest from work, a festive Sabbath meal, and a synagogue service. No meal in Jesus' home would take place without a blessing before and another after the meal. At the outset of the meal, Joseph would recite this over the bread: "Blessed are you, Lord our God, King of the universe, you who have brought bread forth from the earth." On feast days and perhaps on Sabbaths, if the family could afford it, Joseph would likewise bless the wine: "Blessed are you, Lord our God, King of the universe, you who created the fruit of the vine."[40] After giving thanks to God and blessing him over the food, the people considered the food duly blessed.

Though Nazareth was a poor community and very small, it did have a synagogue, and it was the custom of Jesus and his family to go there for Sabbath service (Luke 4:16). We have no written outline of the Sabbath service from that time, but it was essentially a service of prayer and readings from both the Torah, the first five books of the Hebrew Scriptures (our Old Testament), and the prophets. The *Shema* would be recited in Hebrew along with some of the prayers we have already mentioned, and a homily of sorts would be given in Aramaic, followed by an Aramaic prayer called the *Kaddish*.

Synagogues at this time were not sacred spaces of worship like the Temple. From what we can tell, they were mainly community centers where the men could study and discuss Torah and pray together, and it seems they were most often led by ordinary laymen rather than by priests or scribes. Any male Israelite over the age of thirteen could have the privilege of reading and commenting on the Scriptures, as Jesus did soon after his baptism in the Jordan (Luke 4:18-30). Jairus, whose dead daughter was raised by Jesus, was such a lay synagogue leader (Luke 8:41).

To read in the synagogue, a man would obviously have to be literate. Did Jesus go to school? It is unlikely that a formal school existed in a hamlet as tiny as Nazareth. There may have been some opportunity for Jesus to advance his Hebrew and Torah-reading skills in the synagogue in Nazareth, but there is no evidence that he studied formally under a master, as did the scribes. The only training in the Torah that we are sure he had was the two days he spent at the Temple at age twelve and the indispensable mentoring he received from Joseph. The primary responsibility for teaching him to pray and read Hebrew was Joseph's. His influence on the intellectual and spiritual formation of his son, and therefore on his son's disciples then and now, is incalculable.[41]

MENTORING IN WORK

We traditionally refer to Joseph as a carpenter. But the Greek word used to describe the trade of both Joseph and Jesus is *tektōn*, which refers to a builder who worked with both wood and stone. This is much heavier work than fine carpentry or furniture making, though that may have also been part of their work.

Jesus would have begun as his father's helper at a quite young age and, when he was older, would have been his father's apprentice. His goal would have been to learn to do everything his father could do.

Men of this occupation would often travel to where the work was. With Nazareth being so small, it is likely that Joseph traveled for work, and Jesus, at least by the time of adolescence, would have traveled with him. One of the largest and most cosmopolitan towns of Galilee was not far from Nazareth, only about an hour's walk. Sepphoris was a capital of Galilee when Jesus was born. When he was about ten, there was an uprising that led to the destruction of the city, which then had to be rebuilt. There would have been lots of work for builders for many years afterward.

One final thing about Jesus' education. Nazareth was entirely an agricultural village. Even people who had a trade, like Joseph, most likely had a garden and some animals. Jesus' teachings display his intimate knowledge of the growing of grain, grapes, and olives and the pastoral life of shepherds and sheep. His familiarity with these things was most likely obtained by work and not just by observation. He would have learned to tend animals and cultivate a garden from both Joseph and Mary.

THE FINAL YEARS IN NAZARETH

After Joseph and Mary find Jesus in the Temple, the Gospels do not mention Joseph again. There is little doubt that he died sometime between Jesus' twelfth year and the beginning of Jesus' public ministry. How many years Jesus had with him we do not know. What we do know is that Joseph was alive through the most crucial years of Jesus' formation in the prayers and commandments prior to his thirteenth birthday.

Jesus was celibate, as was his cousin, John the Baptist. Jesus would have lived with and provided for his widowed mother before his baptism. The closeness between mother and son that began in Jesus' infancy must have developed considerably during those years together.

THE MEANING OF INCARNATION

"And the Word became flesh" (John 1:14). The term *incarnation* literally comes from the word "flesh." Sometimes we think of the Incarnation primarily as the divine Word being joined to a human body. But the Incarnation means much more than that. It means that the Word of God unites himself with a full human nature, including a human mind and personality that needs to grow just as a body does.

This means that the Son of God fully entered into every aspect of human experience, including the relational experience of being a son, a grandson, a cousin, a friend, a student, and a worker. It means he passed through and experienced each of the many stages of life.

The Incarnation did not simply make it possible for the Son of God to die on the Cross to reconcile the world. Redemption means atonement: "*at-one*-ment." From the beginning of human history, men and women have chosen to walk away from God (Genesis 3). Sin is not so much an offense on a lawbook as it is the rupture of a relationship, when one party turns its back on another. The gulf between God and humanity opened up through the sin of the first man and woman, and the alienation widened with each person's decision to make the same sort of choice. What was needed was reconciliation, the restoration of unity between God and mankind, between the divine and the human. While the sacrifice of the Cross would have a critical role to play, Fathers of the Church such as St. Irenaeus saw "at-one-ment" as having begun even before the Cross, in the very act of the Son of God uniting himself to human nature in the womb of Mary.

The work of redemption and atonement continued as the "Word made flesh" walked through all the stages of human life, healing, sanctifying, and ennobling each of them. Family, learning, work—to all these things Jesus gave new meaning and beauty through the obedient years of silence and hard work in Nazareth.

The Second Vatican Council put it well. Through what happened in Bethlehem and Nazareth, "the Son of God has united Himself in some fashion with every man. He worked with human hands, He thought with a human mind, acted by human choice and loved with a human heart. Born of the Virgin Mary, He has truly been made one of us, like us in all things except sin."[42]

CHAPTER 4

IN THE DESERT
PREPARE THE WAY

THE JUDEAN WILDERNESS

The Holy Land is a place of dramatic contrasts. The hill country of Judea, a few miles west of Jerusalem, is lush and green with pines, vineyards, and almond trees. But the ancient name of Jerusalem, Zion, means "dryness." Less than a mile from the Jerusalem Temple, on the east side of the Mount of Olives, the desert begins. From half a mile high, the wilderness gradually descends for sixteen miles until it reaches the lowest place on earth, the Dead Sea.

For most, "desert" brings up images of the Sahara, a sea of sand rippled with waves of dunes. The Judean wilderness is not at all like that. It is wild, rough country, with plunging ravines and craggy peaks. It is this rugged, bleak desert that the prophet Isaiah had in mind as he proclaimed this oracle:

> A voice cries: "In the wilderness prepare the way of the LORD, make straight in the desert a highway for our God. Every valley shall be lifted up, and every mountain and hill be made low; the uneven ground shall become level, and the rough places a plain. And the glory of the LORD shall be revealed, and all flesh shall see it together." (Isaiah 40:3-5)

A VOICE IN THE DESERT

For many, these words immediately call to mind John the Baptist. But John was not the first to make this passage his motto. Less than ten miles from the place John baptized the multitudes, there lived a mysterious community made famous by the sensational discovery of their library, known to the world as the Dead Sea Scrolls. They called themselves the Yahad, meaning "the community." From about 162 BC to AD 68, they lived an intense life of prayer, work, and study at Qumran, some twenty miles from Jerusalem on the northwest shore of the Dead Sea.[43]

The reason these men had withdrawn to such a harsh, desolate place is that they viewed the Temple and its chief priests as hopelessly corrupt. The community was founded about the time that Judas Maccabeus' brother Jonathan proclaimed himself high priest and king. He was of the wrong family to be high priest. This, together with his love of money and political power, caused great scandal. Some priests of the traditional high priestly clan, the line of Zadok (descendants of Moses' brother Aaron), refused to attend sacrifices and feasts in Jerusalem. They and their followers fled to the desert to live a life of purity and penance, preparing the way for the Lord and fulfilling, they believed, the words of Isaiah 40:3-5.[44]

There is a certain eerie beauty about Qumran, and there was a certain beauty about the community that lived here.[45] These men loved prayer and loved God's word, studying it day and night. In their devotion to learning, they collected and copied not only the inspired books of what we now call the Old Testament but also biblical commentaries that show us how some Jews interpreted the Scriptures at that time. They also collected other books of spiritual wisdom written between the times of the Old and the New Testaments that shed great light on Jewish life and hopes at the time of Jesus.

Something else is also striking about this community. Its members were preoccupied with ritual purity. This was a broad tendency that had been developing among Jews in Palestine over

The Discovery of the Dead Sea Scrolls

For centuries, people knew that ruins existed in a desolate area near the northwest shore of the Dead Sea. Many assumed they were remains of a Roman fortress. But shortly after World War II, some Bedouin shepherds ventured into one of the natural caves in the hills above the ruins. The scrolls they discovered there were determined to be biblical texts about two thousand years old. The news of this discovery sparked a race between Bedouins and archaeologists to explore 273 holes and caves in the nearby cliffs, searching for any writings and artifacts they might contain.[46]

Decades of exploration and study revealed that the scrolls included copies of at least part of every book of the Old Testament except Esther. These texts were about nine hundred years older than any other surviving copy of the Hebrew Scriptures. Many writings from the community, the Yahad, that had assembled this library were also found, detailing their way of life and their beliefs.

The ruins near the caves were simultaneously excavated. As the desert sands were removed from the surface, an ancient community complex was revealed, complete with a dining room, rooms for studying and copying texts, and an extensive network of ritual baths, cisterns, and water channels.

The idea that the ruins had been a Roman fort was not completely mistaken. When the Jews of Palestine revolted against Rome in AD 66, the Romans sent several legions to Palestine to quell the rebellion. Before the Roman armies arrived in AD 68, the Yahad evidently hid their library in the nearby caves, expecting to retrieve the scrolls after the enemy had been defeated.

But it was the Romans, not the Jews, who proved victorious; any community members who survived the massacre at Qumran would have perished with the last holdouts in Jerusalem or at Masada. There was probably no one left to return and recover the library. And if any had returned, they would have found their beloved community transformed into a Roman fort. So the trove of documents lay hidden for nearly two thousand years.

the two hundred years before Jesus. Ritual washing of some kind had been prescribed in the Old Testament in a general sort of way for women after childbirth (Leviticus 12:1-8), for priests before officiating in the Temple (Exodus 30:17-21), and for all Israelites after touching a corpse (Numbers 19:11-12).

But oral traditions that had developed since about 200 BC vastly increased the requirements for such washing, requiring full immersion in special baths filled with water collected in particular ways. The members of the Qumran community took this to an extreme, requiring all members—priests, Levites, and laymen— to fully immerse themselves in a *mikveh*, or ritual bath, before each meal. As a result, the Qumran complex is full of ritual baths.

The preoccupation with purity had another consequence. To remain pure, the members of the community had to stay aloof from everyone who failed to live up to its standards, including Gentiles, sinners, and people with physical blemishes—indeed, from anyone who did not belong to the community.

It was actually considered a solemn duty at Qumran to curse sinners and a duty of the righteous to swear "everlasting hatred for all the men of perdition."[47] When Jesus said, "You have heard that it was said, 'You shall love your neighbor and hate your enemy.' But I say to you ..." (Matthew 5:43-44), he was referring to sentiments such as these.

The piety of the Qumran Yahad was unusually rigorous, but the emphasis on protecting oneself from ritual contamination, a kind of holiness by segregation, was widespread in Israel at this time, especially among the Pharisees. The messages of John the Baptist and Jesus were radically different.

JOHN THE BAPTIST

In or about AD 28, a dramatic figure with an urgent message appears on the banks of the Jordan River less than ten miles north of Qumran. His theme is the same theme as that of the

Qumran community. He sees himself as a voice crying out in the wilderness, "Prepare the way of the Lord!"

Luke tells us that this is John, the son of the priest Zechariah and his wife Elizabeth, who had conceived him in her old age through a special intervention of God. The family home is in the hill country of Judea, on the west side of the mountain range. It is verdant, with terraced hillsides covered with grapes. Yet Luke makes a curious statement immediately after the account of John's birth, saying, "And he was in the wilderness till the day of his manifestation to Israel" (Luke 1:80).

What would a child be doing growing up in the desert? We are told by Josephus that the Essenes were known to take "other men's children, while yet pliable and docile ... and mould them in accordance with their own principles."[40] There are other curious facts about John to consider: He was born of elderly parents who may have died during his childhood, he was a priest but is never mentioned as functioning as such in the Temple, he has exactly the same biblical motto as the Qumran community, and he launched his ministry less than ten miles from Qumran. All things considered, it is likely that he had some significant contact with the group that many associate with the Essenes, and perhaps he lived there for a season of his life.

ELIJAH THE PROPHET

There had been many sages in the two centuries before John's appearance. The author of the book of Sirach was a wise man of the second century BC. Rabbinic literature tells us of Hillel and Shammai, great teachers in Jerusalem in the time of Herod the Great, and Gamaliel, the Jerusalem rabbi who was a mentor to Saul of Tarsus. But no one is recognized during this period as a prophet. In fact, there was a widespread perception that prophecy had died out in Israel. It was an evil age, the age of Belial, as the Qumran documents put it, and most people thought God's Spirit had withdrawn because of Israel's sin.

Yet John comes clothed like the prophet Elijah (2 Kings 1:8), in camel hair with a leather belt around his waist. Jews were aware of the promise at the very end of Malachi (4:5), that the Lord would send Elijah back before the Day of the Lord. It is significant that the spot where John was baptizing, opposite Jericho, near the Jordan's ingress to the Dead Sea, is where Elijah was assumed into heaven (2 Kings 2:4-14).

The Gospels, and Josephus as well, testify that large crowds flocked to see this new prophet.[49] Many came from Perea,[50] the Jewish region along the east bank of the Jordan, and some even made the twenty-mile journey from Jerusalem to be baptized by him.

SADDUCEES AND PHARISEES

Representatives of two Jewish groups are specifically mentioned as coming to see John (Matthew 3:7). The Sadducees assembled around the high priest and his family and around a group known as the chief priests—the permanent, full-time clergy in charge of running the Jerusalem Temple. The Sadducees included laymen too, landed gentry who belonged to a small group of the leading families of Israel.

So the Sadducees were the official clerical and social elite, centered in Jerusalem. Controlling the Temple and its treasury, they were the wealthy Jewish aristocrats who served as the liaison between the people and their Roman overlords. As one might imagine, the common people were generally cool to them, sometimes cynical and even hostile.[51]

Then there were the Pharisees, a renewal group largely of lay people, whose name most probably comes from the word meaning "separated" or "holy." They did not go to the same lengths as the Qumran community in physically sequestering themselves from sinners. However, they too sought to uphold uncompromising standards of piety, ritual purity, and tithing and to call all Israel to ever-greater holiness. They disagreed with the Sadducees on the theology of the afterlife and on such things as

Priests and Levites

In reading the Gospels, we run across various leaders in Jewish life. Priests and Levites, who served in the Temple, were among the most important. The main role of the priest was to offer sacrifices for the people, while the Levites assisted as singers, doorkeepers, and guards in the Temple precincts.

In ancient Israel, the vocations of priest and Levite were strictly hereditary. There was no need for seminary training. If your father was of the tribe of Levi, you were born a Levite. If you could prove that your father was also a descendant of Aaron and your mother was an Israelite of pure ancestry, you were a priest from birth, as was John the Baptist.

Both the priests and the most important Levites, the singers, had to demonstrate their privileged lineage back four or five generations. When a young priest reached the age of twenty, he would bring his genealogical documents to the Sanhedrin, the governing political and judicial assembly made up of eminent Jews, which met in the Temple. They would examine the documents and would also make sure that the young man was without physical deformity. If everything was in order, the young man would be ordained by being vested with priestly robes. Then he could begin fulfilling his priestly functions. His father or another experienced priest would show him how to carry out the rituals.

Israel's sacrificial worship could be carried out only in the Jerusalem Temple. About eight thousand priests and ten thousand Levites lived in the Holy Land at the time of Jesus; they were organized into twenty-four groups that took week-long turns in Temple service. Each group would travel to the Temple twice a year and serve from one Sabbath to the next. During the three annual pilgrimage feasts, all the priests and Levites would report to the Temple.[52]

During any normal week, then, there would be about three hundred priests and four hundred Levites on duty. During festivals, the number would be close to eighteen thousand! Obviously, there were too many clergy on duty at any given

(continued)

---

time for everyone to be given a function. So each morning, lots were cast as a way to apportion the various liturgical tasks. Those who were not selected to serve turned in their vestments for the day and went home.

Only priests could offer the animal sacrifices on the altar and enter the Holy Place, the central and most sacred building of the Temple complex. The area immediately around the altar and the Holy Place, called the court of the priests, was also restricted to priests. Levite singers would stand on a platform bordering the court of the priests and lead psalms and hymns during the sacrificial service. Levite doorkeepers opened and closed the Temple doors at sunrise and sunset. Other Levites cleaned and policed the Temple area, keeping unauthorized people, like Gentiles, from entering restricted parts of the complex. The Temple guards who arrested Jesus in Gethsemane would have been a detachment of such Levites.

Priests and Levites received a share of the tithes and a portion of sacrificed animals. But since this was not enough to provide them with a living, virtually all of them plied a trade during the forty-six weeks that they were not on Temple duty. We have records of priests who were butchers, builders, stone masons, and professional secretaries or scribes. The latter were obviously educated, but not all priests had advanced training in the Scriptures and the oral "traditions of the fathers."

---

the proper traditions to follow regarding Sabbath observance and purification rites.

Since the time of the Maccabees (around 164 BC), the Pharisees had been a voluntary association of pious Jews, mostly from the merchant and artisan classes, who were dedicated to meticulous observance of the law. In addition to the Law of Moses, they were also zealous for the oral law, the "tradition of the fathers," which laid out precise norms for observing the Sabbath, ritual washing, tithing, daily prayer, and works of charity. Josephus says there were only about six thousand full-fledged Pharisees a generation after the time of Jesus, and this estimate is probably on the high side. But the influence of the Pharisees far exceeded their numbers. They saw themselves as the spiritual elite of the nation, and it appears the people saw them in that light as well. By the time of Jesus, the spirituality and theology of the Pharisees had become the standard for many pious Jews, including those who were not full members of the association.

So the Sadducees were the official leaders of the Jews in Palestine, with ritual and financial power. The Pharisees were the popular leaders, who had the confidence of the people. But these two very different groups had this one thing in common: When they arrived at the Jordan to be baptized by John, he called them a "brood of vipers" (Matthew 3:7).

REPENTANCE IN ISRAEL

John, in the spirit of Elijah, is announcing an imminent judgment of God. If the people are to survive the fiery judgment of the Day of the Lord, they need to make a sincere break with their past lives and be baptized as a sign of their determination to begin anew in total dedication to the will of God. The Greek word used in the Gospels to describe this is *metanoia*, which literally means a change or transformation of mind. John appears to mean by this a profound interior change of heart and mind that finds expression in concrete changes in behavior.

In the Old Testament, there were very specific rules for making reparation for sins committed knowingly or unknowingly. First, complete and total restitution was required. Over and above what was taken, an additional fifth of that total must also be restored plus an expensive animal sacrifice called a sin offering must be made in the Temple, with a portion of the payment going to the priests on duty (Leviticus 5:14–6:7). All this had to be done before forgiveness was obtained.

Certain classes of sinners were considered unable to fulfill these conditions and therefore could never be forgiven. For example, tax collectors typically overcharged so many people so often that, if they wanted to repent, they would never be able to do so. If they could accurately tally up all they owed, which was next to impossible, it would be certainly impossible to pay it all back. So they were hopelessly alienated from God and from the covenant community of Israel.

But John accepts the repentance of tax collectors (Luke 3:12-13), something the Qumran community, the Pharisees, and the Sadducees would never think of doing. And John does not press on them the requirements imposed by the book of Leviticus. Neither does he mention anything about maintaining ritual purity. He calls instead for a true and sincere change of heart expressed outwardly not in ritual action but in justice and charity to one's neighbor. Sharing one's goods with the poor and refraining from overcharging and bullying people—these are the kinds of thing that John recommended as fruits befitting repentance (Luke 3:10-14).

John certainly did not get such a gracious, merciful attitude from Qumran. Could he have gotten it from his father, Zechariah, whose great prophetic canticle (Luke 1:68-79), issued on the day of John's circumcision, spoke of the forgiveness of sin and the tender mercy of our God? Or perhaps John had given the book of Isaiah a deeper reading than his neighbors at Qumran, whose motto and John's own was Isaiah's call to "prepare the way of the Lord." Perhaps John had noticed this text just a few verses before: "Comfort, comfort my people, says your God. Speak tenderly to Jerusalem, and cry to her that her warfare is ended, that her iniquity is pardoned" (Isaiah 40:1-2). We don't know for sure. But while most of Israel believed that the Spirit of God had been quenched, the Holy Spirit had moved John to leap in his mother's womb. He is a prophet and, says Jesus, more than a prophet (Matthew 11:9).

And so the prophet sent by God speaks a stern word to the failed leaders of God's people. They take great pride in their status as sons of Abraham. Rabbinic literature shows that Jews expected Abraham's merits to be accredited to his descendants.[53] Many counted on these merits to stand them in good stead on the Day of Judgment. But God, says John, can raise up children for Abraham from the stones (Luke 3:8). He is not impressed with children of Abraham who have hearts of stone. For all their focus on ritual compliance, the Pharisees and Sadducees who come to the banks of the Jordan show neither a desire for a true change of heart nor a willingness to change their pattern of life. Ironically, tax collectors and sinners do.

HUMILITY AND JOY

Jews had been waiting a long time to see a prophet once more arise in their midst. This would be a sign that the evil age was drawing to a close and God's deliverance was drawing near. John's ministry heightened expectation and enkindled great excitement.

John could have taken advantage of this situation. He could have ridden the wave of popular acclaim right into Tiberias, Herod's great city, or Jerusalem, the city of prophets and kings. But he would not do so. When a delegation of priests and Levites from the Temple came to ask John who he was, he made clear he was neither the messiah, nor the prophet Moses promised in Deuteronomy 18:15, nor Elijah back from the dead (John 1:19-23). He was preparing the way for someone else, a person whose sandal strap he was not worthy to untie (Mark 1:7). He was baptizing merely with water, but the one coming after him would baptize "with the Holy Spirit and with fire" (Luke 3:16).

The extraordinary humility of John comes into even greater focus when Jesus appears in the crowd coming to be baptized. John protests that he should be baptized by Jesus (Matthew 3:14). When some of John's disciples leave him to follow his cousin, his remaining disciples are alarmed and seek to arouse John. But John refuses to be provoked to jealousy. The one who leapt for joy in his mother's womb replies that he is not the bridegroom but the best man. His task has been to lead the bride to her spouse. Mission accomplished, he now rejoices to make a tactful exit and leave the spouses together, united. "This joy of mine is now full. He must increase, but I must decrease" (John 3:29-30).

Decrease he will. Not long after Jesus' encounter with John at the Jordan, John is taken prisoner by Herod, whom he had publicly condemned for stealing Herodias, Herod's brother's wife. In fulfillment of a rash promise made to his stepdaughter, Herod then has John beheaded and John's head presented to his wife on a platter.

At first glance, it might seem strange to regard John as the patron saint of joy. His strident call for repentance and his severely ascetic lifestyle paint a dour picture. There is no hint of the mirth and cheerfulness that we find in a figure like St. Philip Neri, yet John exhibits a profound spiritual joy. Humility has freed him from the frantic compulsion to exalt himself. Both at the beginning and at the end of his life, he is free to delight in the presence of the younger cousin who is his master (John 1:30). Humility gives him the inner peace to spend his entire life preparing for the one "who is to come" (Luke 7:19) and then, when he arrives, to step out of the spotlight and fade from the picture.

CHAPTER 5

BAPTISM AND BATTLE

Matthew tells us that John recognizes one person in particular among the crowds who wade into the Jordan to be baptized. When Jesus comes to be baptized, John objects: "I need to be baptized by you, and do you come to me?" (Matthew 3:14). Jesus' response seems puzzling, "Let it be so now; for thus it is fitting for us to fulfil all righteousness" (Matthew 3:15).

Another word for righteousness is justice. How is it just for someone with no sin to submit to a baptism that is a sign of repentance?

FULFILLING ALL RIGHTEOUSNESS

The divine Word lowered himself to be born in an especially messy place in this very messy world of ours. He now lowers himself even further. In the lowest spot on earth, he submerges himself under the Jordan's waters in a sign of repentance.[54]

We have seen that the Incarnation does not mean simply that the divine Word assumes a human body, but that he completely enters into our life and experience. In justice, humanity needs to humble itself before God and repent of its sin. Jesus so identifies with us that he does this, in the name of all of us, and shows us the path of lowliness and repentance that we ourselves must tread. The early Christian teachers called the Fathers of the Church love to point out that he was not sanctified by the waters. Instead, the Fathers teach, he sanctified the waters of what would become a new kind of baptism, baptism not only with water but also with the Holy Spirit. Some see this as the moment when the sacrament of Baptism is instituted. Before his ascension, Jesus will command that his disciples go and baptize. Here, he inaugurates the sacrament in action by stepping into the waters.

It is just and right that "the pioneer and perfecter of our faith" (Hebrews 12:2) go before us, in perfect solidarity with sinful humanity, a penitent in our place even though he did not sin (Hebrews 4:15).

THE DESCENT OF THE HOLY SPIRIT

When Jesus rises from the water, as countless others have already done, something unique transpires. All four Gospels note that the Holy Spirit can be seen descending upon him like a dove. Matthew, Mark, and Luke add the detail that "the heavens opened" (Matthew 3:16; Mark 1:10; Luke 3:21).

We have seen with the Qumran community that that era was thought to be an evil one, under the dominion of Belial, or the Devil (compare 1 John 5:19). Prophecy, it was thought, had vanished. The Holy Spirit, like the cloud of glory that had once filled the Temple, had withdrawn.

The opening of the heavens and the descent of the Spirit upon Jesus is a sign not only of his unique vocation but also of a dramatic shift in salvation history. It means that the evil age is drawing to a close and the new messianic age is finally dawning. The Holy Spirit is back, descending and remaining upon a person who is therefore most certainly a true prophet and more than a prophet. For though all prophets were inspired by the Spirit, none before Jesus had baptized or immersed other people in the Holy Spirit. Perhaps the prophecy of Joel is about to be fulfilled: "I will pour out my spirit on all flesh" (Joel 2:28).

ANOINTED MESSIAH

In a speech recorded in the Acts of the Apostles (Acts 10:38), Peter makes it clear that he regards the baptism of Jesus as Jesus' anointing.

Jericho, City of Palms

The place where John was baptizing was on the Jordan River opposite Jericho. Eight miles north of Qumran, Jericho is a town with a unique history. We learn from archaeology that it is one of the oldest cities in the world, one of the first places human beings learned to raise crops so they could stop wandering and settle down in one place. It boasts one of the oldest surviving human structures, a tower dating to 8,300 BC, which was already thousands of years old when the Pharaohs built the pyramids. Located just a few miles from the Dead Sea, it is also the lowest city on earth, at 846 feet below sea level.

Joshua was not the first to destroy the town or the last. Jericho, called "the city of palm trees" in the book of Deuteronomy (34:3), was destroyed and rebuilt multiple times over the centuries. It boasts a freshwater spring that gushes abundantly. Made pure and fresh by a miracle worked by the prophet Elisha (2 Kings 2:18-22), this spring makes Jericho an oasis of green in the midst of the unforgiving Judean desert. Moses and Joshua must have recognized it as fitting the description of the land promised by God to the Israelites. Its grass could be converted by sheep and goats into abundant milk, and its palm trees yielded dates that could be boiled down to produce a sweet, thick syrup known as date honey. Truly Jericho appeared as "a land flowing with milk and honey" (Exodus 3:8). To tribes struggling to survive in the brutal conditions of the desert, it would have been a tempting prize.

About six miles to the east is the Jordan River and the place Jesus was baptized by John. The setting sun casts the shadow of a lofty mountain on the town. Known as the Mount of Temptation, it is where, according to an ancient tradition, Jesus was shown the kingdoms of the world by Satan.

Jesus sees it this way as well; after his baptism, at the synagogue at Nazareth, he refers back to his Jordan experience when he says that the words of Isaiah 61 have been fulfilled: "The Spirit of the Lord is upon me, because he has anointed me" (Luke 4:18).

In the Old Testament, priests, kings, and at least some prophets, like Elisha, were literally anointed with a specially perfumed olive oil (Exodus 30:22-33) that Christian tradition came to call chrism. A person so anointed was especially consecrated for God's service and given power for that service by the Holy Spirit. Soon after Saul was anointed king, he prophesied, filled with the Holy Spirit. The oil which Samuel used to anoint David was placed in a horn, a symbol of the strength that would be conferred through the anointing. From the moment that the chrism touched his head, "the Spirit of the LORD came mightily upon David" (1 Samuel 10:6-13; 16:1-13).

But doesn't Jesus already have the Spirit? After all, he was conceived when his mother was overshadowed by the Holy Spirit, the power of the Most High (Luke 1:35). The Spirit has indeed dwelt in him ever since. Yet this Jordan anointing is a new filling with the Spirit, a new empowering of his humanity to inaugurate a specific threefold mission, the mission as Priest, Prophet, and King.

We have seen that all of Israel was on edge, expecting God to act in a decisive way through some sort of special figure. In Hebrew, *meshiach* ("messiah") literally means "anointed one," which translates as *christos* in Greek and *Christ* in English. Most people, when they thought of "messiah," imagined a figure like David, a warrior king. Others expected a prophet like Moses or Elijah. The Dead Sea Scrolls reveal that the Yahad of Qumran were expecting both of these end-times figures and also a third—a messianic priest who would offer sacrifices once again in purity and righteousness.[55] Yet we have no evidence than the Jews of Qumran or anywhere else expected all three messianic roles to be assumed by the same person.

"MY BELOVED SON"

Matthew, Mark, and Luke all attest that at the moment of Jesus' baptism a voice comes from heaven, saying, "This is my beloved Son, with whom I am well pleased" (Matthew 3:17).

After centuries of silence, God once again speaks, revealing this man, anointed by the Holy Spirit, to be his Son. In John's Gospel, John the Baptist, following Jesus' baptism, gives witness that Jesus is the "Son of God" (John 1:34). This indicates, for starters, that Jesus is the anointed King, and it echoes what the Lord said to David: "You are my son, today I have begotten you" (Psalm 2:7).

But Jesus' sonship goes beyond the adopted sonship of David and the kings of Israel, as the angel revealed to Mary when he explained that her child would be begotten of the Holy Spirit (Luke 1:35). The voice of the Father and the descent of the Spirit upon the Son is a theophany, a manifestation of God. What makes this theophany unique is that it is an explicit manifestation of the Trinity, the three divine persons in one God, although the Trinitarian implications were not necessarily apparent to John or the others present. Icons in the Christian East reflect this Trinitarian theophany.

God has not only spoken; he has spoken his final and complete Word in Jesus of Nazareth, his anointed Son.

THE SERVANT OF THE LORD

The second part of the Father's pronouncement reveals something more. The phrase "with whom I am well pleased" (Matthew 3:17) brings us back to a text from the prophet Isaiah that offers another clue to the surprising mission for which the Son is anointed. He is the mysterious Servant of the Lord (Isaiah 42:1-6) who is to be a covenant to the people of Israel and a light to the nations, but who is to fulfill his mission through suffering (Isaiah 53:1-12). He is to be a lamb led to the slaughter (Isaiah 53:7). It is no accident that after Jesus' baptism, John the

Baptist points him out twice as "the Lamb of God, who takes away the sin of the world" (John 1:29, 36).

This illumines what it means that Jesus, through the descent of the Spirit, is anointed priest. He is to offer the sacrifice of perfect love and obedience to God, expressed in his entire life but most especially in his own death. Most priests offer sacrifices of animal victims to God. Jesus will offer himself. He will be both priest and victim.

Baptism in water is undoubtedly a symbol of cleansing. But immersion in water in the Old Testament is also a sign of death, as we see in the stories of Noah's flood and the Exodus (Genesis 6–9 and Exodus 14:21-31). During the time of his public ministry, Jesus will refer to his upcoming death as a baptism (Luke 12:50). His submersion under the waters of the Jordan is a sign of his acceptance of his role as the perfect penitent and also his acceptance of death as the necessary path to the fulfillment of his mission.

Suffering is also an inevitable consequence of his anointing as prophet. The text of the Old Testament is clear that a prophet is the mouthpiece of God. Yet God often desires to speak a word of correction that his people, and particularly their leaders, do not care to hear. So prophets don't tend to win popularity contests. Amos and Jeremiah were both persecuted by the chief priests of their day (see Amos 7:10 and Jeremiah 20:1-2). Jeremiah was thrown in a cistern, narrowly escaping with his life (Jeremiah 38:1-13). The prophet Uriah, the son of Shemaiah (Jeremiah 26:23), and the prophet Zechariah, son of Jehoiada (2 Chronicles 24:21), were executed by the kings of Judah in Jerusalem. In accepting the prophetic anointing, Jesus is accepting suffering, persecution, and even death at the hands of the authorities of God's own people.

ANOINTING FOR BATTLE

In the pagan world, athletes were anointed with oil as a preparation for an arduous athletic contest. This relates to the Israelite notion of kingly anointing. The king is a shepherd who leads his people to pasture but also puts himself between his flock and their predators. Soon after his anointing, David courageously volunteered for single combat with the Philistine giant Goliath (1 Samuel 17). The idea of the king as warrior derived from his duty to defend his sheep. The goal, of course, was victory. But kings of Israel could and did die in the line of duty (2 Kings 23:29).

Most Jews identified their enemies as foreign oppressors, such as the Philistines or the Romans. Jesus sets his sights on unmasking the ultimate enemy at the root of human suffering and rebellion. This is the enemy, symbolized by the serpent in Genesis 3, who had led the first man and woman into sin and therefore alienation from God and from each other. The result had been corruption leading to death.

And so, soon after Jesus' baptism, the Holy Spirit who descended upon him leads him into the nearby wilderness to be tempted by the devil.

Israel had once been led into the desert by the luminous cloud and the pillar of fire and had there faced temptations. Israel had repeatedly succumbed. God's decision to lead the people of Israel into the desert was to humble them and test their resolve to be faithful to the covenant which they had made with him on Mount Sinai. Jesus' entrance into the desert and undertaking of a lengthy fast are further expressions of his humility. God allows him, like Job, to be subjected by Satan to what Matthew and Luke tell us are three principal temptations.

The first temptation takes advantage of Jesus' physical vulnerability. He is fully human and as susceptible as anyone else would be to the pangs of hunger. Satan's strategy is to induce Jesus to abandon the fast and to use his wonder-working power to gratify himself and prove himself. "If you are the Son of God, command these stones to become loaves of bread" (Matthew 4:3). After all, what harm would it do? You've deprived yourself enough. Such miracles could relieve your suffering; but more than that, think about how much suffering you could wipe out in the world if you would just focus on what people *really* need— food and other material things—instead of being preoccupied with spiritual things no one really cares about.

But Jesus is secure in the Father's love and has no need to prove himself. Physical bread is a wonderful thing but not the only or the greatest good. He deflects the temptation with Scripture: "Man shall not live by bread alone, but by every word that proceeds from the mouth of God (Matthew 4:4, citing Deuteronomy 8:3).

The next temptation is for Jesus to wow the crowds with a spectacle. Satan brings Jesus to the pinnacle of the Temple and says, "If you are the Son of God, throw yourself down; for it is written, 'He will give his angels charge of you,' and 'On their hands they will bear you up, lest you strike your foot against a stone'" (Matthew 4:6, citing Psalm 91:11-12). The pinnacle of the Temple was the southwest corner of the complex and towered above a very busy traffic area. It was the place where the trumpet was sounded at the time of the sacrifices, calling the people of the city to stop and worship. It would have been the best place to impress the most people with a show.

Jesus recognizes the ruse. Satan is twisting Scripture to use it against the One whose Word it is. From the place where people are called to worship God, Satan wants Jesus to distract people from worshipping the Father and focus instead on him. If he did so, Jesus would be acting out of pride, presuming on God's protection when he was doing the opposite of God's will. Jesus responds to this misuse of Scripture with Scripture wielded as the sword of the Spirit (Ephesians 6:17): "It is written, 'You shall not tempt the Lord your God'" (Matthew 4:7, citing Deuteronomy 6:16).

Finally, the Enemy leads Christ to the summit of a high mountain, traditionally identified as the peak located immediately west of Jericho, and shows him the entire world. The temptation goes like this: Are you not destined to be king of the world? Why not choose a shorter, easier path to lordship than suffering and death? All you need to do to assume your rightful role as king is to make a small adjustment in the object of your loyalty and worship. Simply switch that from your overbearing Father to me, and all will be done for you instantly and painlessly! Jesus commands Satan to begone, "for it is written, 'You shall worship the Lord your God and him only shall you serve'" (Matthew 4:10, citing Deuteronomy 6:13).

Luke makes a notable comment at the end of his account of the temptation: "And when the devil had ended every temptation, he departed from him until an opportune time" (Luke 4:13). The first thing that often comes to mind as the opportune time is the garden of Gethsemane and the entire Passion. Jesus certainly is extremely vulnerable during his passion and has numerous opportunities to evade death. Satan uses Herod to tempt Jesus to entertain him with some marvel (Luke 23:6-12). One of the thieves crucified with him as well as the bystanders at Golgotha taunt him to get himself down from the Cross (Mark 15:30).

But there is more to the opportune time than this. We need to understand that the three temptations in the desert return again and again in the course of Jesus' public ministry, in the people's demands for yet another spectacular sign to prove his authenticity (Matthew 12:38), in Peter's attempt to dissuade him from the Cross (Matthew 16:22-23), and through the people who would have carried him off to make him a political king (John 6:15). His initial victory in the desert ordeal foreshadows the entire ministry and the final ordeal—the same temptations, the same victory.

RECAPITULATION

One of the Fathers of the Church, St. Irenaeus, loved to expound on a principle he saw in this story as well as all throughout the New Testament. The leaders of God's people, like the people generally, had all failed to fulfill their mission. It is a common maxim that you don't get do-overs in life. But that does not apply to Israel. Jesus assumes headship of God's people, relives its history, and does things over again, right. In the desert, even Moses, the leader of the covenant people, failed at one crucial moment, losing his temper before Israel at the waters of Meribah instead of showing them God's holiness and patience (Deuteronomy 32:51-52). For that reason, Moses was not allowed to enter the Promised Land. In Jesus, Israel is finally found perfectly faithful in the desert. Irenaeus called this reliving and re-heading up of Israel "recapitulation" (*caput* is the word for "head" in Latin).

There is an even wider recapitulation that takes place in the desert. If we go further back in the Old Testament, there is the story of a more primordial temptation, the temptation in the Garden. It was Paradise; Adam and Eve lived in a luxurious garden with luscious fruit hanging everywhere. Wild beasts were their companions with whom they lived in harmony. They were given everything they needed and more. Only one fruit was forbidden, and it was exactly this fruit that the tempter induced them to eat. Their communion with God and each other was ruptured. They were exiled from the Garden to a land choked with thorns and thistles. A stern angel with a fiery sword barred their return. Their harmony with creation was also ruptured. The wild beasts became predators.

Finally, in Jesus, the situation is reversed. A Son of Man walks into this wilderness and vanquishes the tempter. Paradise begins to be restored. Mark hints at this when he writes, "And he was with the wild beasts; and the angels ministered to him" (Mark 1:13).

Jesus is not just the new Moses, head of the new Israel; he is the new Adam, head of a new humanity. His forty days in the desert are like the forty weeks that a woman is with child; through his public ministry, a new era is about to break forth, and ultimately a new humanity will be born. Jesus, the new Joshua, has crossed the Jordan. He is about to lead God's people into the Promised Land, a new paradise.

CHAPTER 6

GOOD NEWS OF THE KINGDOM OF GOD

Whenever a regime change occurred in the Roman world, an *evangelion* (gospel) was issued to carry the good news throughout the empire. When Jesus returns to Galilee, he has such an announcement to make. God, not Herod or Caesar, is becoming King. "The time [Gk., *kairos*] is fulfilled, and the kingdom of God[56] is at hand; repent, and believe in the gospel!" (Mark 1:15).

John had announced that the time was soon coming. Jesus is now announcing that the time has finally come.

THE KINGDOM OF GOD

But one could ask, was not God already King, from all eternity?

Naturally, God has always been King—in heaven. But a quick look around tells us that things are quite different than they ought to be on earth. The suffering and evil that exist in the world were as apparent in the first century as they are now. Amid so much misery, the cry "Where is God?" can often be heard.

Jesus' message is that God is right here, right now, with us in an entirely new way. It is now *kairos*, God's chosen moment, the moment he asserts his sovereign lordship over his rebellious creation. He has come to take charge, to straighten things out, to make things right.

Sometimes Jesus uses the phrase "the kingdom of heaven." People have often gotten the wrong idea from this expression—that God's kingdom is a place far away that we will enjoy only after we die, in heaven. But "heaven" in the phrase "kingdom of heaven" is a reverent Jewish way of saying "God" without directly using his name.

So "kingdom of heaven" is another way of saying kingdom of God. This kingdom is not so much a place. Probably a better translation for it is "reign" of God. Jesus is soon to teach his disciples a prayer that will, in one of its petitions, give us a simple definition of this kingdom, or reign, of God: "Thy kingdom come" means "Thy will be done, on earth as it is in heaven." The kingdom of God means God's reign, his sovereignty, appearing now right in the midst of our troubled world, God having his way on earth as he has his way in heaven.

The passing of time in history is known as the *chronos* of everyday time. It's measured in seconds, minutes, days, and years. With the beginning of Jesus' public ministry, a different time has finally arrived, and Jesus uses a different word for it. This moment, this "inbreaking," is *kairos*, God's time, a critical, decisive moment that changes everything and calls for a decision. The coming of God's kingdom means that a completely new era has arrived. The final act in the drama of salvation history has begun. Like John the Baptist, Jesus insists that the necessary response is repentance, *metanoia*, a change of heart leading to a change of life.

The only appropriate response is to get with the program and yield to the King's way of doing things. It entails a joyful surrender to the new fact that things have changed and that God is indeed taking over now.

Jesus' announcement is a call not only to repent but to "believe in the gospel" (Mark 1:15). In the entire New Testament, the word *faith* and the related verb *to believe* occur over and over again. To believe in the gospel of God means to decide to accept the message as true, to welcome it with joy, to allow it to sweep you up into its momentum and carry you forward on a new path. It is a combination of the receptive "let it be" of Mary's trust (Luke 1:38) and the active faith of Joseph, who keeps walking even through trials. In contrast, not to believe in the gospel can mean to put up active resistance to the message—to close your eyes, stop up your ears, harden your heart, and plant your feet firmly in the same spot where they have always stood. Or it could mean paying lip service to the gospel but failing to respond with a changed life (Matthew 7:21-23).

JESUS' NAZARETH MANIFESTO

Soon after beginning his preaching in Galilee, Jesus pays a visit to his hometown. He attends the Sabbath service in the synagogue, as he had so many times throughout the years when he lived in Nazareth (Luke 4:16). On this day he serves as a lector. After opening the scroll of the prophet Isaiah, he reads this portion:

> The Spirit of the Lord is upon me, because he has anointed me to preach good news to the poor. He has sent me to proclaim release to the captives and recovering of sight to the blind, to set at liberty those who are oppressed, to proclaim the acceptable year of the Lord. (Luke 4:18-19; and see Isaiah 61:1-2)

Then he sits down and, as is his privilege as a man of Israel, gives the homily: "Today this Scripture has been fulfilled in your hearing" (Luke 4:21).

This text is a sort of manifesto. It is Jesus' mission statement. But it is less a statement of his goals than a statement of fact. The future promise has come. The kingdom of God is here in the form of a Jubilee (Leviticus 25), the acceptable year of the Lord that Isaiah foretold.

One experience we moderns have in common with the ancients is the experience of debt. Anyone saddled with school loans or credit card bills knows what a crushing burden debt can be. Debt bondage is bad enough today. In ancient Israel, if you couldn't pay your debts, you could lose not only your home but also your freedom; being sold into slavery to pay off your bills was a very real possibility. God, in his mercy, commanded Israel that every fiftieth year, the Jubilee year, all property would be restored to its original owners and Israelite slaves would be granted their freedom. On the basis of a mysterious prophecy in the book of Daniel (9:20-27), Jews in the time of Jesus were looking for a super-Jubilee that would put a definitive end to Israel's total bondage, including the guilt of its sin. Jesus says that he is here to bring it. Now.

DEEDS OF POWER

Jesus did not just talk about the Jubilee of the kingdom. He came to inaugurate it, to set it in motion. Luke said that he returned to Galilee "in the power of the Spirit" (Luke 4:14). Many people today are used to religion as inhabiting the realm of ideas and noble sentiments. If they have any experience of religion, they typically would not describe it in terms of "power" that makes a dramatic difference in everyday life. But if anything is clear from the Gospel records, it is that Jesus immediately began to do powerful deeds that caused a sensation by solving seemingly unsolvable problems.

The epicenter of the divine earthquake was not Nazareth but a town about twenty-five miles farther north and east called Capernaum. It was a fishing village on the shore of the Sea of Galilee and a border town, a customs' stop for travelers before they crossed from the jurisdiction of Herod Antipas to that of his half brother Philip. Because Capernaum lay on the major trade road from Egypt to Mesopotamia, constant parades of people passed through with their pack animals, and they had to stop before leaving the city in order to pay their import/export taxes.

The beginning of Mark's Gospel provides us with a vignette of one day in the life of Jesus in Capernaum (Mark 1:21-34). It is a Sabbath and, as he did in Nazareth, Jesus takes the opportunity to teach in the synagogue. Suddenly a man tormented by a demon disrupts the assembly. With a simple word of command, Jesus expels the demon, and the man is free. "Immediately," Mark writes, Jesus leaves the synagogue and walks thirty yards to the home of Simon Peter and his brother Andrew. Finding Simon's mother-in-law ill with a high fever, he once again "immediately" takes her by the hand and lifts her up. At that moment, the fever leaves her, so she just as matter-of-factly begins serving food for Jesus and his companions. At sundown, when the Sabbath is over, virtually the whole town shows up at the door with their afflicted family members and friends, and Jesus heals them all.

Mark, in his repeated use of the word "immediately," is trying to get across the point that Jesus wastes no time. He is in a hurry to draw people into this new realm of the kingdom. Mark is also highlighting the drama, the surprise, the suddenness, and the excitement that surround the entire public ministry of Jesus, and especially Jesus' miracles. The Gospels typically call them *dynameis*, deeds of power (from which comes our English words "dynamic" and "dynamite"). They are also called *teras*, or wonders. The evangelist John prefers to call them *semeion*, or signs, since they are indicators, signposts pointing beyond themselves to deep and profound truths concerning the kingdom and Jesus. They illustrate what God's reign means, who God is, and who Jesus is. The Word of God in the Bible does not just mean what we call words. The Hebrew term for "word," *dabar*, means total communication taking place through both words and deeds. Actions, so the saying goes, speak louder than words. These mighty deeds of Jesus are God speaking loud and clear to his people.

EXORCISM AND HEALING

It is no accident that the first mighty deed recorded in the Gospel of Mark is an exorcism. In the desert battle, Jesus "binds the strong man"; now he sets about plundering the strong man's house (Mark 3:27). What we see in the ministry of Jesus is an assault on the kingdom of darkness, a clash of kingdoms. The usurper who has seized God's world and oppressed his people is now confronted with the world's rightful sovereign reclaiming what is his, liberating his subjects.

There appear to have been a good many aspiring Jewish exorcists in the first century (see Mark 9:38). In fact, a miracle that the historian Josephus reports from the period, one that he himself witnessed, was an exorcism performed by a Jew named Eleazar. This was carried out as a sort of spectacle observed by Vespasian, the Roman general who became emperor. To get the job done, Eleazar used a ring containing special roots. He put the ring up to the nose of the possessed man. Eleazar was able to pull forth the demon by way of the man's nostrils while the man sniffed the roots. He then employed numerous secret incantations, going back to King Solomon, to command the demon never to return. Finally, to prove that the demon had left the man, he ordered the demon to tip over a bowl of water set up for that purpose.[57]

This sort of exorcism, a spectacle relying on potions and incantations, borders on magic. It is the kind of thing people apparently expected from exorcists in those days. This could not be farther from the method of Jesus. Coming face-to-face with the reality of evil, he simply confronts it with a firm word of rebuke, and the battle is over. There is no showmanship, just a simple command. The people are amazed: "What is this? A new teaching! With authority he commands even the unclean spirits, and they obey him" (Mark 1:27).

Jesus' healings of people with various infirmities exhibit the same noble simplicity along with the added note of compassion. Take, for example, the lepers. In Jesus' day, all flaking, scaling sorts of skin diseases, from Hansen's disease to psoriasis, were categorized as leprosy. Once a leper was certified as such by the priests, he or she became a social outcast, obliged to stay away from human society.

The isolation of lepers was at least as great a suffering as their physical malady. The first chapter of Mark's Gospel records a poignant incident when a leper came and knelt before Jesus, begging him for healing: "'If you will, you can make me clean.' Moved with pity, he stretched out his hand and touched him, and said to him, 'I will; be clean.' And immediately the leprosy left him" (Mark 1:40-45).

There is an important detail in this story that a modern reader may miss. To touch a leper was to become ritually contaminated and in need of purification. So lepers in Jesus' day were used to being shunned. Jesus could have healed him with a verbal command, just as he drove out demons with a command. But he deliberately chose to reach out to the outcast—and touch him.

Many of the accounts of Jesus' healings and exorcisms are equally brief and understated. Even the lengthier accounts, such as the raising of Lazarus, exhibit the same compelling quality of an interpersonal encounter—Jesus' compassion and authority on the one hand, and the petitioner's faith, sometimes even bold, persistent faith, on the other. The petitioners vary. They include the crippled, parents of dying children, blind men, desperate women, a synagogue leader, even a Gentile centurion.

From a purely historical point of view, it is indisputable that Jesus, as the Jewish historian Josephus puts it, is a "doer of startling deeds."[58] In his own day, not even his enemies disputed this fact. They just said that it was "by Beelzebul, and by the prince of demons [that] he casts out the demons" (Mark 3:22). Jesus points out how ridiculous it would be for Satan to fight against himself. What he says next underlines clearly what these exorcisms and healings mean: "But if it is by the Spirit of God that I cast out demons, then the kingdom of God has come upon you" (Matthew 12:28). The kingdom of God is the liberating, healing power of the Holy Spirit flowing from Jesus into the people who welcome the kingdom by faith.

 **Miracles and Magic**

In the second century AD, two famous critics of Christianity, Trypho and Celsus, dismissed Jesus as just another magician, of the same ilk as the magicians of Greece and Egypt. In recent years, this interpretation has been popularized by several scholars, such as John Dominic Crossan, who have received much coverage in the popular media.

There is an extensive published collection of Greek magical papyri that date from the second century BC to the fifth century AD. The collection contains page after page of magic spells—recipes for exotic concoctions, strings of names of disparate deities, and chains of nonsense syllables.

A magician's goal is very pragmatic. The magician is a professional who is paid for results. He or she is not partial to any one deity or religious system. Each spell is a mishmash of incantations, divine titles, and rituals from many cultures and religions. The magician is not sure which of these will push the right button and get the desired result from the right deity. So lots of alternatives must be included, in a shotgun approach. The motto of the magician is "whatever works!"

This bears no resemblance to the miracles worked by Jesus as recorded in the Gospels. In fact, a careful study of both the Gospel miracles and the surviving Greek magic spells allows us to compare the general characteristics of miracles and magic.

Magic involves these elements:

- Impersonal, superhuman forces are harnessed by a magician.

- The magician uses secret formulas and rituals.

- The rituals work by bending those forces to the magician's own will.

- The magic is to achieve quick fixes for practical problems.

Magic is marked by individualism and entrepreneurship: the magician is a paid practitioner who is interested in guarding his secrets, not sharing them with a community of disciples.

A miracle, as shown in the Gospels, has these elements:

- It is characterized by faith and submission to a personal God.

- It takes place within a distinctive faith tradition.

- Its purpose is to build up the community of faith.

- It does so by a public manifestation of God's power.

- It is not dependent on any set ritual or formula.[59]

The contrast between magic and the miracles of Jesus could not be starker.

THE BAPTIST, ELIJAH, AND ELISHA

The Gospel accounts of John the Baptist line up well with what Josephus tells us about him: John drew large crowds and had great influence yet did not work any signs. So when he sent messengers to Jesus from prison, asking if Jesus was the one who is to come, Jesus sent this message back to him:

> Go and tell John what you have seen and heard: the blind receive their sight, the lame walk, lepers are cleansed, and the deaf hear, the dead are raised up, the poor have good news preached to them. (Luke 7:22)

The deeds, in other words, tell the story. The kingdom of God has arrived. This is what it looks like when God is in charge.

Keep in mind that in the Old Testament, such works were rare. The great miracles of the plagues of Egypt, the parting of the sea, and the manna were associated with Moses, though he was not a miracle worker per se. The kings of Israel, including David, the greatest of them, also were not miracle workers, and so there seems to have been no idea that the coming Davidic messiah would work miracles. The great "writing" prophets like Isaiah and Jeremiah worked no miracles. Only the prophets Elijah and Elisha were wonder workers, and these are precisely the figures Jesus identifies himself with in terms of his mighty works.[60]

This can be seen in Jesus' comments in the synagogue in Nazareth in Luke 4. After he issues his manifesto, Jesus is aware of what the people are thinking. They have heard of the mighty works he performed in Capernaum and wonder why they haven't seen any themselves. In response to their unspoken objection, Jesus points out that Elijah was sent to raise the son not of a widow of Israel but of a pagan (1 Kings 17:8-24)—and that Elisha healed not an Israelite leper but a foreign one (2 Kings 5). This hint that the benefits of the Jubilee are to be given to the pagans is more than the people of Nazareth can take. This is not the kind of Jubilee—and Jesus is not the kind of messiah—they are expecting. Part of what they were looking forward to on the Day of the Lord was

God's vengeance on their foreign enemies. There is actually a verse in Isaiah 61 that mentions it, which Jesus decided not to read aloud.[61] Enraged by his failure to live up to their expectations, they try to kill him (Luke 4:28-29).

This story, set by Luke at the beginning of his account of the public ministry, shows that it is possible to reject the kingdom of God and thereby shut oneself away from the amazing blessings that it brings. Unbelief is the choice to opt out, and Jesus apparently respects that choice. The Lord will not force his healing love on anyone. In Mark's account of Jesus' hometown visit, he says Jesus "was not able to perform any mighty deed there. ... He was amazed at their lack of faith" (Mark 6:5 NAB).

So this is the ultimate answer to the unspoken question of the people of Nazareth: "Why have you not worked the miracles here that they say you've worked in Capernaum?" It's because Jesus finds an openness of faith among people in Capernaum, including the Gentile centurion (Luke 7:1-10). In Nazareth, he meets a door firmly shut and bolted.

TEACHING WITH AUTHORITY

Jesus draws large and excited crowds everywhere he goes. His miracles, of course, have a lot to do with this. But they are not the entire reason for his magnetic effect on people. Jesus also teaches everywhere he goes. People seem to hang on his words. His teaching has the power to arouse hope and expectation. And this message is delivered in an entirely new way, just like his exorcisms and healings.

The scribes of Jesus' time, who enjoyed great prestige among the people, commonly taught with reference both to Scripture and to famous sages who went before them, such as Shammai and Hillel, two teachers from the first century BC. "Shammai interprets it this way, but we agree with Hillel, who understands it like this."[62] It is much like the way a college student will substantiate every point in his or her term paper by footnoted quotes from scholars.

Jesus' teaching method is totally different. Mark expresses the people's reaction succinctly: "They were astonished at his teaching, for he taught them as one who had authority, and not as the scribes" (Mark 1:22). Jesus asserts his authority not only over previous teachers but even over Moses. This is seen in a striking way in Jesus' Sermon on the Mount (Matthew 5–7). Again and again, on topic after topic, he frames his teaching this way: "You have heard it said ... But *I* say to you ... " Throughout the sermon, while he disagrees with common established tradition, he actually extends and even amends Moses' teaching on such matters as divorce (Matthew 5:31-32), retaliation for injuries (5:38-41), and the swearing of oaths (5:33-37).

The kingdom of God is the final stage in the history of salvation. As the herald of the kingdom, Jesus brings revelation to its final completion. For this reason, he speaks and acts as if he is in charge, as if he has the right and duty to step in and take over. No scribe or rabbi before or after him would ever think of conducting himself in this way.

NOT WITHOUT PARABLES

It is not just the authority of Jesus' teaching that is distinctive. It is his vivid, compelling style as well. He largely teaches by means of colorful symbols and metaphors taken from everyday life, which he sometimes weaves into intriguing stories. The prophets and sages of the Old Testament had used images and symbols to a great degree, as did the later rabbis of the Talmud. Still, in comparison to these other teachers of Israel, Jesus' creativity in imagery and story stands out in a striking way.

The word used for the sort of story made famous by Jesus is *parable*. It is our English translation of the Hebrew word *mashal* (pl. *meshalim*), meaning "comparison." In a broad sense, *mashal* covers any simile or metaphor, any figurative, symbolic language expressed in a saying or proverb. In this wide sense, it could be said that all of Jesus' teaching on the kingdom of God is given in parables (Mark 4:11).

One of the properties of a symbol is that it cannot be reduced to just one clear and simple meaning. A symbol is like an onion: peel back one layer of meaning and another one appears. Symbolic language, then, is particularly suitable for Jesus' use: what he has come to reveal is so rich that abstract language can never properly convey it. Neither can just one image or symbol suffice to express it, no matter how rich and inexhaustible that image might be.

So Jesus uses many symbolic comparisons, one after another, a veritable kaleidoscope of figures. He uses them to tease, stimulate, even shock the minds of his hearers. The paradoxes in his comparisons and the surprise endings of his stories are intended to have the same effect as riddles. They leave the listener wondering—questioning and probing long after hearing his teaching. After two thousand years of commentaries and homilies on them, his parables still retain a certain freshness and disclose new dimensions of meaning to those who ponder them.

Some of Jesus' "comparisons" are simply brief similes. Others are more extended metaphors, like his teaching on the vine and the branches in John 15. But sometimes Jesus knits metaphors and images together into stories that don't end as you would expect. These have no real precedent in the Old Testament, except for the parable of Nathan in 2 Samuel 12:1-23.[63] A variety of these stories, like the Good Samaritan (Luke 10:25-37), are preserved for us in the Gospels. Several of them will be examined in detail in subsequent chapters. Here we will just focus on a few of the shorter ones that illustrate important features of the kingdom.

ALREADY HERE AND YET TO COME

The expectation of the messianic era prevalent at the time assumed that God's power would be exercised all at once through military confrontation. But this was not the way Jesus was going about things as he inaugurated the kingdom of God. True, the kingdom was dramatically evident in Jesus' mighty deeds. But these things were transpiring in a modest town of a backwater region of the empire. The beneficiaries were little people of no importance; the most important among them were Jairus, a leader of a Galilean synagogue (Mark 5:22), and a centurion, a noncommissioned army officer (Luke 7:1-10).

Some of the parables Jesus tells about the kingdom address the fact that everything isn't changing all at once, from the top down. The kingdom of God is like a mustard seed, he says, the smallest of seeds, which grows into the largest of shrubs, providing shelter for the birds of the air (Matthew 13:31-32). Things are starting small and from the bottom up. But there is a dynamism of growth at work that will ultimately exceed all expectations.

It is interesting just how many of his parables are about seeds and their surprising growth. The seed of the kingdom is planted, and at first you really can't see any results; everything looks exactly the same. So you walk away only to come back a few days later to find that something has mysteriously changed, seemingly all on its own. A plant has broken the surface and is rapidly growing (Mark 4:26-29).

The kingdom of God changes things. It is inserted like leaven right in the middle of the heavy, seemingly immovable realities of everyday life, and before you know it, these things have been elevated, raised up, and transformed into a new reality—from inedible dough to a light, airy bread that gives life (Matthew 13:33).

So the kingdom has come already and is not a future reality to look forward to? Actually, the presence of the kingdom is not either/or; it is both/and. The liberation has begun and is yet to come. The kingdom is coming in phases. God, through Jesus, is already opening up zones of freedom. It is much like D-Day in World War II. The liberation force has successfully landed on enemy-occupied territory, and every day the liberated area is extended. But much more territory needs to be taken. Until then, there will undoubtedly be setbacks, suffering, and many casualties. But ultimate victory is assured; it is just a matter of time.

In many parables, Jesus lets his hearers know that the final and definitive victory of the kingdom is yet to come. No one knows when it will come (Matthew 24:36). In fact, it will come like a thief in the night, after a time of tribulation (Mark 13:24) when we least expect it (Matthew 24:42-44).

For those who have accepted the new regime, the final coming of the kingdom will be a time of reward and rejoicing after the turmoil that precedes it. For those who have either actively resisted it or neglected to prepare for it, time will have run out. The final coming, for them, will mean judgment. The need to watch, to repent, and to prepare is communicated by Jesus in such stories as the parable of the five foolish virgins, who fail to bring extra oil for their lamps as they wait for the bridegroom. They miss the joyful wedding procession and wind up left out of the party (Matthew 25:1-13).

CHAPTER 7

THE CALL TO DISCIPLESHIP

Jesus' gospel of the kingdom of God is for everyone who is willing to hear. But in a special way, from the very beginning, Jesus is looking to call and train leaders, people who will come to know him intimately and share in his work of proclaiming the kingdom. These people he calls disciples. Among the first are two brothers who live in Capernaum. They are fishermen when they meet Jesus, but they quickly undergo a career change.

"Follow me," he says to Peter and Andrew, "and I will make you become fishers of men." "Immediately," Mark notes, "they left their nets and followed him." In the next verse, the same firm, authoritative call is issued to James and John. They promptly drop their nets, leave their father in the fishing boat, and follow after Jesus (Mark 1:16-20).

Had they ever met him before? John's Gospel notes that Peter and Andrew had some prior contact with Jesus in Perea[64] around the time of Jesus' baptism. But even if they were already acquainted, Jesus' call to drop everything to follow him seems sudden, abrupt, and radical.

THE CALL

In both the Greek and Jewish worlds of Jesus' day, there were renowned wise men who surrounded themselves with bands of students. The Jewish wise man was called a sage or, in the Gospels, a scribe or lawyer. The scribes were experts in the written Law of Moses and the unwritten "traditions of the elders." A few hundred years later, they would come to be known as rabbis.[65]

In the Gentile world, a wise teacher was called a philosopher. Philosophers like Socrates and Plato had been attracting disciples for hundreds of years.

The usual approach in both worlds was for a student to seek out and present himself to a teacher, who would decide whether or not to take him on as a disciple.

Jesus' approach is significantly different. It is he who generally takes the initiative, not the prospective disciple. "You did not choose me, but I chose you" (John 15:16). The outward, audible call by Jesus is only part of the story, though. It is simultaneously accompanied by inward attraction to Jesus, a powerful grace that can only be given by the Father. Jesus notes this when he says, "No one can come to me unless the Father who sent me draws him" (John 6:44).

A few do volunteer for discipleship. But generally, this does not end well, as we see in the case of the rich young man (Matthew 19:16-22; Mark 10:17-22). There is a cost of discipleship, in his case quite a significant one, since this young man is wealthy and reluctant to part with his wealth. One of the beautiful things in this encounter is that Jesus knows from the start that the young man does not have it in him to leave all behind. But instead of looking at him with disdain or impatience, Mark tells us that Jesus looks upon him with love (Mark 10:21). It is comforting to know that he looks upon us in the same way in our moments of greatest failure.

THE UP-FRONT COST

The kingdom of God is not just good news; it is an invaluable treasure, a pearl of great price. As such, it is worth selling everything to obtain it (Matthew 13:45-46). Those Jesus calls to literally walk with him (John 6:66) all over Palestine for three years are required to leave everything behind. But all those who accept the Good News and want to be followers of Jesus also need to be ready, at any time, to let go of everything, even home and family.

This may seem harsh, but we have to stop for a moment to examine what it means to be a follower of Jesus. The literal meaning of the Greek word used, *mathetes*, is "pupil" or "student."[66] The English word we use to translate it, "disciple," connotes a bit more. It indicates coming under the *discipline* of a master, which means not only learning information from him but also being trained by him to become like him.

To embark on the great rescue mission that we call the Incarnation, the Divine Word had left behind the glory he had from all eternity at God's right hand (Philippians 2:5-7). Then the Word made flesh, Jesus of Nazareth, has to leave behind his mother and kin when it comes time to be baptized and launch his public ministry. If Jesus is the master and if discipleship entails imitating the master, then discipleship naturally includes the willingness to imitate Jesus in his own leaving behind of home and family. He requires of his disciples no more than what was required of him.

There is nothing more precious in this world than family bonds and friendship, but the kingdom of God is not of this world at all. It is a matter of the remaking of this world, and Jesus' time is God's *kairos*, the moment God had chosen to inaugurate it. It was urgent to train men who would extend the mission and extend the zone of liberation that is the kingdom of God.

The kingdom has to come first, before all other goods. It has to be announced with great haste. Jesus has a great sense of urgency that will permit no excuses, no delays. When Elisha was called by Elijah to follow him, Elisha asked if he could return to say goodbye to his family. Elijah said yes. When a prospective disciple asks Jesus the same question, Jesus says no. He is greater than Elijah, and his mission, this kingdom moment, is more urgent (see 1 Kings 19:19-21 and Matthew 8:21-22).

Some may breathe a sigh of relief, thinking that such sacrifice, in context of the gospel story, was for the Twelve only. Or they may think that today it is required of priests and religious but not, thankfully, of us ordinary Christians.

Keep in mind that the disciples who traveled with Jesus were a much bigger group than the Twelve. Jesus had selected the twelve apostles from this larger group of disciples. The radical demand to give up everything is a general requirement for *all* disciples, not just the Twelve. Jesus makes this crystal clear: "Whoever of you does not renounce all that he has cannot be my disciple" (Luke 14:33). Jesus says this not to the Twelve but to the great multitudes who are traveling with him at the time (Luke 14:25).[67]

The word Jesus uses here, *renounce*, is interesting. It means that the legal title to all we own must be signed over to the Lord. Our property and our relationships are no longer ours but his. We renounce sovereignty over them and the right to dispose of them as we wish. Our motto is now "Your kingdom come, your will be done on earth," in my life, "as it is in heaven." You are not renouncing your love for your family. But you are showing that you are willing, if necessary, to let go of the enjoyment of your family's company. Your family, your interests, your home, your possessions are henceforth on loan to you. God may call in the loan at any time. He may call it all in at once—or he may call in the loan of some things right away and other things later or not at all.

We can see this in the experience of the followers of Jesus in the Gospels. When Jesus calls them, Peter and Andrew in principle leave all behind. But the next thing you know, Jesus is at their house healing Peter's mother-in-law (Mark 1:16-18, 1:29-31).

And it is quite likely that Jesus stayed there whenever he and his disciples were back in Capernaum (Mark 2:1).[68] So we see that Peter and Andrew continue to enjoy home and family, at least occasionally, for some time. Eventually, however, Peter will have to leave them behind for Antioch and then Rome.[69]

The same holds true of friendships. The two pairs of brothers— Peter and Andrew and their friends John and James, the sons of Zebedee—who were formerly business partners, are still together as disciples. Now, instead of fishing together, they are following Jesus together. We are not sure when, but sometime after Jesus' death, it presumably comes time for them to separate, as they are called to different places to lead the early Church and preach the gospel.

Another example is Mary of Bethany, the sister of Martha and Lazarus. Though the word "disciple" is not actually used of her in the Gospels, she is nonetheless put forward as a sort of model disciple. She appears three times in the Gospels, each time at Jesus' feet (Luke 10:39; John 11:32 and 12:3). But Jesus apparently never calls her to leave her home or her siblings in Bethany to follow him on the road. Rather, with Martha, her role is to welcome Jesus and the disciples into her home whenever they come to Jerusalem (Luke 10:38; John 12:2).

Each of us is called by Christ to be his disciple, to follow him. This always involves repentance, a radical change of life, a change of heart, and the willingness to leave all behind for him. But just as the Master has a unique plan for each of our lives, so the outward form of discipleship will vary from person to person, as it did for Jesus' first followers. To understand the unique role that each of us is called to play requires listening intently to the Master's voice, as Mary of Bethany did, who sat at the Lord's feet and gave him her full attention (Luke 10:38-42).

THE BENEFITS

After the rich young man declines to give away his property to follow Jesus, Peter speaks up and says, "Behold, we have left everything and followed you." Jesus replies, "Truly, I say to you, there is no one who has left house or brothers or sisters or mother or father or children or lands, for my sake and for the gospel, who will not receive a hundredfold now in this time, houses and brothers and sisters and mothers and children and lands, with persecutions, and in the age to come eternal life" (Mark 10:28-31).

Because the kingdom is both present and to come, the rewards of discipleship are both present and future. Jesus does not just open up new insights into the Law, as a scribe would do for his disciples. Rather, he opens up for his disciples a whole new world. This includes new brothers and sisters, one's fellow disciples. It also includes a new mother, Mary, since he will give all his disciples to her when he entrusts the Beloved Disciple to her, and her to him, from the Cross (John 19:27).

In terms of lands, they will go places they had never dreamed of going. Jesus, unlike the sages of his day, does not settle down in one place to provide his disciples a tranquil course of study. He is constantly on the move, with a large retinue of disciples moving along the road with him. It is adventure, full of all the things that make us love adventure stories, including danger and risk, triumph and glory. Imagine watching Jesus open the eyes of a man born blind, raise the dead, feed five thousand people with five loaves and two fish, and walk on water!

IMMERSION

Discipleship means more than attending liturgy and Bible study once a week. It means living with Jesus, being immersed in his presence as well as his teaching.[70] Living and traveling with him means spending massive amounts of time with him. You pick up more this way than you ever could attending a university course. Living with him allows you to watch Jesus interact with people. You observe things that you never could just through reading. When he speaks to people, you can hear the tone in his voice and see the expression on his face. You see him slip away in the evening to pray all night. You watch him as he copes with hunger, weariness, and setbacks. Much is absorbed, picked up, as it were, by osmosis. Jesus is passing on to his disciples all that he has received from his heavenly Father and from his earthly, adoptive father, who had discipled him in the tradition of Israel.

This handing on of a whole life, an entire vision and legacy, is what we mean by Tradition. It really cannot be imparted any other way than this sort of immersion. The goal is to learn to see things through the eyes of the Master, to learn to think, pray, and love as he does.

BELIEVING *INTO* HIM

But discipleship means something even more. There is a personal bond formed with Jesus himself that goes beyond just learning *from* him. Jesus calls his disciples to believe *in* him (John 3:16, 3:18, 3:36, 6:35, 6:40, 12:44), even to abide or remain in him (John 6:56, 15:4, 15:7). No prophet, king, or sage of Israel had ever spoken in such a way. Not Moses, not Elijah, not David.

We are very used to this call of Jesus to "believe in" him. But in the Greek of the New Testament, a very strange grammatical construction is often used to express it, something that didn't previously exist in Greek literature. We find it only in the New Testament, mainly in John and Paul. It seems that Christians developed this new grammatical usage to convey a distinctly Christian concept. Faith, in the Old Testament, is basically a matter of trust, of relying on God. That is certainly involved when it comes to "believing in" Jesus. But more literally, for the early Christians "believing in" Jesus means to "believe *into*" him, to lean into him, to plunge into him.[71] The idea is of a dynamic movement, a journey of love not just into his ideas but into his very heart.

KNOWING HIM

So this "believing in" is not just "accepting as true." It is not just an intellectual thing, something separate and distinct from loving. "Believing in" necessarily includes loving. The goal is to come to know and love him in an ever deeper and more intimate way, not just to know facts or truths about him.

As mentioned in the introduction, some languages have two different verbs to differentiate two different kinds of knowing. In Spanish, for example, *saber* is to know facts; *conocer* is to know a person. *Conocer* means acquiring a familiarity, an acquaintance, a personal experience of the person. When people talk about having "a personal relationship with Jesus," they are talking about this most fundamental characteristic of discipleship. When Paul speaks about his passion to "know him" (Philippians 3:10), this is what he is referring to.

In fact, in John's Gospel, there is a person who exemplifies this but is never named. Tradition identifies him as John, son of Zebedee. But in John's Gospel, he is simply called "the Beloved Disciple." He is probably called this because he is intended to be a model of the ideal disciple; we are invited to aspire to his role and write our own names in the blank left by the absence of his. The Beloved Disciple always wants to be as near Jesus as he possibly can be. At the Last Supper, we find him leaning on the Lord's breast. On Good Friday, he is the only disciple standing at the foot of the Cross. To him, the Lord entrusts his mother (John 19:27).

A PERSONAL RELATIONSHIP WITH JESUS

Knowing Jesus is quite different from what many people think Christianity is all about. The very noun *Christianity*, like the noun *Catholicism*, is an abstraction. From these terms, you could get the idea that Catholic Christianity is mainly a "belief system," along with a code of ethics and a few required religious practices. It's a total package that you buy into. You subscribe to the beliefs, as you would to a political platform, and you try to keep the rules, which of course you can't do perfectly. You go to Confession and attend Mass on Sundays and holy days. Check off all the boxes, and you are good to go.

That is not the idea here. *Believing* is primarily in a person. Personal attachment to him comes first. Correct ideas about him, about God, about the kingdom, about the Bible—this is all involved and is important, but it flows from and depends on the person. Jesus' disciples actually came to know, love, and follow him before they truly understood who he was. The revelation of his identity only gradually unfolded, and they didn't exactly "get" it until after his resurrection. In the words of Pope Benedict XVI, "Being Christian is not the result of an ethical choice or a lofty idea, but the encounter with an event, a person, which gives life a new horizon and a decisive direction."[72]

MAKING JESUS THE CENTER OF YOUR LIFE

I will always remember the shock I experienced when I first ran into a group of Catholics who were living this adventure called discipleship. I was a practicing Catholic who would never think of denying the tenets of the Creed or missing Sunday Mass, though I found it rather dull. For excitement, I played bass in a professional rock band.

Yet the excitement of the people I met was so much greater than what I was experiencing in the music world. And it seemed very different from what I had experienced of religion till that moment. The people I'd met sincerely believed that Jesus had a plan for each of their lives. He was leading them, day by day, speaking to them, using them to touch others and using others to touch them. They seemed to be living the adventurous lives of the disciples who walked with Jesus from town to town in Galilee.

It was authentic and attractive. I just couldn't figure out why, after so many years as a practicing Catholic, I hadn't even known that such a thing was possible, much less actually experienced it.

One of the leaders of the group, a nun, talked this over with me and shed some light on the subject. "God's always been a part of your life, right?" she asked. "Exactly!" I replied. "He's *always* been a part of my life." Sister Fran said, "That's precisely the problem."

"What?" I replied, confused.

"If you want the adventure that these people are experiencing, you have to make a shift from having Jesus as a *part* of your life to making him the *center* of your life. You've been running the show. You need to give him permission to take over. Give him the reins!"

I made the decision to do that. It is a decision that I have found must be renewed each day. In fact, that's why I make the Sign of the Cross so often. Every time I do, I renew my decision to live no longer for myself but for him "who loved me and gave himself for me" (Galatians 2:19-20).

REFORMING YOUR LIFE

To be a disciple is to give Jesus free rein in your life. The call to repentance, to *metanoia*, is a call to reform your life, which is to say, to reorient your entire life around Jesus as its new center. It means priorities are shifted. New things, like more prayer and service to others, may need to be added. Other things may need to go to make more room for the Lord. If you want to know whether Jesus is the center and top priority in your life, examine how you spend your time and your money.

My life was a very noisy one when I first made the decision to make Jesus the center of my life. Television, radio, and recorded music filled and cluttered up most of the available space. It became clear that these were like weeds choking out the wheat and keeping it from bearing fruit (Matthew 13:1-9). So I began to clear some ground. In the new space opened up by this tilling, I made new plantings of daily prayer and Scripture. I began to listen to broadcasts and audiobooks that helped me grow spiritually. I began to attend the Eucharist more than just once a week, lingering for a while after in adoration and prayer. I began to read the lives of the saints and tried to hang around more with some saints-in-the-making.

The reorientation and fine-tuning is ongoing, the clearing and planting continues. It continues because discipleship is never finished; as long as we are still breathing, the dynamic quest of discipleship is ongoing. It is a journey of constant change called conversion. St. John Paul II, in his very first encyclical, explains what discipleship is about:

> From the outset, conversion is expressed in faith which is total and radical, and which neither limits nor hinders God's gift. At the same time, it gives rise to a dynamic and lifelong process which demands a continual turning away from 'life according to the flesh' to 'life according to the Spirit' (cf. Rom 8:3-13). Conversion means accepting, by a personal decision, the saving sovereignty of Christ and becoming his disciple.[73]

MISSIONARY DISCIPLES

The disciples are not called simply for the sake of their own spiritual perfection. As disciples, they are to become like the Master, and the Master is on a mission.

During the public ministry, Jesus' mission is to announce and inaugurate the kingdom of God. He brings the light of truth to a world of darkness, and he brings the power of the Spirit to overthrow the power of the Evil One. He is impelled, driven by the Spirit, to bring truth, healing, and deliverance to as many places in Israel as possible.

His disciples are to come with him and are even being trained to be his instruments, his representatives in announcing and ushering in the kingdom of God. They are to be "kingdom bringers." All are called to be peacemakers (Matthew 5:9). All are called to be washers of feet (John 13:14-15). At least eighty-two of the disciples are specifically sent to heal, preach, and drive out demons (Luke 6:12-16; 10:1). There is no question of mission being optional; if you are not a missionary disciple, you are simply not a disciple.

THE ROAD AND THE JOURNEY

Both the dynamic, ongoing spiritual journey of discipleship and the urgency of mission are graphically presented to us in what the three-year public ministry of Jesus actually looks like.

Many people have the impression that Jesus and the disciples spent three years in the rather limited region of Galilee and then undertook one great journey to Jerusalem for the last Passover of his life.

This misunderstanding is corrected by a closer inspection of the four Gospels. John helps us a great deal, since he makes it clear that Jesus and his disciples regularly travel to Jerusalem for the great annual feasts, as required of Jewish men by the Torah, and at least once go to Jerusalem for the Feast of the Dedication (Hanukkah) in December.[74] Mark and Matthew tell us that at least once he travels fifty or more miles west from Capernaum to the region of Tyre and Sidon, where he exorcises the daughter of a Syrophoenician (Canaanite) woman (Matthew 15:21-28; Mark 7:24-30). Jesus and the disciples go north about twenty-five miles from Capernaum to the foot of Mount Hermon at Caesarea Philippi (Matthew 16:13). They go to the Decapolis, a pagan region to the south and east of the Sea of Galilee, where Jesus heals a deaf-mute man (Mark 7:31-37), and further south to Perea, across the Jordan to the east of Samaria and Judea. This is all on foot—and for five or six months of the year, in unbearable heat under a blazing sun.[75]

Discipleship is not for the faint of heart. For Jesus and his followers, it entailed rigorous discipline and constant exertion. The travel was just about nonstop. Stagnation was not an option. If you lingered in an area and failed to move with the Master, you'd soon find yourself quite a distance away from him.

In the beginning, we don't find the abstract term "Christianity." The Acts of the Apostles records that at first the Jesus movement was simply called "the Way" (*hodos*), which can also be translated as "the journey."[76] Jesus declares himself to be "the way" (John 14:6). To be a disciple is to embark on a never-ending journey with him, into him, and through him to the Father.

CHAPTER 8

THE TRUTH
ABOUT GOD

On the last day of his earthly life, Jesus comes face-to-face with the Roman governor, Pontius Pilate. In that momentous exchange, Pilate is obviously perplexed. He demands to know who Jesus is (John 18:33) and where he came from (John 19:9). So Jesus responds, "For this I was born, and for this I have come into the world, to bear witness to the truth" (John 18:37). This seems to confuse Pilate even further. He responds with yet another question: "What is truth?" (John 18:38).

THE TRUTH

People often think of "truth" in abstract terms—big concepts and noble ideas. Perhaps that's one reason that many dismiss the question of truth as theoretical and remote from real life. Philosophy is the discipline that is traditionally dedicated to the pursuit of truth. It is not a popular choice these days for students selecting a major course of study at a university, especially in America. Speculative matters can wait; real life demands something more practical.

It is the ancient Greeks who gave philosophy to the world. If the Greeks could be said to have a favorite image for truth, it would be light. The Hebrew mind, on the other hand, is much more graphic and concrete. In the Hebrew Scriptures, the predominant image for truth is a rock, and "the Rock" is also a favorite designation for God (Psalm 95:1, 144:1).

Truth is basically reality. It is firm, reliable, something that you can count on, build on, stake your life on. That's what *amen* means in Hebrew. It does not mean, as many have been taught, "So be it." Rather, it is a confident acclamation meaning "It is firm! It is certain—you can stand on it!"[77]

For Jesus, a true Israelite, truth is eminently practical. Knowing and acting on the truth of his teaching is like building a house on rock. Those who hear him and ignore his teaching are building their houses on sand (Matthew 7:24-27).

Jesus' announcement of the kingdom of God brings up a very good question: Who is this God, this eternal Rock (Isaiah 26:4), whose kingdom is now coming? What the reign of God is going to look like has a lot to do with what God is like. For this reason, the most important truth that Jesus came to bring is the full and final revelation of God.

THE PROPHET LIKE MOSES

Israel relied on its prophets for much of what it knew about God. Our English word *prophet* comes from two Greek words that mean "speaks for." A prophet is God's spokesman; he speaks on behalf of God.[78] His word is God's word. His teaching about God is God's teaching about himself.

Israel had not seen a bona fide prophet in about five hundred years. The appearance of any new prophet would be a signal that God was once again on the move and that the final phase of salvation history had begun. But many were expecting not just any prophet: Moses had promised that God would one day raise up a prophet like himself (Deuteronomy 18:15, 18:18). Moses had been the preeminent prophet in their history. God not only had worked great marvels through him but had given Israel the covenant and the Torah through him. Moses was, then, a unique mediator between God and Israel. Through Moses, God had even revealed to Israel his sacred name: Yahweh, I AM WHO I AM (Exodus 3:14). Many incredible prophets, like Elijah, had come after Moses, but none were really quite like him.

Part of Moses' uniqueness is explained in the book of Deuteronomy: "And there has not arisen a prophet since in Israel like Moses, *whom the LORD knew face to face*" (Deuteronomy 34:10, emphasis added).

Moses could play his unique role as deliverer and covenant mediator because of the extraordinary intimacy he had with God. The Lord spoke to Moses "face to face, as a man speaks to his friend" (Exodus 33:11), yet that intimacy had its limits. When Moses asked to see God's glory, the Lord agreed to let his glory pass by him, but he allowed Moses to see only his back, not his face (Exodus 33:18-23).[79]

When Jesus is anointed at his baptism in the Jordan and the Spirit descends upon him in the form of a dove, the voice of God is heard identifying Jesus as his beloved Son. It is interesting that no such title was given by God to Moses or any other prophet of the Old Testament. Only regarding the future son of David in the oracle of Nathan had God said, "I will be his father, and he shall be my son" (2 Samuel 7:14).

In the four Gospels, Jesus calls God "Father" 170 times. And he uses a very Jewish sort of saying to explain what it means that he is called "son."

As we've seen, a father in ancient Israel mentored his sons in a very complete way. Teaching his son to read the Torah, to say his prayers, to keep the Law—this was a great part of the knowledge a father typically handed on to his son. But a father typically mentored his son in his trade as well, which included passing on trade secrets. This made the bond between father and son intimate and unique. No one knew another better in ancient

The Clockmaker God of Deism

The 2008 U.S. Religious Landscape Survey by the PEW Research Center found that while 97 percent of American Catholics said they believed in the existence of God, only 48 percent of them were absolutely certain that God is a Person and that it is possible to have a personal relationship with him.[80]

One factor explaining this is a religious philosophy that swept Europe and America in the eighteenth century called Deism. In response to the horrible wars between Catholics and Protestants in the previous two centuries, Deists promoted a more rational, "scientific" religion. God, for these thinkers, set up the world to operate on moral and natural laws. He is like a clockmaker who creates a magnificent timepiece, winds it up, and then lets it run on its own. He then steps away to attend to his own pursuits.

So, for Deists, God is majestic but remote. He does not reveal himself or work miracles or intervene. We owe him honor and obedience, but we can expect no authentically intimate relationship with him. There is no original sin or need for grace. "God helps those who help themselves" is a principle of this commonsense, pragmatic approach to religion.

Even Christians and other theists whose creeds formally profess a personal God have been deeply influenced by this tendency to think of God as "the man upstairs," a remote sovereign who deserves our respect but who has little influence on our day-to-day lives.

Such a vision of God is very far from the face of the merciful Father revealed by Jesus.

Israelite society than father and son. Nothing was held back from the son—all was shared, all was conveyed. This was Jesus' relationship to Joseph.

But, says Jesus, this is also his relationship with God, his Father in heaven. "All things have been delivered to me by my Father;

and no one knows the Son except the Father, and no one knows the Father except the Son and any one to whom the Son chooses to reveal him" (Matthew 11:27).[81]

Jesus, then, is the prophet like Moses, but he is much greater than Moses. His own intimacy with God is greater than Moses': Moses was God's servant; Jesus is God's Son.[82] For a father holds nothing back from a son—the son sees not just his father's back but his father's face. Because Jesus has seen the face of God, he can reveal God's face to us as no one before him ever could.

JESUS' INTIMACY WITH GOD

Jesus can, then, bring the final and complete revelation of the truth about God, because he knows God perfectly, directly, and intuitively. In the Old Testament, it was assumed that no one could see God's face and live. Yet *seeing* is precisely how John describes Jesus' familiarity with God and why he can bring the full revelation of God to humanity: "No one has ever seen God; the only-begotten Son, who is in the bosom of the Father, he has made him known" (John 1:18).

In a graphic way, Jesus' profound intimacy with God is illustrated in his practice of slipping away from the crowds, and even from his disciples, to spend a long time in quiet communion with his Father. Amid all the excitement of the events of the first chapter of Mark's Gospel, the morning after the healing of Simon's mother-in-law, Jesus gets up long before dawn and goes out to a lonely place to pray, only to be followed by Simon and the others (Mark 1:35-36).

All the Gospel authors note that this is the habit of Jesus, with Luke pointing it out most often. Luke obviously is making this point, among others—if it is necessary for Jesus to make time for quiet prayer, how much more necessary is it for us?

Luke notes that Jesus spends extended time in solitary prayer at most of the great junctures in the gospel story. Before he chooses the Twelve from his larger group of disciples, Luke mentions, he heads to the hills and spends the entire night in prayer (Luke 6:12-16).[83] And Matthew, Mark, and Luke give us extensive reports of Jesus' moments with the Father in Gethsemane on the night before he died.

We need to remind ourselves of the substantial daily prayer life that Jesus and the disciples would already have as devout Jewish men of their time: grace before and after meals, the *Shema* early in the morning introduced and concluded by various blessings and the great *Tefillah* ("the prayer"), the *Tefillah* prayed again at the hour of the evening sacrifice, and finally at sundown the *Shema* and *Tefillah* once again.[84] Yet this extensive liturgical prayer life is not enough for Jesus; he has a yearning for intimate and continual communion with his Father, a longing we first see in him when he lingers behind in the Temple at the age of twelve instead of joining the caravan returning to Nazareth (Luke 2:41-51).

The disciples would pray the traditional Jewish daily prayers with Jesus, as Jesus had prayed them with Joseph. But on one occasion, after seeing Jesus alone at prayer, one of the disciples wants to go further in prayer. Wanting to share in Jesus' special intimacy with God, he asks Jesus to teach them a special prayer that would set them apart as disciples of Jesus and heralds of the kingdom of God (Luke 11:1). After all, John the Baptist's disciples had been given their own special prayer that identified them as his followers.

Jesus responds by teaching them what we call the Our Father, or the Lord's Prayer. Most of us in Western culture, especially those with a Christian upbringing, have heard it so often that it has become routine and commonplace. We need to try to understand just how shocking it must have sounded at first to the disciples' ears. We can only appreciate it if we better understand how they were used to praying.

OUR FATHER

First of all, the language Jesus uses jolts them. He and the disciples speak Aramaic in their daily conversation, but they have learned from childhood to recite the *Shema* and say their daily prayers in Hebrew. The *Tefillah*, the *Shema*, and all the blessings that surround the *Shema*—all are recited reverently in the ancient liturgical language of the Torah.

Faithful Jews were expected to say these prayers at fixed times throughout the day. In these prayers, Jews delighted in stringing together different names for God—Lord of Wonders, Our Redeemer, Shield of Abraham, Lord of Heaven and Earth, God of Abraham, God of Isaac, God of Jacob, God Almighty, God Most High. But the most typical way to address God, still the classic introduction to most Jewish blessings, was "Lord our God, King of the Universe."

God is the almighty, the King. Israel's daily liturgical prayer was laden with the sense of God's transcendence, God's infinite and unspeakable majesty. Therefore, the recitation of these lengthy prayers was carried out with great formality and solemnity. It was quite beautiful. But it also ran the risk of becoming formalistic and routine, like the ceremonial at a royal court.

The prayer Jesus teaches them is, in contrast, amazingly brief, simple, informal, and direct. And as noted earlier, he does not teach it in the exalted language of the Temple but in the humble, ordinary language of everyday life, Aramaic. The very first word of the prayer is one of the most striking and revolutionary things about it—for he teaches them to invoke God simply as Father. Only Jesus, the Son in a unique and incomparable sense, could dare to address God in this way. But he is now teaching his disciples to address God in the same way, thereby giving them a share in his very special relationship with God. He is inviting them to share in his sonship.

In the entire Old Testament, God is called Father less than twenty times.[85] No one in the Old Testament or in other Palestinian Jewish literature had ever, before Jesus, addressed God in prayer as Father. In Jewish thinking up to Jesus' own time, such an approach would have been considered far too familiar, too informal, even presumptuous and disrespectful.

The proper word for father in formal Hebrew and Aramaic is *abhi*. But by Jesus' time, addressing your father like this would have been considered overly formal and distant, even fawning. You might address the king this way when you wanted to butter him up and obtain favors; but not your dad. Your own father you would call *abba* (accent on the last syllable). This term originated in the babble of small infants. It would be one of the first words said by a little child, together with the Aramaic word for "mamma," *imma*. In Jewish society in Jesus' day, adult children continued to call their aging parents *abba* and *imma*, much as we would use Dad and Mom. *Abba* was used, without a pronoun, to address one's father directly and also to talk about him to others. Our father, my father, the father—all would be covered by the simple word *abba*.

We have no evidence that any Jew before Jesus ever dared to refer to God, much less address him, in such a way.[86] But Jesus addresses God as *abba*[87] and teaches us to address his Father with the same utter confidence, the unselfconsciousness and unpretentiousness, of a little child. *Abba* is the exclamatory word that a child spontaneously cries out when running up to his father and leaping into his arms. Children instinctively know that when they cry out and raise their arms, they will be lifted up and embraced. It seems to be this kind of abandonment and confident assurance that Jesus is referring to when he says, "Unless you turn and become like children, you will never enter the kingdom of heaven. Whoever humbles himself like this child, he is the greatest in the kingdom of heaven" (Matthew 18:3).

I have fond childhood memories of my father returning home from a business trip and my grandfather coming to town to spend a holiday with us. Not only would I be picked up, but my father would repeatedly throw me in the air. Not once did I fear he would drop me or that I'd hit my head on the ceiling. My grandfather would squeeze me with a bear hug, growling in my ear that he was going to eat me up. Rather than being afraid, I squealed with delight and could sense his delight in me.

This is the kind of relationship with himself that God offers in the era of the kingdom of God, the final and ultimate stage of salvation history. The almighty judge, the fearsome King, the powerful one, comes with a strength that turns out to be tender and affectionate, gentle and meek. The King, through his rightful and only Son, approaches us as if we too were his sons and daughters.

It is incomprehensible that this should be the case. But it is one of the great surprises of the kingdom. This is the meaning, ultimately, of the deliverance and the healings worked by Jesus. He is making war on Satan not merely to take his territory back. He comes to take his children back. We were kidnapped, and he is fighting to free us and take us home. As in the Exodus from Egypt, he is bringing us out of bondage to make us his very own.

But it is not just on the level of the nation. It is not just Israel as a people that is his child. He brings it down to the level of each one of us, intimately, personally. He delights not just in the human race. Not just in Israel. Insofar as I am joined to his Jesus, his Son, he delights also in me.

PARABLE OF THE PRODIGAL SON

In the Old Testament and the rabbinic literature of the Mishnah and Talmud, there is a sense of God as Father who takes delight in his people. But the accent is most often that of Psalm 147:11— "The LORD takes pleasure *in those who fear him*" (emphasis added). The Talmud records that Rabbi Judah (ca. AD 150) said, "If you behave like children, you are called children. If you do not behave like children, you are not called children."[88]

This was the problem with Jesus, as far as the Pharisees were concerned. Jesus befriended people who did not fear the Lord. They had not kept the Law, did not behave like God's children, and therefore had no right to consider themselves God's children. You could not expect to be the recipient of God's love if you did not first do all that God commands.

To answer these objections, Jesus tells three parables (Luke 15), including one of the best known of all gospel stories, the parable of the Prodigal Son (Luke 15:11-32).

The traditional name for the story comes from the younger of the two boys born into a prosperous family. The two receive all good things from their father and stand to inherit a sizable estate. But brashly and offensively, the youngest suddenly demands his inheritance while his father is still alive and well. It is like telling one's father, "I wish you were dead!" The father amazingly agrees to the boy's insolent request. The son then effectively thumbs his nose at his father, takes the money, and runs. He quickly squanders the entire fortune on partying and prostitutes. At this point, he finds himself broke, empty, and alone. He is reduced to having to take a job tending swine, the most unclean and disgusting of animals. However, the pigs eat better than he does. Having hit bottom, the boy wakes up and comes to his senses. He can pick himself up and return to his father's house where, he is confident, he can at least get work as a hired hand and be better off than he is among the hogs.

So he begins the journey back. His rehearsed speech asking forgiveness is motivated more by his hunger than by love for his father.

From a long distance off, the father sees the boy on his way back. The father cannot wait for the son to arrive; he runs out to meet the son and embraces him. He does not appear to care about the son's motivation for returning. The fact that his son has returned is all that matters. He commands his servants to exchange the boy's tattered rags for the most luxurious robe and to put a ring on his finger and sandals on his naked feet. He orders the slaughter of the fatted calf, the most valuable animal on the estate, which has been reserved for the most important of occasions. It is time for high feasting, complete with music and with dancing.

The older son, who hears the din made by the merrymakers, comes in from the fields to discover what has happened. He is aghast. In expressing his outrage to his father, he refuses even to refer to the prodigal as his brother: "This son of yours," he says, has eaten through the family's wealth and blown it all on sin, and now his father squanders on him yet more of the family's goods? The older son complains bitterly. He has never done anything but honor and obey his father, yet he has never received so much as a goat to butcher and enjoy with his friends.

The father's tender patience with his indignant older son is almost as moving as his gracious response to the prodigal. He gently reasons with him: We have to celebrate—your brother was dead and has now come back to life. The story leaves us in suspense: Will the elder son come around?

The question we are left with at the end of the story is the real question of the moment. The Pharisees are deeply disturbed by the careless favor shown by Jesus to sinners. Will they get over their indignation and join the celebration? Can they ever accept the fact that God is not quite as they had pictured him?

Unlike the Pharisees, God had never closed the door to the prodigals. Yes, they had squandered their inheritance and the family's property as well. Yes, they had dragged themselves through the mire. Yes, they had objectively offended heaven. But heaven is now ready to run out and meet those making their way back, lifting them up as a father raises up a fallen child.

God is the Lord, the King of the Universe. But he now comes as Father. Yes, he is the mighty, all-powerful One. But his omnipotence is chiefly manifest in this: There is no sin too great for him to forgive.[89]

God: Father or "Force"?

In recent decades in Western society, increasing numbers of people consider God an impersonal force that penetrates, envelopes, and energizes all things. In 2008, nearly a third of U.S. Catholics described God in these terms.[90] The influence of religions from the East along with elements of popular culture, like the *Star Wars* saga, have reinforced this tendency: "May the force be with you."

The God of Jesus is Spirit; Jesus' disciple Paul quoted a Greek philosopher, Epimenides, to say as much: "In him we live and move and have our being" (Acts 17:28). God is present everywhere and is "immanent" in all things, most definitely a creative and energizing *force*. But God is not a *force field*, like gravity or radiation. Such realities are powerful, to be sure. But they are impersonal.

Our concept of personhood involves a few important things—self-consciousness and freedom are two of them. A person is free to love and to withhold love. A person has the capacity to give himself or herself to another. A person is also unique and unrepeatable.

A free, unique person, capable of love, is the highest reality that we know. We human persons may be subject to powerful and impersonal forces of nature. But in a certain sense, we are greater than any of them, in that we are free persons. To conceive of the Supreme Being as an impersonal force would therefore be a contradiction in terms. We human beings, in our personhood, would be superior to such a reality.

In his teaching that God is Father, Jesus is saying that God is more, not less, personal than we are. He is completely free and uses that freedom to love in a way that is extravagant, unlimited, and overwhelming. He is not limited in knowledge, time, and power as finite creatures are. In his omnipotence, he is able fully to appreciate, know, and love the unique beauty of each person whom he has made.

In our experience of human fathers, we all have encountered disappointments. Curiously, we nevertheless have a concept of what true and ideal fatherhood looks like: strength and authority combined with tenderness and gentleness. This is exactly the God whom Jesus reveals as Father.

PERSONAL AND FAMILIAR

In the few texts in the Old Testament where God is spoken of in terms of Father, this particularly carries with it the idea of tenderness and mercy. In Hosea 11, God compares himself with a father who teaches his child to walk, who raises him to his cheek, feeds, loves, and heals him. Even though the child spurns his love, God refuses to repudiate him. "My heart," says the Lord, "recoils within me, my compassion grows warm and tender" (Hosea 11:8).

Jesus, in the stories of Luke 15, makes clear that the Father's compassion is not directed just to the covenant people as a whole. Rather, it reaches out even to the isolated, defeated individual who has failed miserably and squandered his inheritance. God is like a shepherd who, some would say recklessly, leaves ninety-nine sheep to pursue the one that strayed; he is like a woman who loses a precious coin and drops everything to look for it in every nook and cranny until she succeeds in finding it.

The message of all three parables is clear—each person is precious and irreplaceable. This is proved by the fact that the firstborn Son, infinitely precious to the Father, has been sent by the Father to seek out and find each wandering and wayward child. Each of the three parables of Luke 15 concludes with great rejoicing and high celebration. God is not an aloof monarch who waves his hand to commute the sentence of his criminal subject. God's mercy is the exuberant love of a father who draws near. "It is hardly an exaggeration," says Pope Francis, "to say that this is a 'visceral' love. It gushes forth from the depths naturally, full of tenderness and compassion, indulgence and mercy."[91]

Perhaps the story known as the Prodigal Son should be renamed. *Prodigal* comes from the Latin term for "lavish." It can mean recklessly spendthrift, like the son, but it can also mean prodigiously generous, like the father. In that case then, this parable is really about the prodigally merciful Father. God's fatherly love is extravagant, lavish, and in the eyes of the elder son, wasteful. This super-abundant generosity and boundless goodness of God is what makes the kingdom of God the "pearl of great price," which is worth selling everything to obtain. Only in the kingdom can we experience what it means to be infinitely loved.

MOSES AND JESUS

In the great sweep of the story of Israel, there is no one greater than Moses. Before Moses, the children of Israel knew some of the truth about God, but oddly enough, they didn't know his name. It was through Moses that God revealed himself by the name of Yahweh, I AM WHO I AM (Exodus 3:14). The Torah, the Law God gave through Moses, was the imprint of this name on every aspect of their life, a new life of freedom from the slavery of Egypt.

In the new era of the kingdom of God, Jesus reveals God's secret name and deepest identity—Father. The fundamental truth, the Rock on which we are to build our lives, is this merciful and infinite love that calls each of us by name. This affirming love of the Father makes us firm, providing us with an unshakable and secure foundation. This new name, Father—the final, ultimate name of God revealed in the last days—colors every aspect of the life and message of the kingdom. This life is most concisely expressed in the kingdom's prayer, the emblem of the new family, the Our Father.[92]

CHAPTER 9

THE FATHER
OF MERCY AND
THE DAUGHTERS
OF ABRAHAM

The words of the Lord's Prayer and the story of the Prodigal Son go a long way toward painting a new picture of the God of Israel as the loving Father who yearns to lavish love on his children. But the disciples want more than to simply hear stories about what God is like. So Philip makes his famous request: "Lord, show us the Father, and we shall be satisfied."

Jesus is disappointed by this: "Have I been with you so long, and yet you do not know me, Philip? He who has seen me has seen the Father" (John 14:8-9).

In his mission to reveal the face of God, Jesus had not started with words. The Pharisees demanded to know the meaning of his actions, especially his scandalous practice of eating with sinners. This is the whole reason why Jesus tells the three parables of Luke 15. They serve as an explanation of the meaning of what he has been doing. His exorcisms, his healings, his dealing with sinners—all of these together serve as a revelation of God as Father, of what God really thinks and what he is really like.

Jesus paints a vivid picture of the Father with his words. But even more so, in his encounters with people, his face reveals the Father's face.[93] When he looks into people's eyes, those who meet his eyes with faith can see in them the loving look of the Father. And in that glance, which is sometimes accompanied with a touch, loving power flows from the Father through Jesus into them. Jesus is "the way" (John 14:6) in the sense that he is the road on which the Father runs to meet the child who is ready to come back home.

MERCY: LOVE'S RESPONSE TO SUFFERING

In the few times that God is referred to as Father in the Old Testament, the idea of God's fatherhood is usually linked with the idea of mercy in response to his people's sin and suffering. Psalm 103:13 says, "As a father pities his children, so the LORD pities those who fear him." In Jeremiah 31:20, God says, "Is Ephraim my dear son? Is he my darling child? … Therefore my heart yearns for him; I will surely have mercy on him, says the LORD."

Sin in the story of the Bible is not primarily a legal infraction, a blot on the heavenly register. It is an act of walking away from God that leads to alienation and misery. A careful reading of Genesis 3 brings this into focus. The forbidden fruit certainly looks good, and its benefits sound very appealing. But in actuality, the fruit is like bait that conceals a hook. Once the bait is taken, freedom is lost. The enemy has been invited in, and he comes to impose his own regime of thorns and thistles, suffering and death. The apple is also a poisoned apple, much like the one given to the fairy-tale princess Snow White. It contains the serpent's venom and begins to poison everything. Innocence is lost. Man and woman find themselves now alienated from one another. There is a loss of transparency; they are suddenly embarrassed to be seen and shield themselves from each other. And they hide from God, who had been their friend, as he walks in the Garden in the cool of the evening. Later, one of their sons, jealous of his brother, kills him. Everything falls apart. God does not impose this as punishment; no, the prohibition of that particular fruit was intended to shield his beloved from just such horrors. Sin injures others, but no one is more grievously damaged by sin than the sinner himself.

The story of the Prodigal Son reveals this perfectly. It is not only money that is lost. The real tragedy is squandered sonship. The sin of the younger son has led him to isolation and degradation. For a Jew, there was no more poignant picture of lost dignity than wallowing in the muck, keeping company with swine.

This is the deepest suffering: the loss of dignity. But it helps us to understand what mercy is—mercy is love's response to suffering. God's mercy is never cool, distant, or condescending. Mercy comes near not only to bind up the wounds but to raise up the wounded. Mercy relieves bodily suffering and at the same time relieves the deeper, aching pain by recognizing a person's unique worth and restoring to the person a sense of value, a sense of personhood. God's merciful love is an affirming love; beneath the mud-caked rags of the one walking toward him, the Father recognizes a precious and irreplaceable son. He sees and rejoices in the value of this prodigal. The elder son can only protest—he has already cost us too much! It isn't fair to waste more on him. He is not worth it!

From the vantage point of strict justice, the Prodigal Son was right to expect no more than to be given a job like a hired hand. He and his brother could at least agree on that. But the Father, in love, refuses to be limited by justice. He is the Father of mercy, who is, in fact, "rich in mercy" (Ephesians 2:4). He lavishes this mercy on the one who had been the prodigal but now, once again, is welcomed as a son.

The centrality of mercy as the heart of the gospel has been emphasized over the last few decades by one pope after another. St. John Paul II called mercy "the most stupendous attribute of the Creator and of the Redeemer." Pope Benedict XVI wrote that "mercy is the central nucleus of the gospel message; it is the very name of God." Pope Francis puts it even more simply: "Mercy is God's identity card."[94]

MERCY AS GRACE

The gospel, the Good News, is that each person is infinitely loved and cherished by an all-knowing and all-powerful Father. For those who accept it, this love comes as a free gift. This is the meaning of the term *grace*, so often used by St. Paul and throughout Christian tradition. Grace is related to our term *gratis*, meaning without cost.

But it is necessary to add that grace, this free gift, consists of God's affirming love that comes to heal, deliver, transform, and elevate. This is not a feeble love of wistful sentiments. It is powerful and efficacious. And this is exactly what we see in the encounters between Jesus and people who dare to open themselves to the kingdom of God, which we now can also call the kingdom of mercy.

We have already seen that Jesus responds to a leper, one of the most marginalized figures in first-century Palestine, with compassion and mercy (Mark 1:40-42). When he heals his skin disease, Jesus also affirms the leper's worth and humanity by reaching out and touching him. That touch ends not only the leper's sickness but also the bitter exile of loneliness and degradation that the disease had imposed on him.

There is another class of people who were pushed down and aside in first-century Palestine. To a startling degree, Jesus is particularly concerned to reveal the Father's mercy to women, whom he considers the daughters of Abraham.[95]

THE SAMARITAN WOMAN

Women in Jesus' time were not accorded the same dignity as men. Women could not serve as witnesses in a court of law because they were not considered trustworthy. The positive precepts of the Law were not considered binding on Hebrew slaves or women because their time was not their own; it belonged to the man of the house. A woman could not divorce her husband, but she could be divorced by him for any reason (at least that was the most popular legal opinion), even if she simply burned his dinner.[96] A woman was not generally an heir to her parent's estate—that would be divided among her brothers. Men did not speak in public to women to whom they were not married. In fact, women were kept at home, out of public view, as much as possible. This rabbinic saying from the Mishnah conveys the prevailing attitude:

> Engage not in too much conversation with women. They said this with regard to one's own wife, how much more [does the rule apply] with regard to another man's wife. From here the Sages said: as long as a man engages in too much conversation with women, he causes evil to himself, he neglects the study of the Torah, and in the end he will inherit gehinnom [hell].[97]

In the Gospel of John, when Jesus arrives at Jacob's Well around midday, there should have been no one there (John 4:5-42). Drawing water was hard work, and it would be done by women early in the morning, in the cool of the day. It was something to look forward to—an opportunity to get out of the house, see friends, laugh, and talk.

But Jesus does not find himself alone at the well. There is a woman who has come at that time presumably to avoid the company of other women. Jesus is tired from the journey and has sent the disciples into town to buy food. He approaches the woman and asks her for a drink. She is shocked. For though Samaritans also are descendants of Abraham, Isaac, and Jacob, Jews usually refuse to have anything to do with them.

To us, it may appear that Jesus is being demanding by asking her to wait on him. But to the contrary, he is honoring her. We already have seen that it was considered spiritually undesirable for a man to make conversation with a woman. Jews, in addition, considered Samaritans ritually impure. A Jew would avoid touching such people or drinking from their cups. In asking for a drink and making conversation, Jesus is seeing her, recognizing her, and saying, "You are not a threat … You are not unclean."

He moves the conversation from well water to living water, then abruptly asks her to fetch her husband. She replies honestly that she has no husband. Jesus then points out that she has actually had five husbands and is not married to the man with whom she is currently living. So she has been rejected by five men and is now being used by a sixth. But the man standing before her does not reject her. In fact, he engages her, and to her, to this woman valued by no one, he reveals the precious secret of who he really is (John 4:26).

When the disciples get back from the town, John notes that "they marveled that he was talking with a woman" (John 4:27).

This encounter involves no physical healing. Instead, it works an even deeper healing. The woman runs off. In her excitement, she forgets that she has no credibility and starts to tell people in the town that they have to come see this one who has told her everything she ever did. Amazed, they listen to her, come, see, and believe. Her dignity is restored. Her neighbors believe her testimony. And even more important, she has experienced in a very deep way the love and acceptance of God.

We are not told whether she changed her way of life. But her heart was surely changed by the love that she had encountered. When Jesus offered living water that would become a spring in her, welling up to eternal life, her response, "Give me this water!" (John 4:15), was her own confession of faith. How could Jesus deny such a request?

THE ADULTERESS

Another story from John's Gospel also famously discloses the Lord's mercy to a suffering woman. While Jesus is teaching in the Temple area, a woman is dragged to him, who, her accusers say, had been caught in the very act of adultery. It is telling that the man with whom she sinned is not also brought to Jesus for sentencing. The scribes and Pharisees remind Jesus that Moses said she should be executed, but they want to know what Jesus will say. Clearly, they don't really care about the adultery. And they don't care about the woman. She is only a pawn to be used to place Jesus in checkmate.

Instead, Jesus puts the scribes and Pharisees in the more difficult position. He says, "Let him who is without sin among you be the first to throw a stone at her" (John 8:7).

They have exalted themselves over the guilty woman they have dragged before him. Jesus is reminding them that, if strict justice were the measure, they too would find themselves condemned. They could have marveled, given thanks, and sought more wisdom from Jesus. But instead they slip away, one by one, leaving the miserable woman alone with Jesus. He speaks to her calmly, looking up at her: "Woman, where are they? Has no one condemned you?" She says, "No one, Lord." And Jesus says, "Neither do I condemn you; go, and do not sin again" (John 8:10-11).

She does not defend herself. She does not deny her sin. And neither does Jesus deny her sin. He simply establishes a fact: she and her accusers have something very fundamental in common— they all are in need of mercy. And God is ready to give mercy as a free, undeserved gift. There is one proviso—if you accept it, you must change. Because it contains within itself God's healing love, mercy received will actually begin to transform you.

KINGDOM OF MERCY

The kingdom of God is the kingdom of mercy. The revolutionary experience of mercy is what characterizes the kingdom and produces the crowds and the excitement. The kingdom breaks out at moments and at places you would least expect—a funeral procession in the village of Nain, right across the valley from Nazareth, for example. A widow's only son is about to be buried, and the wailing of the bereft and now destitute woman moves Jesus deeply. In Hebrew, the word for mercy is related to the word for womb. It is something deeply felt, in a visceral way. In compassion, Jesus touches the bier and calls the woman's son back to life (Luke 7:11-17).

Luke tells yet another story that shows the mercy of the Father encountered in the Son. Jesus is invited to the home of a Pharisee for a festive meal. Suddenly a woman, known to be a sinner, barges in uninvited. Sobbing, she makes her way to Jesus and begins to wash his feet with her tears. Then she loosens her hair and lets it down in public, something a reputable woman would never do. She uses the loosened hair to dry his feet so that she can anoint them with precious ointment (Luke 7:36-50).

Simon, the hosting Pharisee, thinks that this man can't possibly be a prophet—a prophet would know what kind of woman is touching him. A prophet would feel the spiritual pollution exuding from such a wretch and dismiss her from his sight.

Since Jesus is a prophet and more, he knows Simon's thoughts and so uses a parable to help Simon understand the meaning of what is happening: Two men owe debts to the same creditor, one debt small, the other large. Neither can pay his debt. So the creditor writes off both debts. Which debtor is more grateful? Obviously, the man with the larger debt, who was forgiven more.

Jesus makes it plain that Simon has been a good host. But Simon's measured hospitality means that, by his own estimate at least, he's not been forgiven much. The woman's over-the-top expression of love reveals that she knows her life has been entirely changed by the forgiveness she has received. Her love does not win her forgiveness; her love is her response to the forgiveness she has accepted and appreciated. When suffering people allow the mercy of God to flow into their lives, it changes everything. It is like being dead and getting your life back—"Your faith has saved you," Jesus says, "Go in peace." Her acceptance of the gift, her yes, is the faith that has saved her.

THE WOMEN FOLLOWERS OF JESUS

In light of what the Mishnah says about conversation with women, it is easy to understand why no sage from the time of Jesus is known to have taken on female disciples—nor to our knowledge did any sage of Israel travel with a band of disciples, teaching in one town and then another.

Luke, however, gives us some important information about Jesus' entourage that is easy to miss. We have already seen that Jesus traveled with a large band of disciples who included, but by no means were limited to, the Twelve. But he also tells us that among these who traveled with him were a number of "women who had been healed of evil spirits and infirmities: Mary, called Magdalene, from who seven demons had gone out, and Joanna, the wife of Chuza, Herod's steward, and Susanna, and many others, who provided for them out of their means" (Luke 8:2-3).

Only three are named. Their "call" is not described, as is the call of Peter and Andrew, James and John. But then again, the "call" to discipleship of most of the other male disciples is not described by the Gospel writers either. What Luke tells us is that their lives had been changed forever by the merciful love of God that had come to them in their suffering and had set them free. We are not told that these women were sinners, like the unnamed woman in Luke 7. The fact that Mary Magdalene had been freed from seven demons says something about the severity of her problem, but it does not necessarily tell us whether or not the demonic infestation was due to personal sin.[98]

But what does seem to come clear is that whatever happened to these women, they, like the woman in Luke 7, responded in gratitude by offering their lives and resources in service of the Lord's apostolic mission. The wife of Herod's steward would have been a prominent and well-to-do woman. Perhaps she was free to give her money to the mission and travel with the team because her husband had died. For a married Jewish woman of Palestine to travel with a group of men without the company of her husband would have been highly unlikely. This fact, and the fact that these women had control over their own finances, argues for the fact that they were widows.

In any case, Jesus includes them among his closest followers. And in the final climax of the story, we will see them faithfully standing at the foot of the Cross, announcing the good news of the empty tomb, and seated with the disciples in the Upper Room waiting for the coming of the Holy Spirit. In this assembly of 120 disciples, one more woman is to be found: Mary, the mother of Jesus (Acts 1:14).

CHAPTER 10

HOLINESS REDEFINED

Throughout the gospel story, the scribes and Pharisees keep popping up as the central villains. They criticize Jesus at every turn. Jesus sometimes returns the fire. As gentle and compassionate as Jesus is, even with notorious sinners, he upbraids the scribes and Pharisees harshly, sometimes vehemently. We must now examine this conflict, for it is essential to understanding Jesus and his teaching about God and about how God's people are to live.

HOLINESS AND THE TORAH

The greatest event in Israel's history, the Exodus from Egypt, was not simply to free Israel from bondage to Pharaoh but to make these liberated slaves God's very own people. At Mount Sinai, the Israelites were set apart for God. At that moment, they were given a special way of life that marked them as God's very own people. They were to reflect his holiness to the world through the holy way of life laid out for them in the Torah. God's command to them was clear: "Be holy, for I am holy" (Leviticus 11:44-45).

Their failure to live up to the standards of the Torah led to the catastrophe of the Babylonian captivity. So after the exiles returned home, holiness became the new focus. The Maccabees made the intensification of Torah observance the unquestioned agenda of the nation. All the Jewish parties that emerged waved this banner. By

Jesus' time, it was the Pharisees who had become the acknowledged leaders in this holiness movement. Though full-fledged members of the movement were only a few thousand, their influence was great. The people generally held them in high esteem.

So it must have come as a shock to his listeners when Jesus proclaimed, "Unless your righteousness exceeds that of the scribes and Pharisees, you will never enter the kingdom of heaven" (Matthew 5:20).

HOLINESS AND PURITY

Holiness meant for the Pharisees being "set apart" in the sense of being separated from the profane and especially from unholy people and things. Their name, therefore, appears to derive from this very principle—*Pharisees* most likely comes from the word meaning "separated ones." The word *Torah* originally meant "teaching, instruction." The Pharisees emphasized the legal dimension of it to such a degree that "the Teaching" became known as "the Law." To the 613 written commandments (*mitzvot*) contained in the Torah, the five books of Moses, the Pharisees and their scribes added a whole body of oral law that meticulously specified how to interpret and apply the 613 written commandments. In effect, this added many more rules to the written 613, some of which had little or no basis in the written Torah.

No wonder trained specialists were needed to help people navigate this complicated maze of regulations. The scribes or lawyers of Jesus' time would become known a few centuries later as rabbis.

The oral law comprised detailed rules on the Sabbath, ritual purity, and tithing. Particular case studies of how, when, and to whom these rules applied in specific situations occupied the scribes' attention. They were appalled that Jesus and his disciples were so cavalier in their approach to such things.

Take purity, for example. The written Torah says nothing about needing to ritually wash one's hands before eating. But the oral tradition of the elders demanded it in many situations. Naturally, the Pharisees are scrupulous about this custom and ask Jesus why he and his disciples neglect it. Jesus replies,

> Hear and understand: not what goes into the mouth defiles a man, but what comes out of the mouth, this defiles a man. ... What comes out of the mouth proceeds from the heart, and this defiles a man. For out of the heart come evil thoughts, murder, adultery, fornication, theft, false witness, slander. These are what defile a man; but to eat with unwashed hands does not defile a man. (Matthew 15:10-11, 15:18-20)

Jesus is passionate about purity—but purity of heart, not purity of hands, cups, and dishes. In his Sermon on the Mount, his renewed law for the renewed Israel, Jesus proclaims the essence of true blessedness in the form of the short, proverb-like phrases of the Beatitudes. These constitute a sort of charter of the kingdom of God, encapsulating Jesus' redefinition of holiness. One of these beatitudes reveals the kind of purity God is really after: "Blessed are the pure in heart, for they shall see God" (Matthew 5:8).

Jesus has come to purify, heal, and renew people from the inside out. The heart of a child is pure. Those who welcome the loving mercy of the Father can experience an inner cleansing that will transform thoughts and behavior, moving them to cry out in the joyful freedom of the children of God, "*Abba*, Father!"[99]

STRAINING OUT A GNAT AND SWALLOWING A CAMEL

Jesus sees some scribes using their knowledge of the fine points of the law to evade the spirit and purpose of the law. The fourth commandment, honor your father and mother, obliged adult children to financially support elderly parents. But through a legal fiction, a man was allowed to "dedicate his property to God," thus exempting it from being used to help his parents.[100] Jesus rails against the hypocrisy of this: the use of a legal tradition of human origin to nullify one of the most important of God's commandments (Mark 7:9-13).

The way the scribes and Pharisees used the oral traditions of the elders was supposed to safeguard the Law—to make a fence around the Torah. Instead it was violating and obscuring the Torah's most fundamental principles.

Take, for example, Sabbath regulations. While teaching in a synagogue one Sabbath, Jesus notices a woman who is bent over, unable to stand erect. Jesus calls her over and lays hands on her. She immediately straightens up. The synagogue leader is indignant (Luke 13:10-14). Healing, according to the tradition of the elders, is work. And work is forbidden on the Sabbath.

Jesus calls this out as moral blindness. The entire meaning of the Sabbath is being overlooked by the synagogue ruler and other like-minded champions of the Law. The Sabbath is a reminder of the past—God's great work of Creation and the gift of rest to his people. But it is also a pointer to the future, to the final, blessed rest of the people of God in the messianic age, when God will give them ultimate rest from their enemies on every side.[101]

The Jubilee year was the Sabbath of Sabbaths, a time when slaves were liberated from bondage and debts were canceled. The Jubilee year also pointed forward to the great Jubilee God's people were hoping for in the age to come (Daniel 9:24). In Jesus, the age to come has arrived. The great Jubilee is here (Luke 4:18-19; Leviticus 25:8-55). The meaning of the Sabbath is now fulfilled. Nothing more appropriate can occur on a Sabbath in the great Jubilee than the liberation of captives. And the one anointed by the Spirit to proclaim the Jubilee has the right and the obligation to do it. "The Son of man is lord of the sabbath" (Matthew 12:8).

Jesus calls out the synagogue ruler's objection as hypocrisy. If an animal owned by the synagogue ruler suffered from thirst on the Sabbath, the synagogue ruler would not think twice about walking it over to the watering trough. Yet the poor woman has been suffering for eighteen years ... and this righteous synagogue ruler wants her to wait still longer for relief? Jesus will not tolerate leaving this precious daughter of Abraham to suffer one more day.

Mercy is what happens when love is brought face-to-face with suffering (Luke 13:10-16), and it is mercy that God desires, not sacrifice (Matthew 12:7, citing Hosea 6:6). God had instituted the Sabbath as a blessing for his people. These blind guides had turned it into a burden (Mark 2:27).

Missing the forest for the trees, majoring in the minors ... our culture has many ways of referring to the problem we see here. Observing the care taken by scribes and Pharisees to pay exact tithes on such small things as herbs, Jesus calls them out: "You blind guides, straining out a gnat and swallowing a camel!" (Matthew 23:23-24).

THE HEART OF THE TORAH

It is a question from a scribe that gives Jesus the opportunity to identify the heart of the Law, what is being overlooked in the legalism of his critics. The question is not asked honestly; the scribe's intent, says Luke (10:25-37), is to put Jesus to the test: "What shall I do to inherit eternal life?" the scribe asks. Jesus turns the question back on him: "What is written in the law? What do you read there?" The scribe answers, "You shall love the Lord your God with all your heart, and with all your soul, and with all your strength, and with all your mind; and your neighbor as yourself." Jesus, in turn, says to the scribe, "Do this and you will live."

The scribe correctly identifies the first and greatest commandment as Deuteronomy 6:5, the second of the two verses that all Jewish men recite at least twice a day as part of the *Shema*.[102] The first verse of the *Shema* is a short creed: "Hear [*Shema*], O Israel, the LORD our God is one LORD" (Deuteronomy 6:4). Jews had a duty to "believe in God," which meant believing that the Lord is the only God. So doctrinal correctness is important. But if the Lord is really God, then the next verse naturally follows. God must not just be "believed in" but must be loved profoundly and totally.

The duty to love in this way could have been simply expressed by saying "with all your heart." In Hebrew, the heart indicates the emotions, which is often how we think of the heart in the English-speaking world, and also the very center of one's being. The Latin word for heart is *cor*, from which we get the English word *core*. Pope Francis explains that

> in the Bible, the heart is the core of the human person, where all his or her different dimensions intersect: body and spirit, interiority and openness to the world and to others, intellect, will and affectivity. If the heart is capable of holding all these dimensions together, it is because it is where we become open to truth and love, where we let them touch us and deeply transform us.[103]

As if this were not enough, Deuteronomy, as quoted by this scribe, commands us to love God with all our soul, mind, and strength. That expression is like adding bold, italics, and underlining to this command. It is a way to insist emphatically on the totality, energy, initiative, and passion that must fuel our love for God. God has given us absolutely everything and does so at every moment of our lives. Thus, what we owe God is an all-out, total sort of love, every minute of every day.

Who honestly can say that they have consistently loved God in this way?

To this commandment, the scribe has joined another from Leviticus 19:18—"Love your neighbor as yourself." This sounds a lot like what we would call the Golden Rule, given by Jesus in the Sermon on the Mount. Probably the most famous sage from the generation before Jesus, Hillel, had voiced a version of it. To a prospective Gentile convert to Judaism who was looking for a simple way to sum up the law, Hillel said, "That which is hateful to you do not do to another; that is the entire Torah, and the rest is its interpretation. Go study."[104]

Notice that Hillel formulates the rule in a negative fashion, to do no harm. It is no accident that Jesus, instead, puts it in a positive way: "So whatever you wish that men would do to you, do so to them; for this is the law and the prophets" (Matthew 7:12).

For Jesus, sin is not just an offense or transgression against a person. The word in Aramaic for sin means debt, and it expresses better Jesus' notion of sin. The idea is that one positively owes active love and mercy to a neighbor. To fail to respond in action to the suffering of another is a sin of omission. It is shocking that, in the only scene of the Last Judgment that Jesus provides us in the Gospels, the "goats" who are sent into everlasting fire are condemned not for offenses they committed (sins of commission) but for duties they neglected (sins of omission): "For I was hungry and you gave me no food, I was thirsty and you gave me no drink, I was a stranger and you did not welcome me, naked and you did not clothe me, sick and in prison and you did not visit me" (Matthew 25:42-43).[105]

The second thing to be aware of is that "neighbor" in Leviticus 19:18, as understood at this time, did not include all people. For example, it did not necessarily apply to women, particularly one's spouse. The same sage who said "Do not do to another what seems to you to be hurtful" also ruled that Deuteronomy 24:1 allowed a man to dismiss his wife for any reason, even if she simply burned his supper.[106]

The neighbor one was commanded to love in Leviticus 19:18 was one's fellow countryman, a faithful Israelite, and the Old Testament broadens this a bit to include the resident alien (Leviticus 19:34; Deuteronomy 10:19). According to the sages, a resident alien meant a Gentile living in the land of Israel who at least followed some Jewish beliefs and customs. But the command to love did not bind a Jew to love Jewish sinners, Samaritans, Gentiles, or his personal enemies. As we have seen, it was in fact considered a duty by the Qumran community to hate and curse sinners. The Pharisees and their scribes appear to have had a similar attitude.

THE GOOD SAMARITAN

We need this background to understand the next question the scribe addresses to Jesus. He is not satisfied with Jesus' affirmation that the command to love God and one's neighbor is the way to eternal life. He wants to know where he can draw the line, whom he can safely exclude from the category of neighbor, whom he is *not* obliged to love. "But he, desiring to justify himself, said to Jesus, 'And who is my neighbor?'" (Luke 10:29).

Jesus answers him with a parable that has become one of the most famous stories in the history of Western civilization (Luke 10:30-37). The scribe gets much more than he bargained for.

A man foolishly travels alone on the desolate road between Jerusalem and Jericho. Predictably, he is beaten, robbed, and left for dead. The criminals even take his clothes, leaving him lying on the road naked. A priest appears, traveling downhill from Jerusalem to Jericho. He is presumably on his way home from his week of Temple service.

Purity laws in the Old Testament oblige a priest to avoid touching a dead body unless the person is a close relative (Leviticus 21:1-2). So as not to transgress ceremonial regulations, the priest moves to the other side of the road and passes the man by. Next a Levite comes by, perhaps also traveling home from Temple service. No law forbids him from helping, but he too would be ritually impure for a week after touching such a man. Plus, he would have to make a sin offering. So he too passes the man by. One would expect the next man to come along to be a Jewish layman. Instead, he is a Samaritan.

Jews and Samaritans have been fighting a family feud for centuries. Samaritans, as far as the Jews are concerned, are heretics, schismatics, and half-breeds. They don't have the right Bible—they accept only the first five books of the Torah—and they don't come to Jerusalem for the feasts. True, they are descendants of Jacob and Abraham, but some Gentiles have contributed to their gene pool.

Bear in mind that, in the preceding chapter of Luke's Gospel, Jesus and the disciples are refused hospitality in Samaria because they are on their way to Jerusalem (Luke 9:51-56). In fact, John and James ask Jesus if he shouldn't call fire down upon the town in revenge. This gives you an idea about how Jews and Samaritans felt about each other.

The Samaritan Bible contains the very same rules about ritual purity as the Jewish Bible. But in Jesus' parable, that doesn't keep the Samaritan from stopping to help the man lying on the road. The Samaritan finds him alive but badly wounded. The Samaritan has packed wine and oil for his own journey, and he uses them to dress the man's wounds. He puts the victim on his own donkey, takes him to a local inn, and gets him a room. The next day, before resuming his journey, he leaves money with the innkeeper to cover the expenses of the recovering man. Plus, he promises to stop by on his return trip to pay any additional expenses that might be incurred.

Which man, asks Jesus, was a neighbor to the unfortunate victim? The scribe can't bear to say the word "Samaritan." Instead he says, "The one who showed mercy on him." Jesus concludes the conversation with this directive: "Go and do likewise."

The primary concern of the priest and Levite in this story seems to be ritual purity. But the second most important commandment after loving God is not about ritual purity. It is the mandate to love your neighbor as your very self. Not only is Jesus showing that mercy trumps ceremonial law; he is saying that the duty to love extends not just to people who are like us but even to our political and theological adversaries.

HOLINESS REDEFINED

Jesus has brought the final revelation of God. God is the merciful Father whose bountiful generosity extends to sinners as well as the righteous, women as well as men, foreigners as well as Israelites. If holiness is being like God, then to be God's holy people means to share in and reflect God's mercy. The perfection of God consists in his perfect love, shown most fully in his love of the unworthy. So true holiness must also manifest this dimension of God's love.

In the sermon on the Mount, Jesus makes clear that he has not come to abolish or relax the law, but to fulfill it (Matthew 5:17). This does not mean simply to observe the law as it is, but to bring the law to its final completion. Jesus, like the Pharisees, is for an intensification of the law—but in an entirely different direction. Instead of intensifying things peripheral, provisional, and transitory, Jesus intensifies and clarifies the Torah's most central precepts, bringing them to full and complete measure. God loves even his enemies. So the love of neighbor required of God's people in the new era of the kingdom can admit of no exception. Shocking as it may seem, it has to include love of enemies:

> You have heard that it was said, "You shall love your neighbor and hate your enemy." But I say to you, Love your enemies and pray for those who persecute you, so that you may be sons of your Father who is in heaven; for he makes his sun rise on the evil and on the good, and sends rain on the just and on the unjust. … You, therefore, must be perfect, as your heavenly Father is perfect. (Matthew 5:43-45, 5:48)

Jesus also puts the same idea a different way: "Be merciful, even as your Father is merciful" (Luke 6:36).

POVERTY OF SPIRIT

The very first line of the Beatitudes, the charter of the kingdom, is this: "Blessed are the poor in spirit, for theirs is the kingdom of heaven" (Matthew 5:3). It is no accident that this comes first in the list. Another name for poverty of spirit is humility. Pope Benedict XVI notes that the present-day entrance to the place of Jesus' birth is a small doorway less than five feet high. He says, "If we want to find the God who appeared as a child … we must bend down … in order to pass through the portal of faith and encounter the God who is so different from our prejudices and opinions."[107] Humility is the doorway into the kingdom of God.

Humility does not mean looking down on oneself or thinking ill of oneself. Instead, it means not thinking of oneself very much at all. The poor in spirit are free to forget themselves because they are secure. They accept the fact that, as creatures, they are small, vulnerable, and not ultimately in control. But they know there is a loving Father who is great, omnipotent, and totally in control. The poor in spirit are content to find their security in God rather than in themselves and to depend on God rather than on themselves. Dependency like this comes naturally to a child, which is why Jesus says, "Let the children come to me ... for to such belongs the kingdom of heaven" (Matthew 19:14).

To illustrate the difference between poverty of spirit and its opposite, Jesus tells a parable about two men who one day go up to the Temple to pray. One is a tax collector, the other a Pharisee. The Pharisee stands up and thanks God profusely that he is not like other sinful men, especially the despicable tax collector who is praying nearby. As part of his prayer, he reminds God of his merits: "I fast twice a week, I give tithes of all that I get."

The tax collector, on the other hand, stands in the back, beating his breast and saying, "God, be merciful to me a sinner" (see Psalm 51:1). Jesus makes it clear that it is the tax collector who leaves the Temple justified, not the Pharisee, "for every one who exalts himself will be humbled, but he who humbles himself will be exalted" (Luke 18:9–14).

THE POISON OF PRIDE

Jesus' audience for this story consisted of "some who trusted in themselves that they were righteous and despised others" (Luke 18:9). The problem with the Pharisee is that he is not in touch with reality. He is impressed with his religious accomplishments and thinks God should be impressed as well.

There is no doubt he did the good works he mentioned plus more. But if he paid attention to the *Shema* he recited every day, he would be aware that fasting twice a week and paying tithes of 10 percent on what he owns is nothing compared to what he owes God, which is 100 percent of every penny and every waking hour. Compared with what he owes, what he offers God is a mere pittance.

Prayer is looking at God and talking to God. This Pharisee is looking at himself and is preoccupied with himself. Attempting to elevate his own standing before God, he has to thrust down those around him. Pride is essentially competitive. And it is an exhausting enterprise, always needing to demonstrate that it is worthier than others and better than others. It is the sin of the gloating mob who were looking forward to stoning the adulteress in John 8.

The horrible thing about pride is just how insidious it is. It is probably the most dangerous temptation of religious people. Sexual sin is flagrant and hard to miss. Pride, however, starts subtly and almost imperceptibly. It flies under the radar and stealthily delivers its lethal payload. A couple of centuries before Jesus' time, the Pharisees arose from the Maccabean heroes who resisted apostasy and saved the independence of Israel. In other words, the Pharisees numbered among the good guys. Before long they, along with the descendants of the Maccabees, had become the bad guys. Pride had done its ugly work.

In the early stages of the disease, there is a chance that the proud person can recognize the peril he is in and take evasive action. But the problem is that pride immediately begins the process of clouding one's vision and hardening one's heart. Pretty soon the proud person becomes blind and heartless. Notice that Jesus calls the Pharisees "blind guides" (Matthew 15:14; 23:24). And what angers Jesus most is their hardness of heart (Matthew 13:15; Mark 3:5).

The publican in the story, on the other hand, illustrates what poverty of spirit means. The Pharisee is under the illusion that God is fortunate to have such a wonderful worshipper as himself. The tax collector is under no such illusion. He is completely aware that he comes to God empty-handed. He has nothing to stand on but God's mercy. The Pharisee is pleased with himself and so looks at himself. The publican can no longer look at himself. Instead he looks away from himself, to God. The poor in spirit are not full of themselves and so can be filled to overflowing with God and with all good things in him. "Blessed are those who hunger and thirst for righteousness, for they shall be satisfied" (Matthew 5:6).

Immediately following the story of the Pharisee and tax collector, Jesus finds himself surrounded by parents bringing little children for him to bless and touch. The disciples rebuke the parents: Jesus is far too important a person to waste his time and energy on infants. Jesus corrects his disciples. There is nothing more important than this moment. What is happening here is prophetic. It illustrates exactly what he is trying to teach them. "Truly, I say to you, whoever does not receive the kingdom of God like a child shall not enter it" (Luke 18:17).

Who is more unselfconscious than a little child? Who is less self-sufficient? Who more excited about receiving presents? The kingdom of God can only be received humbly and joyously as a free gift. The kingdom of God is the joy of children who delight in their Father's embrace.

THE RIGHTEOUSNESS OF THE PHARISEES

The simplicity and ingenuousness of the little child is the antithesis of the complicated, self-righteous legalism of the scribes and Pharisees. When Jesus says that unless your righteousness exceeds that of the scribes and the Pharisees, you will not enter the kingdom of heaven, this is precisely what he is talking about.

But Jesus issues a warning that we overlook at our peril: "Beware of the leaven of the Pharisees" (Matthew 16:6). Leaven, mixed with dough, slowly and imperceptibly causes the dough to rise. Pride puffs up, and pride can turn beautiful rituals and devotions bad by making them lifeless routines that we use to justify ourselves and exalt ourselves over others. If you find yourself getting oversensitive to criticism or seething with outrage over the failings of others, beware. If you think what happened to the Pharisees could never happen to you, it could already be happening.

CHAPTER 11

THE TRUE ISRAEL

Salvation, according to the thinking of many in the modern world, is a personal thing. It is about going to heaven when you die and perhaps about interior peace of soul. Some in the history of Christianity have interpreted Jesus' saying "The kingdom of God is in your midst" (Luke 17:21) to mean that the kingdom is within a person's heart.

The kingdom of God inaugurated by Jesus has a deeply personal impact, for it is characterized by a personal intimacy with God as Father that goes beyond anything previously known in the history of Israel. But it is not about private, individual salvation. The special prayer Jesus teaches is one he teaches his disciples together, a prayer that is intended to distinguish them as a community. The very phrase "our Father" implies that those who pray it are brothers and sisters. It is a personal prayer that inaugurates a family relationship.

Israel began literally as a family, the family of Abraham, Isaac, and Jacob. But the family had been fragmented over the years. Not all groups of Jews in Jesus' day had the same idea of what sort of messianic figure would usher in the end times. But all agreed that one of the promises that would come true in the final age would be a restored Israel, not just renewed in holiness but reunited, reconstituted as one people again.

ISRAEL REGATHERED AND REUNITED

The history of God's people, indeed the history of humanity, had been the sad story of strife and division. Cain killed Abel. Joseph was sold into slavery by his brothers. The twelve tribes split into two rival kingdoms. Both the Northern and the Southern Kingdoms went into exile. Some people lost their identity as God's people and were assimilated into Gentile culture; hence the "ten lost tribes of Israel." Others remained faithful but wound up scattered in small communities in Babylon, Rome, and other cities around the world. These were the Jews of the far-flung Diaspora (meaning "dispersion"). A small remnant returned home (in 538 BC) only to face renewed hostilities with their relatives and neighbors, the Samaritans, and oppression by pagan Gentiles.

In the last days, promised the Lord, the twelve tribes would be somehow gathered together again. The number of biblical texts where this gathering in is either promised or prayed for is staggering. The regathering of the twelve tribes is a motif woven throughout all different classes of biblical literature, from the earlier to the later prophets, from Maccabees to Sirach.[108] It is an indispensable ingredient of the hope of Israel.

This gathering into the new and true Israel of the last days is, therefore, a key focus of Jesus' public ministry. He is gathering a select group of disciples around himself and calling them to labor with him in the work of gathering. As he notes, "He who does not gather with me scatters" (Matthew 12:30; Luke 11:23).

ASSEMBLE THE OUTCASTS

Though all Jews looked for the regathering of Israel in the last days, not all were agreed as to who would be included. The Qumran community identified their little sect with the end-times community of salvation. The Pharisees were at least a bit more inclusive—they hoped to convince other Jews to qualify for membership through ever-more-rigorous observance of the law. But how about those who had not kept the law, adopting Gentile ways? Tax collectors and other sinners were considered beyond the pale by most pious Jews. They would not be invited to the party.

John the Baptist appears to have been the first to think otherwise. Just a few miles from where he baptized tax collectors lies the town of Jericho. One day Jesus and his disciples happen to be passing through Jericho on the way to Jerusalem. A man named Zacchaeus, identified as the city's chief tax collector, is anxious to get a look at Jesus (Luke 19:1-10).

We need to note here that Jericho was part of Judea and therefore under direct Roman control. All tax collectors were shunned by pious Jews because the profession was known for dishonesty and extortion. But at least Galilean tax collectors worked for a Jewish sovereign, Herod Antipas. Tax collectors in Jericho worked directly for the pagan Roman occupiers. The chief tax collector actually bid on the tax franchise in an auction. To get the contract, he would have to pay the Romans up front for all the tolls required from the district for the entire term of the contract. To get his money back and make his profit, he would then have to send out the tax collectors, accompanied by police, to collect their pound of flesh. He had to be quite wealthy to buy the franchise in the first place. The more he and his staff squeezed the population, the more money they could keep and the wealthier they would become. Surely there could not be too many people in Jericho more resented than the town's tax-collector-in-chief.

Now, imagine the spectacle of a well-dressed man, one of the wealthiest in town, running as fast as he can to find a good place to stand along the road. Unfortunately, a waiting crowd already lines the route, stretching far ahead of Jesus' entourage. The man is short and so will never be able to see over the heads of the people in front of him. So this privileged, dignified businessman resorts to climbing a tree to see the celebrity. Imagine the amusement of the crowd. The big shot is making a fool of himself.

Jesus catches sight of the little man perched in the large sycamore and calls him by name: "Zacchaeus, make haste and come down; for I must stay at your house today." Zacchaeus hurries down and receives him with joy.

The reaction of the crowd is predictable. They begin to grumble and object: "He has gone in to be the guest of a man who is a sinner."

In response to their grumbling, Zacchaeus addresses Jesus. "Behold, Lord, the half of my goods I give to the poor; and if I have defrauded any one of anything, I restore it fourfold." John the Baptist had told the crowds to give some evidence that they meant to reform. But he didn't require the strict restitution demanded by Leviticus—giving back what was taken plus 20 percent. Zacchaeus has gone above and beyond the strict measure of the Law, offering to make fourfold restitution to people he has overcharged and even give 50 percent of what he has acquired honestly to the poor! The Law doesn't demand this. Neither does Jesus. What Zacchaeus gives, he gives freely, from the heart.

Nowhere in this account is faith mentioned. Instead, faith is demonstrated. The Father, in an invisible way, nudges Zacchaeus from within by the Holy Spirit. Grace is given in the form of a desire to see Jesus. Zacchaeus responds to this grace by pursuing Jesus, quite literally and avidly. He will allow no obstacle to get in his way, even if he has to make a spectacle of himself by climbing a tree like a child. "Unless you turn and become like children, you will never enter the kingdom of heaven" (Matthew 18:3). Here the word "turn" is the turning around of repentance. "Whoever humbles himself like this child, he is the greatest in the kingdom of heaven" (Matthew 18:4).

Bold, active pursuit of God. Willingness to humble oneself like a child. Welcoming Christ joyfully, receiving him into your house and life. Jesus' call at the start of his public ministry was "repent, and believe in the gospel" (Mark 1:15). There is no better example of what this means than Zacchaeus.

Jesus' inviting himself to dinner is a sign of the Father's acceptance and love. It comes as a grace, an undeserved gift. But Zacchaeus' response illustrates another dimension of the faith and repentance that are the doorway to the kingdom—the acceptance of the gift spontaneously leads to a changed life. The kingdom is a pearl, a treasure. For the one who recognizes its value, no price is too great to pay. Whatever he holds in his hands is a trinket in comparison. So it makes total sense to let it go.

As far as Jesus is concerned, Zacchaeus cannot be written off or excluded from the kingdom. He is a son of Abraham by birth and now a son of Abraham by faith. He is one of the family who has strayed and been brought back, a real person who puts flesh and bones on the fictional tax collector praying near the Pharisee in the previous chapter of Luke. In that chapter, Luke also tells us that the rich ruler goes away sad. Unable to part with his possessions to follow Jesus, he shows how hard it is for the rich to enter the kingdom. Now Zacchaeus, in contrast, shows that "what is impossible with men is possible with God" (Luke 18:27).

THE TWELVE

Jesus apparently does not invite Zacchaeus to join the band of disciples traveling with him to Jerusalem. But at the start of the public ministry, Jesus calls many to literally follow him. Among the first is a despised tax collector who probably worked the toll road, the Via Maris, which passed through Capernaum. Called Levi by Luke and Mark (Mark 2:13-17; Luke 5:27-32), he is identified as Matthew in the Gospel that bears his name (Matthew 9:9-13). Jesus notices him, looks at him, and issues the command, "Follow me." Luke notes that he leaves all behind, rises, and follows Jesus.

What is shocking here is that Jesus does not just pardon a sinner but invites him to become a member of his inner circle.

It soon comes time to take yet another critical step in the public ministry. As is his custom, Jesus goes up on a hill one evening and passes the entire night in prayer. As he comes down the mountain, he has in his mind the names of twelve men chosen from his larger group of disciples. The number twelve is no accident. Twelve is the symbolic number for the people of God, Israel, who are organized into twelve tribes, named for the sons of Jacob (who is also called Israel). The choosing of twelve to lead his band of disciples is a prophetic action. These twelve are to be the new foundation of a renewed people of God, the new patriarchs who will one day "sit on twelve thrones, judging the twelve tribes" of the new Israel (Matthew 19:28).[109] An august and exalted role, for sure. And on one of these thrones, beside the fishermen from Capernaum, will sit Matthew, the tax collector.

We know very little for sure about most of the Twelve. Peter and his brother Andrew were fishermen from Capernaum, as were James and John, the sons of Zebedee. And we know that Matthew was a tax collector. The others were Philip, Bartholomew, Thomas, another James (son of Alphaeus), Simon the Zealot, and two Judases—Judas son of James (sometimes identified as Jude Thaddeus), and Judas Iscariot, who betrayed the Lord. The fact that one of them was a tax collector speaks volumes about Jesus' plan. So does the fact that another is called Simon the Zealot.[110]

Often people assume that Simon the Zealot was an anti-Roman revolutionary. There are two problems with this misconception. The first is that it is an anachronism. Galilee was ruled at this time by the Jewish tetrarch, Herod Antipas. There were no Roman legions stationed in Galilee to rebel against. And the Zealot party of anti-Roman insurrectionists apparently did not get started in Palestine until about thirty-five years after Jesus' ministry.

The second problem with this misconception is that it distracts us from the real significance of what "zealot" meant in Jesus' time, which sheds light on why a zealot was called to the inner circle. *Zealous* meant jealous—jealous for the rights of God and outraged over offenses committed by fellow Jews against the Lord and the Torah. Zealots in Jesus' time were those who vehemently opposed compromises with pagan culture. The legendary model for zeal was Phinehas, Aaron's grandson, who, seeing an Israelite take a pagan woman into his tent to make her his wife, went into the tent and slew them both with his spear.[111]

The Qumran sectarians considered it a duty to hate sinners, but they withdrew to the desert, leaving sinners to be destroyed in the Lord's wrath in the last days. Pharisees exhorted sinners, urging them to compliance with the Torah. Zealots went beyond mild persuasion; they were for compelling sinners or punishing them. At the very least, they would publicly shame backsliders and those who were flirting with pagan culture.

Paul is a great example of a zealot in this sense and calls himself such: "As to the law a Pharisee, as to zeal a persecutor of the Church" (Philippians 3:5-6). He obtained a legal mandate from the chief priests to arrest Christian heretics and drag them to prison (Acts 9:14, 26:12), but at least he operated within the law. Some zealots took matters into their own hands and dealt "street justice" to sinners.

The point here is that Simon the Zealot was not an enemy of Rome so much as an enemy of tax collectors and sinners, compromisers and slackers. Simon's sort of people hated the Matthews of the world. And Matthew's sort of people resented the condemnation they got from Simon's sort. But Jesus calls both—the tax collector and the zealot—to live not only with him but with one another. Both had to leave behind not just their possessions but their attitudes, their resentments, and their grievances.

FAMILY MEALS

During the public ministry of Jesus, few things irk Jesus' critics more than the festive meals that Jesus has with tax collectors and sinners. The party that Matthew throws at his home, crowded with a throng of his sinful friends, is just the beginning (Luke 5:29-30). The public ministry is one festive meal after another. His enemies recognize this. Jesus reports that he, unlike his ascetical cousin John, is known so well for eating and drinking that his enemies accuse him of being "a glutton and a drunkard, a friend of tax collectors and sinners!" (Luke 7:34).

Like the calling of the Twelve, these festive meals are prophetic acts. They manifest the joyful celebration taking place in heaven over the return of sinners (Luke 15:1-10). Table fellowship is a sign of acceptance, peace, and friendship. These are homecoming meals in which the Father, through Jesus, is welcoming back the prodigal sons. But they are also family meals where repentant tax collectors eat together with former zealots, learning to accept each other as members of God's family and as part of the wider family of the renewed Israel. The challenges this entails are hinted at in the story of the Prodigal Son where the elder brother is reluctant to join the feasting (Luke 15:25-32).

MERCY AS FORGIVENESS

The bond that holds this renewed community together is the common experience of being touched, through Jesus, by the loving mercy of the Father. To welcome this mercy is to allow oneself to be transformed by it. Resentment against others is inconceivable for those who accept the Father's mercy. This is so central to Jesus' teaching that he repeatedly hammers it home to his disciples during the public ministry and inserts it into the Our Father.

There is a fascinating fact about the Lord's Prayer that is often overlooked. In Matthew's account, the Lord teaches us to ask God to "forgive us our trespasses as we forgive those who trespass against us." This, of course, all Christians know and can rattle off without thinking. However, the meaning of the petition is rather jolting. We are asking God to forgive us to the same degree, in the same measure, as we forgive those who have offended us. To pray this prayer while holding a grudge is to pray a curse upon oneself.

If this were not enough, Jesus, immediately after concluding the prayer, repeats only one of its petitions, and it is this very one. In case we miss the strict requirement embedded in this petition, he points it out: "If you forgive men their trespasses, your heavenly Father also will forgive you; but if you do not forgive men their trespasses, neither will your Father forgive your trespasses" (Matthew 6:9-14).

Finally, in case people still fail to get just how critical forgiveness is, Jesus tells the parable of the unmerciful servant. The servant's incredibly large debt is forgiven by the king. Nevertheless, he immediately throttles a fellow servant and has him thrown in jail for an unpaid debt that is nothing compared to the debt that he has been forgiven. When the king hears about this, he throws the unmerciful servant in prison (Matthew 18:21-35). God's forgiveness comes as a free gift; but it will be rescinded if it is not extended in turn to others.

As far as Jesus is concerned, reconciliation is a duty that comes before offering sacrifice to God. Or to put it another way, offering God a pure sacrifice is so important that one must not dare pollute it by having unforgiveness in one's heart. Either way you look at it, the directive is clearly given in the Sermon on the Mount that "if you are offering your gift at the altar, and there remember that your brother has something against you, leave your gift there before the altar and go; first be reconciled to your brother, and then come and offer your gift" (Matthew 5:23-24).

To Jesus' hearers during his public ministry, this places forgiveness before Temple sacrifices. Jesus alludes to this when Pharisees obsessed with ritual and cultic purity criticize his meals with sinners. He says to them, "Go and learn what this means, 'I desire mercy, and not sacrifice'" (Matthew 9:13, quoting Hosea 6:6). By the time the Gospel of Matthew was written, Christians had already applied this command to the Eucharist, the new sacrifice of the new Israel. As a reminder of the duty to forgive before approaching the altar, the Our Father and the exchange of peace were recited before Communion, as they are today.

One of the few things we know about the Twelve is that all this talk about forgiveness is not just theoretical—the Gospels make no attempt to hide their weakness and foibles. They frequently let Jesus down and presumably irk each other as well.[112] If this were not the case, Peter wouldn't have to ask how many times he is obliged to forgive his brother. Peter suggests seven times, which perhaps he had heard from the lips of Jesus on another occasion (Luke 17:4). Jesus replies that the proper number is rather seventy times seven, which is to say without limit (Matthew 18:21-22).

The renewed, regathered Israel, the community of the kingdom of God, is meant to be a community of the forgiven, who reflect the grace of mercy in a way of life founded on forgiveness and mutual acceptance. The culture of the kingdom is a culture of mercy.

BOUNDARIES OF THE NEW ISRAEL

During the public ministry of Jesus, the nucleus of the new, true Israel of the last days is being formed. Its leaders, the Twelve, are themselves a community of missionary disciples, forgiven sinners who express in their very composition the fact that the new Israel is a community of mercy and reconciliation.

The wider community of Jesus' followers represents even more clearly the all-embracing character of the renewed Israel. Children, who are usually kept out of the way, are celebrated as the model of discipleship, for "to such belongs the kingdom of heaven" (Matthew 19:14). And we have already seen the extent to which Jesus goes out of his way to include women. The healing power of the kingdom is also made available to the afflicted and the downtrodden—the blind, the lepers, the mute, and the lame (Isaiah 35:6, 61:1-3).

But some people of higher social stature are invited to the feast—at least one wealthy member of the Sanhedrin, Joseph of Arimathea; one Pharisee, Nicodemus; an unnamed scribe who Jesus says is not far from the kingdom (Mark 12:34); a synagogue ruler named Jairus; and the wife of Herod's steward (Luke 8:3). Above all, Jesus goes out of his way to reach out to those alienated through sin, "the lost sheep of the house of Israel" (Matthew 15:24) like Matthew, Zacchaeus, and the woman caught in adultery.

But what about those not of the house of Jacob? Like Samaritans and Gentiles?

All the Gospels testify to the fact that Jesus, though focusing on the Jewish population of the land, bumps up against outsiders at various places. On the road to Jerusalem from Galilee, Jesus and the disciples would pass through either Samaria or the pagan Decapolis. We have already looked at Jesus' poignant encounter with the Samaritan woman. But Jesus also delivers a demoniac in the Gerasene region, a pagan occupant of the Decapolis, and a deaf-mute in the Decapolis (Mark 5:1-20, 7:31-37).[113] And the sole leper of ten who returns to thank Jesus for his healing is a Samaritan (Luke 17:11-19).

The colorful story of the bold Syrophoenician (Canaanite) woman who begs Jesus to deliver her daughter reveals the missionary approach of Jesus. Her daughter has "an unclean spirit," and the mother asks Jesus to cast it out. His response to her is telling: "Let the children first be fed, for it is not right to take the children's bread and throw it to the dogs." He is referring here to the children of Israel, to the Jews. But she boldly replies, "Yes, Lord; yet even the dogs under the table eat the children's crumbs" (Mark 7:24-30). How can Jesus resist such insistent faith? Of course he cannot. In the Our Father, he has taught his disciples to ask for the bread of the kingdom.[114] Though this bread will be offered first to the children of Israel, it will be denied to no one who asks for it.

The irony is that Jesus finds more faith outside Israel than within. This is his observation when he is taken aback by the faith of the Capernaum centurion: "Not even in Israel have I found such faith. I tell you, many will come from east and west and sit at table with Abraham, Isaac, and Jacob in the kingdom of heaven, while the sons of the kingdom will be thrown into the outer darkness" (Matthew 8:10-12). The children of the kingdom may have first claim, but "many that are first will be last, and the last first" (Matthew 19:30). This is the same theme that Jesus sounded in the synagogue of Nazareth early in his public ministry, which elicited the violent outrage of his hometown audience (Luke 4:28-30).

When the infant Jesus was presented in the Temple, Simeon spoke of the child as "a light for revelation to the Gentiles" (Luke 2:32), alluding to a prophecy in Isaiah that shows the horizons of the true Israel:

> And now the LORD says, who formed me from the womb to be his servant, to bring Jacob back to him, and that Israel might be gathered to him … : "It is too light a thing that you should be my servant to raise up the tribes of Jacob and to restore the preserved of Israel; I will give you as a light to the nations, that my salvation may reach to the end of the earth." (Isaiah 49:5-6)

The renewed, regathered Israel, the true Israel of the final age, will have marked boundaries that clearly distinguish those inside from those outside. But those markers will not be circumcision, physical ancestry, and dietary laws. They will be mercy, forgiveness, and faith.

CHAPTER 12

THE TRUTH ABOUT JESUS

Who is this Jesus? Herod asks the question and so does Pilate. Is he Elijah? The prophet like Moses? The messiah? Even God? If he is the messiah and is divine, why, during his public ministry, does he not just come out and say so?

As a Jew speaking to Jews within Middle Eastern culture, Jesus would often communicate indirectly and gradually, since this approach is what his hearers would expect.

Jesus' audience is not expecting God to come personally as the promised messiah, nor are they expecting a suffering messiah. Most people are yearning for a kingly warrior like David. They are hoping the messiah-king will beat the Gentiles, not save them. But Jesus himself is the messianic King, prophet, and priest, and no one expected that.

When it comes to his own identity, if Jesus had explained it to his followers all at once, they would not have understood. So he teaches them slowly through parables and actions. His words and his miracles must be seen against the background of the Old Testament and Jewish culture, the way his first audience saw them.

When we carefully examine his teaching and his actions, we can see that he actually does disclose his identity quite clearly, at least to those who understand the Jewish Scriptures and heritage. Ironically, his opponents often appreciate the implications of his deeds and words better than his own disciples do.

THE SABBATH AND THE POOLS OF BETHESDA

Regarding the future time of salvation, Isaiah foretold, "Then shall the lame man leap like a deer" (Isaiah 35:6).

On several occasions, this prophecy is fulfilled when crippled individuals encounter the healing power of God's love in Jesus. The woman who had been bent over for eighteen years is one (Luke 13:10-17). Another of those encounters happens just outside the city walls of Jerusalem. Near the Sheep Gate, one of the major entrances to the city, there once stood two massive pools of water separated by a portico. The entire double-pool complex was surrounded on all four sides by a covered colonnade. The double pool was reputed to have special healing powers at certain rare moments when the waters were suddenly agitated. The name of the place, Bethesda (also rendered Bethzatha), means "house of mercy." Afflicted people lined the edge of the pools along the five porticos, hoping that their turn for a miracle would soon come. One man had been waiting a very long time but was still unprepared when mercy finally found him (John 5:1-18).

Jesus asks the crippled man a direct question: "Do you want to be healed?" The man answers indirectly, in typical Middle Eastern fashion. Rather than simply saying yes, he explains how unfortunate he is because no one ever helps him get into the water at the special moments of healing. Of course, the man implies by this that he wants nothing more than to be healed. Jesus responds by issuing a matter-of-fact command—"Rise, take up your pallet, and walk"—as if this would be the easiest thing in the world for a crippled man to do. Yet "at once the man was healed" (John 5:8-9).

The day this occurs happens to be the Sabbath. As when the crippled woman was healed on the Sabbath (Luke 13:16), the response of the religious leaders is not joy over the man's good fortune but a stern rebuke to him for carrying his pallet, or empty bed; he and the one who healed him have violated the Sabbath regulations. In the oral law of the elders, later written down in the Mishnah, thirty-nine activities are deemed to be work and therefore are forbidden on the Sabbath. One of them is to carry something from one location to another, including a pallet.[115]

Jesus could have appealed to the greater duty of mercy that outweighs Sabbath regulations. Or he could have disputed the authority of the oral tradition, noting that Scripture does not forbid either healing or carrying on the Sabbath. He has approached his debates with his critics from these angles on other occasions, since he heals often on the Sabbath and is regularly taken to task for doing so.

This time, Jesus instead takes a much more radical approach. He says that even on the Sabbath, "My Father is working still, and I am working" (John 5:17).

The scribes of the day admitted that God, through Divine Providence, continues to work on the Sabbath. Babies are still born as God continues his creative work. If God ever ceased working, everything would lapse into nothingness.

But the scribes say that working on the Sabbath is an exclusively divine prerogative. Jesus, by claiming the right to work on the Sabbath and by calling God his Father, is implicitly saying that he is divine and equal to God. It may have taken Jesus' disciples a while to fully understand the significance of this, but the scribes get the point immediately. John tells us, "This was why the Jews sought all the more to kill him, because he not only broke the sabbath but also called God his Father, making himself equal with God" (John 5:18).[116]

LOWERED THROUGH THE ROOF

Another famous encounter of Jesus with a crippled man occurs in Galilee. One day in Capernaum, Jesus is staying most likely in Peter and Andrew's house, where he had healed Peter's mother-in-law. So many people crowd around the house that men carrying a paralyzed man on a pallet are not able to get him to Jesus. So they hoist him up on the one-story structure, break open the thatched roof, and lower the man down into the room where Jesus is. Jesus says to the man, "Child, your sins are forgiven." He can sense what the scribes are thinking: "It is blasphemy! Who can forgive sins but God alone?" Jesus immediately says to them, "Which is easier, to say to the paralytic, 'Your sins are forgiven,' or to say, 'Rise, take up your pallet and walk'? But that you may know that the Son of man has authority on earth to forgive sins," he turns to the paralytic and says, "I say to you, rise, take up your pallet and go home." And so the man does. Mark describes the reaction of the crowd: "They were all amazed and glorified God, saying, 'We never saw anything like this!'" (Mark 2:1-12).

Mark preserves in this account not only the fact of the marvel but the weighty question of the scribes. That's because this is a question the evangelist wants us, his readers, to ask ourselves. Who can forgive sins but God alone? The evangelist is teaching us here by what is commonly known as the Socratic method. As if we didn't already know the answer, Jesus provides the answer implicitly, indirectly, by what he does. Yes, the normal place to obtain forgiveness of sins is the Temple, where the sinner makes the appropriate sin offering. Yes, the only one who can forgive sins committed against God is God himself. Somehow, Jesus is the new Temple, the place to meet God and experience forgiveness and mercy. He bears God's authority because through him people are brought face-to-face with God.

THE CALMING OF THE STORM

Bad weather can quickly turn a boat ride into a nightmare. This is particularly true on the Sea of Galilee, a freshwater lake resting almost seven hundred feet below sea level. Also known as the Sea of Tiberias, it sits in a bowl with mountains surrounding it. Wind blowing across the land accelerates as it goes downhill and flows through a narrow valley into the lake. The cool wind from this valley hits the lake as if it were blown in by a bellows. So when conditions are right, massive waves can quickly arise and wreak havoc on the flimsy wooden boats used by the fishermen.

One evening Jesus and the disciples are making their way across the lake when such a storm appears out of nowhere. As the boat fills with water, Jesus remains asleep in the stern. The disciples frantically wake him. He calmly rebukes the wind and commands the sea to be at peace. A great calm ensues, and the disciples are dumbfounded. Mark concludes the section with another rhetorical question: "Who then is this, that even wind and sea obey him?" (Mark 4:35-41).

A Jew steeped in the Hebrew Scriptures could easily offer an answer. No prophet or king in the Old Testament commanded nature. God commanded Moses to lift his staff, and God, through Moses, parted the sea; Moses did not command the sea to be opened (Exodus 14:16-31). Another example occurs after the famous contest on top of Mount Carmel between Elijah and the prophets of Baal. This confrontation vanquished idolatry and cleared the way for God to end the drought and famine that had afflicted the land for years. Elijah, the victor, did not command the rain to return. Instead he prayed fervently and waited. After Elijah's prolonged prayer, God finally answered his plea. It is God who sends the rain (1 Kings 18:41-46).

The closest thing in the Old Testament to the story of Jesus rebuking the wind and the waves is a story in Psalm 107 of mariners caught in a storm:

> They cried to the LORD in their trouble, and he delivered them from their distress; he made the storm be still, and the waves of the sea were hushed. Then they were glad because they had quiet, and he brought them to their desired haven. (Psalm 107:28-30)

In the Old Testament, command over nature is exclusively a divine prerogative. Mark sees the implications of Jesus' actions and wants his readers to come to the obvious conclusion.

THE SHEPHERD

Abraham, Isaac, and Jacob were all shepherds. So were Moses and David. It was natural, then, that the leaders of Israel from the beginning came to be regarded as shepherds. But as we have seen, the shepherds of Israel had regularly done a poor job. Even David, the greatest of Israel's kings, had failed miserably to care for the sheep and instead had become a sheep-stealer, to use the image employed by Nathan the prophet in his famous parable (2 Samuel 12:1-4).

In Scripture, then, the true shepherd, the perfect shepherd, is God himself (Genesis 49:24). Probably one of the best-known psalms expresses this beautifully: "The LORD is my shepherd, I shall not want" (Psalm 23:1). In a famous oracle, the Lord, through the lips of the prophet Ezekiel, expresses his outrage over the way the shepherds of Israel have fed themselves rather than the flock. They have ruled the sheep harshly instead of caring for them: "The weak you have not strengthened, the sick you have not healed, the crippled you have not bound up, the strayed you have not brought back, the lost you have not sought" (Ezekiel 34:4).

Thus, says the Lord, he is against the shepherds and will rescue the sheep from their mouths. He will seek out and gather the sheep who have been scattered and feed them with good pasture on the mountains of Israel. "I myself will be the shepherd of my sheep, and I will make them lie down, says the Lord GOD. I will seek the lost, and I will bring back the strayed, and I will bind up the crippled, and I will strengthen the weak" (Ezekiel 34:15-16).

When Jesus speaks to Zacchaeus, he makes a brief but critical reference to this passage. It explains why he reaches out to the chief tax collector: "The Son of man came to seek and to save the lost" (Luke 19:10).

God himself coming to bring back the strays—this is what is happening in Jesus' ministry. Jesus' work of gathering the fragmented, scattered flock is exactly what God promised to do when he himself would come as the shepherd of Israel. In Luke 15, Jesus tells the parable of the shepherd who leaves ninety-nine of his sheep to search for the one who is lost. This is not just what Jesus is doing but what God promised to do himself.

The Good Shepherd discourse (John 10:1-21), one of the major discourses in the Gospel of John, is given by Jesus in Jerusalem. Immediately before it, a blind man whom Jesus has healed is thrown out of his synagogue by the Pharisees. In Jesus' speech after this episode, he echoes the condemnation of the predatory shepherds found in Ezekiel 34, and he speaks of the false shepherds as strangers, thieves, and bandits.

Jesus is the Good Shepherd. There are different words for "good" in Greek. The term used here means the ideal or model shepherd. Ancient shepherds often had a pet name for each of their animals. Jesus says that he calls each of his sheep by name (John 10:3). He knows and cares for each of them intimately. And unlike the bandits who steal the sheep or the hireling who runs away when the wolf approaches, Jesus lays down his life for them. He has come that they might have abundant life and be gathered back together. He alludes to the fact that this gathering will ultimately include even more than the lost sheep of the house of Israel. He seems to be speaking of the Samaritans and the Gentiles when he says, "I have other sheep, that are not of this fold; I must bring them also, and they will heed my voice. So there shall be one flock, one shepherd" (John 10:16).

The promise God made to come himself and do what the false shepherds of Israel had failed to do is fulfilled in Jesus, the true Shepherd.

BREAD FROM HEAVEN

Although numerous miracles occur throughout the Gospels, only one of them is recorded in all four: the multiplication of the loaves and fish.[117] The traditional site of this miracle is called Tabgha, which is about two miles from Capernaum. The features of this site reflect some important things noted in the various accounts. Tabgha is located on the Sea of Galilee at the foot of the Mount of Beatitudes. John mentions that Jesus takes his seat on "the mountain" before feeding the people.[118] It is a deserted place but watered by springs and therefore lush with abundant green grass. Jesus makes the people recline on the grass.[119] Mark's Gospel specifically notes that Jesus, looking upon the vast crowd, has compassion on them, "because they were like sheep without a shepherd" (Mark 6:34).[120]

This comment by Mark is one of the keys to understanding that this miracle is a fulfillment of Ezekiel 34 and Psalm 23. Through Jesus, the Good Shepherd, God is about to gather his neglected, scattered flock and feed them rich fare on the mountains of Israel (Ezekiel 34:14-16). "The LORD is my shepherd, I shall not want; he makes me lie down in green pastures. He leads me beside still waters" (Psalm 23:1-2).

Jesus teaches them (Mark 6:34) and heals their sick (Matthew 14:14). When the people are hungry, rather than dismissing them to go into nearby towns in search of food, as his disciples suggest, he takes five loaves and two fish, multiplies them, and feeds a crowd of thousands. They eat until they are satisfied—"I shall not want." And twelve baskets are left over, a sign of the abundance of the messianic age and the regathering of the twelve tribes.

A few previous miracles in the history of Israel are recalled here. John mentions that the loaves Jesus multiplies are made of barley. This recalls that it is Passover time, the time of the barley harvest.[121] It also recalls an event in the life of the great prophet Elisha:

> A man came from Baal-shalishah, bringing the man of God bread of the first fruits, twenty loaves of barley, and fresh ears of grain in his sack. And Elisha said, "Give to the men, that they may eat." But his servant said, "How am I to set this before a hundred men?" So he repeated, "Give them to the men, that they may eat, for thus says the LORD, 'They shall eat and have some left.'" So he set it before them. And they ate, and had some left. (2 Kings 4:42-44)

Elijah had multiplied oil and flour to feed himself and two others (1 Kings 17:8-16). Elisha had fed one hundred. Jesus feeds a crowd of five thousand. Clearly, Jesus is a new Elijah and a new Elisha, but he far surpasses them both.

THE BREAD OF LIFE

It is notable that Jesus multiplies the loaves in a "deserted place" (Matthew 14:13 NAB; Mark 6:32 NAB) and produces bread that comes out of nowhere, as if from heaven. This recalls the miracle of the manna when God, through Moses, fed Israel in the wilderness with bread from heaven. No wonder people in the crowd say, "This is indeed the prophet who is to come into the world!" (John 6:14). They recognize Jesus as the prophet like Moses who was promised in Deuteronomy 18:18.

When God gave Israel the manna,[122] Moses never identified himself with that heavenly bread. But on the day after the multiplication of the loaves and fish, in the synagogue in Capernaum, Jesus tells the people that he himself is the bread that comes down from heaven and gives life to the world (John 6:22-59).

In saying this, Jesus is affirming what John tells us in his prologue (John 1:1-14), that the existence of Jesus did not begin in his mother's womb. "He was in the beginning with God" (John 1:2), and he has descended from heaven, sent into the world by the Father. When Jesus identifies himself as the Bread of Life, he takes us back to the town of his birth, Bethlehem, the "house of bread," and to the manger, a food trough, that was his first bed. But he takes us back even further, to an important Old Testament motif: Wisdom's invitation to come, eat and drink:

> Come to me, you who desire me, and eat your fill of my produce. For my teaching is sweeter than honey, and my inheritance sweeter than the honeycomb. ... Those who eat me will hunger for more, and those who drink me will thirst for more. (Sirach 24:19-21)

The speaker here is none other than the book of the covenant, the Word of God, the Torah.

And in a prophecy that is clearly related to the messianic times of a new David to come, Isaiah writes of a nourishment, a bread which comes down from heaven that is the Word of God:

> Why do you spend your money for that which is not bread, and your labor for that which does not satisfy? Listen diligently to me, and eat what is good, and delight yourselves in rich food. ... For as the rain and the snow come down from heaven, and do not return there but water the earth, making it bring forth and sprout, giving seed to the sower and bread to the eater, so shall my word be that goes forth from my mouth; it shall not return to me empty, but it shall accomplish that which I intend. (Isaiah 55:2, 55:10-11)

So Jesus in the multiplication of the loaves and the Bread of Life discourse manifests who he is: the new Elijah, the new Elisha, and the new Moses. But these designations can't express the fullness of who he is. For he somehow is also the personified Word, Wisdom, and Torah of God, who comes as a nourishment that communicates to us God's very life. The "eternal life" that Jesus gives to those who believe is not just a life that goes on and on in endless duration. It is a qualitatively different kind of life, far surpassing biological life or natural human life. It is eternal life in the sense that it is divine life, the very life of God, which through him and in him we begin to taste even now.

THE BRIDEGROOM AND THE WEDDING FEAST

The entire public ministry of Jesus has been characterized by feasting. Again and again, we see the Lord reclining at table with newly repentant sinners and his disciples. These "homecoming meals" are joyous occasions that reflect the celebration going on in heaven. But there is even more significance in them.

The Pharisees typically fasted twice a week. John the Baptist, the ascetic that he was, also taught his disciples a regular discipline of fasting. This is what people would expect from devout Jews.

So Jesus' continual feasting seems, to some, to be scandalous. Jesus quotes his opponents as referring to him as "a glutton and a drunkard, a friend of tax collectors and sinners" (Matthew 11:19). He follows this with a line that should now make sense to us: "Yet wisdom is justified by her deeds." He is Wisdom incarnate, and Wisdom has set a table:

> She has slaughtered her beasts, she has mixed her wine, she has also set her table. She has sent out her maids to call from the highest places in the town, "Whoever is simple, let him turn in here!" To him who is without sense she says, "Come, eat of my bread and drink of the wine I have mixed. Leave simpleness, and live, and walk in the way of insight." (Proverbs 9:2-6)

The Pharisees and the scribes ask Jesus point blank why he and his disciples don't fast while the followers of John the Baptist and those of the Pharisees do. Jesus' response is extremely significant:

> Can you make wedding guests fast while the bridegroom is with them? The days will come, when the bridegroom is taken away from them, and then they will fast in those days. ... No one puts new wine into old wineskins; if he does, the new wine will burst the skins and it will be spilled, and the skins will be destroyed. But new wine must be put into fresh wineskins. (Luke 5:34-38)

The comment cannot help but call to our minds a sign recorded only in the Gospel of John. Jesus, his mother, and his disciples are at a wedding feast where the unthinkable happens: The hosts run out of wine. The request of Mary leads Jesus to take action. Nearby are six massive stone jars for the Jewish purification ritual, each with a capacity of twenty to thirty gallons. Jesus tells the servants to fill them with water. When they are full, Jesus instructs the servants to draw some of the liquid out and take it to the steward of the feast. The steward, not knowing where the wine has come from, compliments the groom: "Every man serves the good wine first; and when men have drunk freely, then the poor wine; but you have kept the good wine until now" (John 2:10).

Jesus transforms the sullied water of Jewish ritual into 120 to 180 gallons of the choice, new wine of the new age, the age of fulfillment.

In the Old Testament, one of the most dramatic signs of the messianic era to come is the abundance of superb wine: "On this mountain the LORD of hosts will make for all peoples a feast of fat things, a feast of choice wines—of fat things full of marrow, of choice wines well refined" (Isaiah 25:6). And from the prophet Amos:

> "Behold, the days are coming," says the Lord, "when the plowman shall overtake the reaper and the treader of grapes him who sows the seed; the mountains shall drip sweet wine, and all the hills shall flow with it. I will restore the fortunes of my people Israel, and they shall rebuild the ruined cities and inhabit them; they shall plant vineyards and drink their wine." (Amos 9:13-14)

Jesus has ushered in the messianic era, the Kingdom of God. The wedding feast of Cana, like the countless homecoming feasts and the sheep returning to the fold, is a sign and anticipation of the final and great feast when the kingdom comes in all its fullness.

One further point cannot be missed. In John's Gospel, Jesus' first sign is performed at a wedding. It is no coincidence that Jesus' cousin, John the Baptist, refers to Jesus in the very next chapter, saying, "He who has the bride is the bridegroom; the friend of the bridegroom, who stands and hears him, rejoices greatly at the bridegroom's voice" (John 3:29). The Baptist's reference here to Jesus as the bridegroom is meant to tell us that the true bridegroom and host at Cana is Jesus. He is the bridegroom of the new Israel. Cana and all the banquets of Jesus' ministry are foretastes and anticipations of the messianic feast, which is a wedding feast (Matthew 22:2, 25:1-3), "the marriage supper of the Lamb" (Revelation 19:9).

Nowhere in the Old Testament is a Davidic messiah or prophet ever called the Bridegroom of Israel. That designation is exclusively reserved for Yahweh, the Lord God.[123] The feasting of Jesus' ministry, the testimony of John the Baptist, and Jesus' description of himself as the Bridegroom reveal him to be not only the anointed one ushering in the messianic age but, in some unprecedented and mysterious fashion, God himself who has come in person.

CHAPTER 13

THE MESSIAH AND
THE MOUNTAIN

Throughout history, the title "Christ" has normally been paired with the name of Jesus, so that one could easily think that it is Jesus' family name. The curious fact is, however, that while Jesus does say "I am the Good Shepherd" and "I am the Bread of Life," he does not get up in the Temple precincts (or anywhere else) and proclaim, "I am the Messiah!"

A few times Jesus refers to himself as a prophet. For example, all four Gospels note that he quotes the proverb "A prophet is not honored in his own country" to explain the rejection he experiences from his own people.[124] But when it comes to the designation "messiah," Jesus shows some reluctance. Once when he is in Jerusalem for the Feast of the Dedication, people brashly say to him, "How long will you keep us in suspense? If you are the Christ, tell us plainly" (John 10:24).

It is Peter who actually comes right out and says it. In an intimate gathering of Jesus and his disciples, Peter finally confesses out loud what many are quietly hoping for and perhaps suspecting. But as soon as he does so, Jesus strictly forbids them to tell this news to anyone (Matthew 16:20).

So why this "messianic secret," as some scholars have called it?

THE MESSIAH THEY WERE EXPECTING

Mashiach ("messiah") is the Hebrew word for "anointed one."
As we've already seen, priests were anointed ones. At least one
prophet, Elisha, had been anointed as well. But what most thought
of when they heard the term "messiah" was a king. Messiah meant
a new David, a king who would do what David did—vanquish
the Gentiles and make Israel a power to be reckoned with once
again. Basically, the idea of a messiah had become wrapped up
with Israel's national ambitions. People thought that political and
military action was the answer to their problems and looked to
God to endorse their program.

There are some prayers composed in the first or second century BC
called the Psalms of Solomon. They did not make it into the Bible
but are very valuable in helping us understand what Palestinian
Jews were thinking at that time. One passage reveals what the
author was looking for in the coming messiah: "He [will] shatter
unjust rulers. … With a rod of iron he shall break [sinners] in pieces
… nations shall flee before him."[125] The Qumran community was
looking for a Davidic messiah. His most important job would be
to lead the army of the sons of light in their great apocalyptic
battle against the sons of darkness. Preparation for holy war, led
by the messiah, was such a central part of their life that one of the
important Dead Sea Scrolls is called the War Scroll. It contains
detailed military instructions for the last battle, down to what was
to be written on the war banners.

But this militaristic messianism was more than just a dream. In
the hundred years immediately after Jesus, the Jews of Palestine
twice put their hopes in armed rebellion. The first uprising ended
in the destruction of the Temple in AD 70. The second was led by a
man who was dubbed Bar Kochba, meaning "son of the star." He
was so called because he was supposed to be the fulfillment of the
prophecy of the star to arise out of Jacob in Numbers 24:17. One
of the most prominent rabbis of the time even proclaimed him the
messiah. That uprising, too, ended in slaughter and humiliation.

Given this popular conception of what a messiah ought to do, Jesus' reticence makes more sense. John's Gospel records just how real this danger was. After Jesus performed the multiplication of the loaves and fish, people were understandably excited. John notes that, "perceiving then that they were about to come and take him by force to make him king, Jesus withdrew again to the hills by himself" (John 6:15).

Jesus could not run the risk of letting anyone identify him as messiah before he had corrected their misunderstanding—until they understood what "messiah" truly meant. The opportunity to do this came when he and the disciples were far away from the crowds, in the remote northern, mostly Gentile, region of the Holy Land, at the foot of the majestic Mount Hermon.

CAESAREA PHILIPPI

Capernaum, the home base of the Galilean ministry, was right on the eastern edge of Herod Antipas' territory of Galilee. Just a couple of miles to the east along the lake shore, you can cross the Jordan and enter the territory of Herod Antipas' half brother Philip. Then about twenty-five miles' walk north and you are at a new town with a towering cliff behind it. This is the town that Philip named in honor of Caesar as well as himself—Caesarea Philippi.

Here, Luke tells us, Jesus slips away for some time alone with God (Luke 9:18), as he does before every important event. After concluding his prayer, he returns to the disciples and asks them who people say he is.[126] They rattle off various opinions they have heard: Some people think Jesus is John the Baptist, Elijah, Jeremiah, or one of the other prophets who has come back from beyond. Then, Matthew tells us, Jesus puts them on the spot: "But who do you say that I am?" Simon takes the initiative and responds, "You are the Christ, the Son of the living God" (Matthew 16:15-16).

Jesus has referred to himself already as the Son, the one with a unique relationship and therefore a unique and total knowledge of God, his Father. Although the disciples do not yet understand fully what this means, at least they have heard the title from Jesus' lips. What is new in Peter's confession is that he identifies Jesus as the messiah, the anointed one of God.

Jesus responds enthusiastically: "Blessed are you, Simon Bar-Jona! For flesh and blood has not revealed this to you, but my Father who is in heaven. And I tell you, you are Peter, and on this rock I will build my Church" (Matthew 16:17-18).

Simon here is serving as the spokesman for the disciples. But even more importantly, he is speaking prophetically. It is God the Father who has prompted this confession of faith in his Son. As a result, Jesus gives Simon a new title, which henceforth becomes the name by which he is called. The Aramaic word Jesus uses is *kephas*, which simply means "rock." The Greek translation is *petros*, which we render in English as Peter.

Simon's new name is more than a nickname. *Kephas* and *Petros* were unknown as proper names at the time in Palestine, and it was unusual for a nickname to replace a person's given name. For example, Jesus calls John and James "the sons of thunder," but the term is just a nickname; they continue to be known as John and James, the sons of Zebedee. In contrast, Peter's new name almost immediately replaces the old; he is rarely called Simon again. Peter's name is tied up with his new role as leader, spokesman, and foundation of this community of the New Israel called by Jesus "my Church." His identity and role have become inseparable from his prophetic recognition and confession of Jesus' identity.[127]

But immediately after he blesses Peter, Jesus forbids his disciples to tell anyone that he is the Christ. Next, he begins to explain that "messiah" does not mean what they think it means. It will not be about riding into Jerusalem on a warhorse with all of Israel lining up behind him. To the contrary, it means going to Jerusalem to be rejected by the leaders of his own people and put to death.

Peter ("the rock") now serves again as the disciples' spokesman. You can understand the horror all of them feel at hearing Jesus say that he will be executed. But Peter's reply is impulsive and rather outrageous. He, the disciple, has the nerve to rebuke his master: "God forbid, Lord! This shall never happen to you." The one who has just called him "the rock" now calls him by another name: "Get behind me, Satan!" The RSV-2CE renders the next line as "You are a hindrance to me." That obscures an ironic wordplay used by Jesus. To "the rock" he says, "You have become a *stumbling stone* [Gk., *skandalon*]," and Jesus continues, "For you are not on the side of God, but of men" (Matthew 16:21-23).

In the story of the temptation in the desert, Luke notes that after failing three times to divert Jesus from his course, Satan "departed from him until an opportune time" (Luke 4:13). This is the opportune moment. Right after being the mouthpiece of God in his confession of faith, Peter becomes the mouthpiece of Satan, who tries to deflect Jesus from the way of the Cross. He tempts Jesus with an easy kingdom of this world that would bypass the road of suffering. This is the great temptation that assails Jesus when he senses that people are about to take him by force to make him king. Now he faces a similar temptation from the leader he has just chosen!

There is no evidence that any Jew before this time had ever put together the idea of the messiah with the kind of redemptive suffering we see in the servant of the Lord in Isaiah 53. But Jesus knows for certain that he is to be a suffering messiah. Simeon had prophesied this about him as a baby (Luke 2:27-35).[128] John the Baptist, calling Jesus the Lamb of God, may have gotten a glimpse of it from the Holy Spirit. It is prefigured in Jesus' baptism when he descends under the waters, an image of death. Jesus hints at it during his public ministry, saying that he has a baptism to receive and is hard pressed until it is accomplished (Luke 12:50). He alludes to it also when he calls himself the Good Shepherd who will lay down his life for his sheep (John 10:11).

If we piece together the Old Testament prophecies, we see that the messiah-king would be anointed by the Spirit. He would be thus authorized and empowered to go into battle to defeat the enemies of God's people and to secure their liberty and well-being. Like a shepherd, he would both defend and feed his flock, leading them to abundant pasture. The long-awaited messiah would do this in a definitive way in the final age, bringing victory, liberty, and an abundance of peace (*shalom*) that would dwarf anything Israel had ever seen.

All this is being fulfilled in Jesus.

The problem is that the people assumed that their enemies were flesh and blood. The messiah would, therefore, naturally accomplish his task by bringing death to Israel's enemies. The people never expected that he would vanquish Israel's enemies by his own death. Victory through the victor's death simply did not make sense to them. Glory through humiliation sounds absurd. If there is any logic to this, it is certainly not obvious. It simply is not the way the human mind works. That is why Jesus says to Peter, "You are not on the side of God, but of men" (Matthew 16:23). Jesus here is echoing the words of Isaiah:

> For my thoughts are not your thoughts, neither are your ways my ways, says the LORD. For as the heavens are higher than the earth, so are my ways higher than your ways and my thoughts than your thoughts. (Isaiah 55:8-9)

A MOUNTAINTOP EXPERIENCE

The news that their master is the messiah is exhilarating; to find out that this means he will have to lay down his life for his sheep is a sort of earthquake. It shakes the disciples' faith to its foundation. They need to understand that a sacrificial death will not be the end of the story. So now that Jesus has revealed to them one side of the mystery of his messiahship, it is time to show them the other.

Matthew, Mark, and Luke tell us that just a few days after Peter's confession of faith at Caesarea Philippi, Jesus takes the inner core of the Twelve—Peter, James, and John—up a high mountain. The mountain is unnamed in the Gospel accounts. But there is written evidence dating to the first half of the third century that the location was Mount Tabor, with Nazareth in a valley in one direction and the village of Nain in another. This summit provides a magnificent view of the surrounding regions of Galilee, and on a clear day you can see snow-capped Mount Hermon about fifty miles to the north.

Luke is the only one to tell us that the purpose of the ascent is to spend some time in prayer (Luke 9:28-36). He is also the only one to suggest that it is nighttime when something extraordinary takes place: The disciples, heavy with sleep (as they would be later, too, in the garden of Gethsemane), wake to an extraordinary sight. As Jesus prays, his appearance is altered, and his clothing becomes "dazzling white." Mark describes his garments as "glistening, intensely white, as no fuller on earth could bleach them" (Mark 9:3). Matthew says his garments become "white as light" (Matthew 17:2).

These details connect us with events and important Scripture texts that help us recognize the meaning of this incident. First, white garments are the raiment of heavenly beings.[129] This means that heaven is Jesus' origin and heaven is his destiny. Second, after Moses spoke with God on Mount Sinai, his face shone with God's glory (Exodus 34:29-35), and he had to veil his face.

In this Transfiguration scene, Moses and Elijah are conversing with Jesus. They are described as being "in glory," but the glory is described as Jesus' glory (Luke 9:31-32). The glory is not a reflection *upon* Jesus; it comes from *within* him. Elijah and Moses share in it. As they talk with him, they reflect Jesus' glory just as Moses' face reflected God's glory on Mount Sinai.

Why are they there? The return of Moses and Elijah has been expected before the end; their presence is a sign that the age of fulfillment has come. Moreover, in Jewish tradition all testimony must be confirmed by at least two witnesses. Moses and Elijah are here as witnesses to Jesus. Moses represents the first five books of the Scriptures, the Law of Moses. The rest of Scripture, for the most part, falls under the heading of "the Prophets." Though there is no prophetic book named after Elijah, the wonder-worker who went up to heaven in a chariot, he is the greatest of the prophets and so represents them all. These two witnesses, then, symbolize the entire body of the Scriptures, all of which witness to Jesus.[130]

Luke is the only evangelist to tell us what Moses and Elijah are discussing with Jesus. They "spoke of his exodus, which he was to accomplish at Jerusalem" (Luke 9:31). Moses and Elijah, the Law and the Prophets, are bearing witness here not simply to the person of Jesus but specifically to Jesus' approaching exodus, as he passes from this world to glory through his death and resurrection. Just as the Exodus from Egypt was the great act of salvation in the past, the New Exodus that will take place in Jerusalem will be the final and definitive act of salvation.

THE LIGHT OF THE WORLD

The light coming from Jesus connects with another Gospel episode. One of the principal images connected with the Feast of Booths is light. We know from the Mishnah that four huge lamps were set up during the feast in the Temple's Court of the Women.[131] These lights illuminated the Temple courts for the seven nights of the feast and cast their light all over Jerusalem. As if that light were not enough, men brandishing torches would fill the Court of the Gentiles and dance in joy before the Lord. Zechariah says that in the great Feast of Booths on the Day of the Lord, "there shall be continuous day … for at evening time there shall be light" (Zechariah 14:7).

In John's Gospel, it is in the Temple court sometime during the seven days of the feast that Jesus proclaims, "I am the light of the world; he who follows me will not walk in darkness, but will have the light of life" (John 8:12). This is the opening of what has come to be known as the Light of the World discourse (John 8:12-20). Though John does not record the episode of the Transfiguration, there are intriguing connections between it and this discourse: the Feast of Booths symbolism, Jesus as the source of light, and even the mention of two necessary witnesses. In John, the Pharisees

Peter's Proposal to Erect Booths

Peter is overwhelmed by the experience of the Transfiguration. His response may seem puzzling to us. "Master, it is well that we are here; let us make three booths, one for you and one for Moses and one for Elijah." Luke adds that Peter did not know what he was saying (Luke 9:33).

To understand Peter's outburst, we need to know that the greatest and most joyful feast of the Jewish year was not Passover but the Feast of Booths or Feast of Tabernacles (Sukkot).[132] It is the great harvest festival, celebrating the autumn gathering of the crops. The grapes have been harvested, pressed, and made into new wine. Olives are to be pressed and made into oil. During the work of the harvest, the people make huts in the fields. Now, they travel to Jerusalem and make festive, decorative huts there. They remember that Israel did not always have the produce of the land; once they wandered in tents in the wilderness. For seven days, the people dwell in the decorated huts, feasting, rejoicing, and giving thanks to God.

The Feast of Booths also has a special connection to the Temple. It was during the feast that Solomon dedicated the first Temple, when a cloud, representing the glory of the Lord, filled the Temple (1 Kings 8:10-11). Alas, when the Babylonians destroyed the Temple (587 BC), the Ark of the Covenant disappeared, and the glory departed.

The Jews believed that in the end times, when God gathered his people again and showed his mercy, the glory would return (2 Maccabees 2:8). What a magnificent Feast of Booths there will be then! The book of the prophet Zechariah concludes with a prediction that in the final days even the Gentiles will come to Jerusalem to worship the Lord and celebrate the Feast of Booths (Zechariah 14:16)!

All of these associations must have overwhelmed Peter when he saw the end-times figures and his own Master resplendent in glory. God's glory had returned. The joy that welled up in Peter would have suggested to him that the final gathering had arrived, the great Feast of Booths. The most natural thing would be to construct booths to celebrate the festival and receive the heavenly guests in proper style.[133]

accuse Jesus of not having the necessary witnesses to back up his claims to be the Light of the World. Jesus points to the tradition of two witnesses and says that the Father and Jesus himself bear witness to who he is (John 8:17-18). Earlier we saw how Jesus is equated with the Torah as well as with Wisdom, both of which are identified in Judaism with God's eternal light (Wisdom 7:26; 18:3-4). But his light is not only for his own people; he has come as the light of the entire world, as a light of revelation to the Gentiles (Isaiah 42:6), as prophesied by Simeon (Luke 2:32).

THE CLOUD AND THE VOICE

No sooner has Peter offered to erect booths for the celebration than a cloud suddenly envelopes Jesus and the disciples. Matthew, Mark, and Luke all use the same word for the movement of the cloud: they all say it "overshadowed" them. This is the same term the angel Gabriel uses in Luke's account of the Annunciation— Mary conceives when the Holy Spirit, the power of the Most High, overshadows her (Luke 1:35).

In the Old Testament, the cloud symbolizes the glory of God, the *Shekinah* that overshadows Sinai and the Tent of Meeting in the desert and later fills Solomon's Temple. With its connection to the Annunciation, the overshadowing cloud can now be recognized as an image of the Holy Spirit.

From the midst of the cloud comes a voice: "This is my Son, my Chosen; listen to him!" (Luke 9:35). The voice of the Father now echoes the voice from heaven that was heard at Jesus' baptism in the Jordan. There the Spirit descended upon Jesus like a dove; here he descends like a cloud of glory. Both utterances of the Father allude to the same text from the Old Testament: "Behold my servant, whom I uphold, my chosen, in whom my soul delights; I have put my Spirit upon him, he will bring forth justice to the nations" (Isaiah 42:1).

To Moses and Elijah are now joined two even more important witnesses to Jesus—the Father and the Holy Spirit. And Moses and

Elijah disappear. It is now Jesus that all must heed, as the Father insists. His command, "Listen to him," echoes the description of the prophet like Moses—"Him you shall heed" (Deuteronomy 18:15).

Like the baptism of Jesus, this episode of the Transfiguration is a theophany, or visible manifestation, of the Trinity: the Father's voice, the Son with the glory of divinity shining through the veil of his humanity, and the Spirit as the overshadowing cloud.

SON OF MAN

The self-description Jesus uses most often in the first three Gospels is Son of Man. The Transfiguration helps us understand what this phrase means. In the book of Daniel, there is a mysterious, heavenly scene. The Ancient of Days, his clothing as white as snow, is seated on his throne. An empty throne is next to his. Then, "with the clouds of heaven there came one like a son of man. … And to him was given dominion and glory and kingdom, that all peoples, nations, and languages should serve him; his dominion is an everlasting dominion" (Daniel 7:13-14). Over time, "Son of Man" came to be associated with the perfect representative of Israel, the chosen one of Isaiah 42:1.[134]

In the Transfiguration, we see the Son of Man, the one destined to sit on a throne next to the Ancient of Days, amid the clouds of heaven. This is a foretaste, an anticipation of his future glory both when, risen, he ascends to the Father's right hand and when, glorious, he returns as Judge and King. It is precisely at these two special times that, once again, Jesus will be seen riding on the clouds of heaven (Acts 1:9; Luke 21:27).

THE EXODUS STILL LIES AHEAD

It is immediately after Peter's confession of faith that Jesus begins to teach the disciples what the notion of messiah really means. His first prediction of suffering includes mention of his resurrection. Peter has reacted against the idea of his death and overlooked the talk of rising again. Now the Transfiguration is part of Jesus' teaching. All the hopes of Israel symbolized by the return of God's glory, the joy of the final, great Feast of Booths, and the conversion of the Gentiles—these are all in the plan. But the booths cannot be erected yet; Jesus and the disciples cannot linger. The only way to glory is the path of the Suffering Servant. And it is time to get back on the road.

CHAPTER 14

FROM TABOR TO BETHANY

The disciples have been on the road with Jesus almost nonstop for about three years.[135] They have kept a grueling pace despite oppressive heat, needy crowds, and constant harassment from opponents. It is not hard to see why Peter wants to linger atop Tabor and bask in the glory.

Yet Tabor is but a moment of vision to strengthen them, a divine rest stop. No sooner have Elijah and Moses disappeared than Jesus leads Peter, James, and John down to the valley, back on the road for the last leg of his journey. He told his disciples a few days before that he would suffer, that they needed to broaden their idea of the messiah. The departure from Tabor, then, means another transition: from the light of glory to the shadow of suffering.

And so Luke tells us that after the Transfiguration Jesus "set his face"[136] in resolute determination and begins his final trip to Jerusalem, the city of destiny, the only place a prophet should die (Luke 13:33).

DISCIPLESHIP AND THE SUFFERING MESSIAH

From the beginning, he tells the disciples that the kingdom of God will cost them homes, friends, and even family. But beginning in Caesarea Philippi, he begins to make it increasingly clear that the pearl of great price will also cost them their lives. If discipleship means becoming like the master, then having a master who is a suffering servant means that they must become suffering servants as well. No sooner does Jesus mention that he will be killed than he declares that each must "take up his cross" and follow after him (Luke 9:23).

We are so used to seeing the cross as a religious symbol that we easily miss how deeply this image must have revolted them. There was nothing religious about the cross in first-century Palestine. It was the ultimate symbol of horror and shame. Jesus, in predicting his passion at Caesarea Philippi, said he would be rejected and *killed*. That was terrible enough. But he had said nothing about *crucifixion*.

Yet now Jesus describes discipleship in terms of carrying your cross? The walk of the condemned from the dungeon to the place of execution is one of the worst things about this cruel form of punishment. A crossbeam is placed over his shoulders like a halter, and he is goaded to carry it through a hostile crowd of people who are jeering, spitting, and pummeling him. The Talmud says it is permissible to curse or strike a condemned criminal, since after his condemnation he is already a dead man.[137] Imagine the shame, humiliation, and rejection such a hopeless soul would feel.

This is what it must have sounded like to them when Jesus declares, "If any man would come after me, let him deny himself and take up his cross and follow me" (Mark 8:34). If that were not harsh enough, Luke records Jesus as saying "take up his cross *daily*" (Luke 9:23, emphasis added).

Persecution and violent death were a distinct possibility for the disciples of an executed master. Jesus has already pronounced blessed those "persecuted for righteousness' sake" (Matthew 5:10-11). Of all eight beatitudes, this one is the grand finale. It is the only beatitude that Jesus repeats. The second time he even tells the blessed ones to "rejoice and be glad" when they are persecuted, since their reward will be great in heaven (Matthew 5:12).

Yet none of his followers wants to hear about the suffering that lies down the road. So Jesus repeats the prediction of his passion even more emphatically: "Let these words sink into your ears; for the Son of man is to be delivered into the hands of men" (Luke 9:44). Luke tells us that the disciples still don't get it and are afraid even to bring up the topic with Jesus.

After the majestic experience of the Transfiguration, James and John have a particularly difficult time remembering the part about suffering and the cross. In fact, having seen the glory of the Son of Man on the mountain, they ask Jesus to grant them the best possible positions next to the King, on his right and his left (Mark 10:35-37).[138]

It is not wrong to aspire to greatness or want to be as close to Jesus as possible. The problem is that James and John don't understand that you can't get to glory with Jesus except by suffering with him. And if you truly want intimacy with Jesus, you must actually desire to share in his humiliation as well as his glory. So he asks the brothers, "Are you able to drink the chalice that I drink, or to be baptized with the baptism with which I am baptized?"[139] (Mark 10:38). Glibly they say they can. But of course they don't know what they are saying, any more than Peter knew what he was saying when he offered to build three booths on top of the mountain. Just a short while later, when their master is seized, all three of them will run away, just like everyone else.

Jesus knows this will happen. Nonetheless, he takes the occasion to teach them what denying oneself really means: "Whoever would be great among you must be your servant, and whoever would be first among you must be slave of all. For the Son of man also came not to be served but to serve, and to give his life as a ransom for many" (Mark 10.43-45).

This choice of words alerts us to an important passage in Isaiah that Jesus has in mind: "My servant, the just one, shall justify the many, their iniquity he shall bear" (Isaiah 53:11 NAB). The amazing point here is that the glorious Son of Man of Daniel 7:13, whose dazzling brightness Peter and the sons of Zebedee have seen on the mountain, chooses to come in the form of a servant (see Philippians 2:7). The King comes as one who waits tables (the literal meaning of the Greek word "to serve").

Since he comes as a servant, his disciples' renunciation of self, their carrying of the cross, means putting to death the worldly desire to be on top and dominate. If they want to be near Jesus, clawing or jockeying their way to the top is the wrong approach. For if they do manage to get to the top, they won't find him there. Jesus goes in the exact opposite direction. He humbles himself. His direction is down—down from heaven to a stable, down to the lowest place on earth, down under the baptismal waters symbolizing death. Those who seek to be with him must therefore go to the lowest place; there they will find him.

This sheds new light on Jesus' words "Blessed are the poor in spirit" (Matthew 5:3) and the call to become a child. It makes sense of the parable about not choosing the place of honor at banquets but rather the humblest place (Luke 14:7-11). Life in "the world," the prevailing culture (1 John 2:15-17), is all about a race to the summit of success. We all know people who are willing to sell their souls and trample anyone who might stand in their way in their relentless climb to the top. Life in the topsy-turvy world of the kingdom of God is also a competition, but it is a race to the bottom.

THE FINAL PILGRIMAGE

We don't know how long it took to go from Tabor to Jerusalem. But Matthew, Mark, and Luke recognize the Transfiguration as a pivotal moment in the public ministry of Jesus. Luke is especially diligent to point out how the rest of the Lord's ministry is one long journey on the road to the City of David where Jesus' exodus will take place. Luke records many encounters, healings, conversations, and teachings during this final pilgrimage, but everything takes place under the looming shadow of the Cross. Jesus' third prediction of his impending death is made toward the end of this long journey. The disciples do not understand it any better than the first two predictions (Luke 18:34).

We do know the general route Jesus takes. The attempt to pass through Samaria has been met with rejection (Luke 9:51-56). That leaves the route through the Decapolis and Perea, called "Judea beyond the Jordan." All four Gospels note that Jesus spends some time here before his final pilgrimage to Jerusalem. This is the place where John the Baptist had preached and where Jesus himself had been baptized. The road to Jerusalem lies on the other side of the river and begins in the town of Jericho.

EYE-OPENING FAITH

Jericho was on a popular route between Galilee and Jerusalem, and Jesus undoubtedly passes through it many times, but this is the only time mentioned in the Gospels. Jesus' fame has preceded him. His approach must be causing a stir, for it catches the attention of a blind beggar known simply as Bartimaeus, literally, the son of Timaeus.

Bartimaeus makes it clear that authentic faith is not reticent. Faith is courageous, sometimes boisterous, even outrageous at times. Unable to approach Jesus in a dignified, somewhat private way, Bartimaeus does what he has to do. He makes a scene. The more people tell him to be quiet, the louder he shouts. Ignoring the rebukes of the crowd, he calls out to Jesus, "Son of David, have mercy on me!" (Mark 10:47-48). By calling Jesus "Son of David," Bartimaeus shows that he believes Jesus is the awaited messiah, the King destined to revive the fortunes of Israel. He has faith in Jesus. And when he finally gets Jesus' attention and is summoned, the text says, he eagerly leaps to his feet, already filled with a hopeful anticipation that Jesus will give him the sight he so earnestly desires. Jesus tells him that it is his faith, in fact, that has saved him, and in that moment Bartimaeus receives his sight.

A frequent theme of Jesus' teaching, particularly after the Transfiguration, concerns the various aspects of faith. In fact, in Mark's account, it is the first thing he speaks about after coming down the mountain (Mark 9:23). Faith gives us a kind of sight that perceives what our physical eyes cannot see. Bartimaeus receives his physical sight by faith. His response to his healing proves that he has received true spiritual vision as well, for he recognizes that the King and the kingdom he brings are alone worth living for. So he leaves all behind and follows Jesus down the road.

John recounts another important event concerning a blind man in the later part of Jesus' public ministry (John 9:1-41). Against the backdrop of the Feast of Booths, Jesus proclaims himself the light of the world (John 8:12). He is not content just to speak about it; he performs an action that is at once a work of mercy and a dramatic symbol of who he is and why he has come. He encounters a man blind from birth and gives him sight. The statement of the healed man has become famous through the hymn "Amazing Grace": "I was blind, now I see!" (John 9:25).

Of course, Jesus heals the blind man on the Sabbath, the day Jesus thinks is the most fitting to give people rest from suffering; the Pharisees, to the contrary, believe it a most inappropriate day to do such a thing. The predictable controversy ensues, but it gets particularly nasty this time, because the Pharisees lash out at the former blind man and throw him out of the synagogue. His offense? He refuses to condemn the man who gave him back his sight and, even more, his life. He now sees all too clearly that the one who healed him is a prophet, regardless of what the authorities say.

Jesus' final commentary on the matter is instructive: "For judgment I came into this world, that those who do not see may see, and that those who see may become blind" (John 9:39). This recalls Jesus' great acclamation of joy following the return of the seventy from their mission: "I thank you, Father, Lord of heaven and earth, that you have hidden these things from the wise and understanding and revealed them to infants" (Luke 10:21).

THE FAMILY AT BETHANY

From Jericho, Jesus and his followers face a grueling uphill climb, almost twenty miles, through the blazing sun and withering heat of the Judean wilderness. The last hurdle is to ascend the Mount of Olives, a two-mile-long ridge about 2,500 feet high, which separates the wilderness from the holy city of Jerusalem.

On the eastern slope of the Mount of Olives lay the village of Bethany, a town where Jesus and his disciples must have stayed often when they came to Jerusalem. It was the first place for travelers to refresh themselves with water and food after the long desert trek and so was a popular rest stop for people traveling from Jericho.

During each pilgrimage feast, for a two- to three-week period three times a year, pilgrims would swell the population of Jerusalem from about 25,000 to nearly 150,000.[140] Most of the visitors could not possibly lodge in the walled city itself, so many stayed in surrounding villages. Bethany was only about a thirty-minute walk from the Temple, so for people coming up for the feasts, it was a convenient place to stay.

The family of Mary, Martha, and their brother Lazarus regularly welcome Jesus into their home in Bethany, and Jesus has a unique love for them (John 11:3-5). While in Perea, Jesus receives the message that Lazarus is seriously ill. Rather than rushing to heal him, Jesus tells the disciples that there is no need to worry. He says this sickness will not end in death. Imagine the disciples' dismay, then, when he tells them a few days later that Lazarus is in fact dead and that it is time to pay the family a visit.

In Bethany, the first person Jesus encounters is Martha. She says to him, "Lord, if you had been here, my brother would not have died. And even now I know that whatever you ask from God, God will give you." To this impressive profession of faith, Jesus responds, "Your brother will rise again." She again speaks with the faith of most Jews of the day: "I know that he will rise again in the resurrection at the last day." To this, Jesus speaks a word that will challenge her to go beyond anything she ever believed either as a pious Jew or even as his follower up till now. He says, "I am the resurrection and the life; he who believes in me, though he die, yet shall he live, and whoever lives and believes in me shall never die" (John 11:21-26).

What could he mean? Lazarus believed in him yet died. And we know that believers in him over the past two thousand years have died. In John's Gospel, Jesus speaks a great deal about "life." He came that we "may have life, and have it abundantly" (John 10:10). He describes himself as the Way, the Truth, and the Life (John 14:6). In John's Gospel, "life" seems to be almost as central a category as the kingdom of God is in Matthew, Mark, and Luke.

The Greek word for "life" used here is not the word for biological life (*bios*) or even human life (*psyche*). It is *zoe*, which signifies real life, the very life of the Living God. *Zoe* is eternal life, and indestructible. Those who can take away *bios* cannot destroy this kind of life. It is powerful, it is free, it is refreshing like "living water," and it is brilliant like light. This Life with a capital L is wholly present in Jesus. He is identical with it. He makes it available. The breaking of this life into our world, transforming everything it touches, is what the kingdom of God is all about.

Jesus asks Martha if she believes what he has said. Martha's response is the strongest, clearest profession of faith in John's Gospel prior to Jesus' resurrection. It is almost identical to Peter's profession at Caesarea Philippi. She says, "Yes, Lord; I believe that you are the Christ, the Son of God, he who is coming into the world" (John 11:27). Nonetheless, she does not seem to grasp fully what he has just said—that the Resurrection and the Life is standing right in front of her, speaking to her, close enough to touch.

LAZARUS, COME FORTH!

We tend to think of death as a natural part of human life, but Jesus sees death as what it is—an enemy. We were never meant to experience death. God forbade Adam and Eve from partaking of the fruit that would make them subject to it. Death came into the world through the envy of the devil, not through the plan of God (Wisdom 2:24). Death cleaves soul from body. It tears families apart. In its presence,

Jesus is angry.[141] In the presence of those wounded by death's sting, Jesus is sorrowful. He weeps (John 11:35). In no other place in his Gospel does John focus so much on Jesus' human emotion.

John calls Jesus' miraculous works "signs" because they point beyond themselves to a greater future reality, his own victory over death for the benefit of all mankind. This is why Jesus delayed, allowing Lazarus to die. In calling Lazarus forth from the tomb, Jesus is now making clear who he is and why he has come. This demonstration of Jesus' power over death is a sign of his own coming resurrection and ours as well.

Imagine how this strikes those who witness the miracle. Three times a day, every day of their lives, they have prayed these words of the *Tefillah*:

> You live eternally, you give life to the dead; you bring back the wind, you pour down the dew; you feed the living, you give life to the dead; in the twinkling of an eye you make salvation send forth its shoots. Blessed be you, Lord, who give life to the dead! [142]

TWO RESPONSES TO THE SIGN

The raising of Lazarus is the last recorded miracle in John's Gospel. Seven is the biblical number of completion. In this seventh sign, John shows us the ultimate meaning of the entire public ministry of Jesus.

The prelude to the seventh sign is Martha's powerful profession of faith. The sequel is her sister Mary's powerful profession of love: When Jesus visits Bethany again soon after, Mary anoints his feet with costly perfume (John 12:1-8). Her dramatic response to a dramatic miracle is itself a prophetic sign that points to Jesus' burial.

News of the miracle is brought back to Jerusalem by many eyewitnesses. We might expect this to lead to Jesus' acceptance. But the Lord knows it will have the opposite effect. Faced with Jesus' extraordinary power and popularity, the authorities in Jerusalem see him not as their savior but as a threat to their tenuous place within the Roman Empire. They have to act quickly to stop Jesus and his followers from getting out of hand.

And so the plotting begins. In the midst of their worried deliberations, Caiaphas makes his famous statement, which the evangelist regards as prophetic: "It is expedient for you that one man should die for the people, and that the whole nation should not perish" (John 11:50). How ironic—it is Jesus' act of giving life that sets in motion the plotting that leads to his death.

While the Jerusalem authorities conspire and scheme, Jesus is the one who is in total control. This is all part of the plan, to willingly experience the humiliating torture of crucifixion, the bitter wrenching of body from soul. He is willing to do this because by means of it, he knows he will accomplish more for us than he did for Lazarus—a lasting victory over death and the gift of eternal life.

CHAPTER 15

THE KING, JERUSALEM, AND THE TEMPLE

From Bethany, it only takes about twenty minutes to walk up the slope of the Mount of Olives and over the crest to where the Holy City comes into view. A few more minutes' walking and you arrive at the village of Bethphage. Matthew tells us that this is where the procession begins (Matthew 21:1).

In the ancient world, the triumph of a conquering hero was celebrated with splendor. The conqueror would ride into town at the head of a grand procession, in a regal chariot or on the back of a stately stallion. Legions of soldiers accompanied him. Elaborate triumphal arches were built to immortalize his valor.

Now it is time for Jesus to enter the Holy City. He has driven out demons, healed the sick, and raised the dead, and the people acclaim him as King. But he is riding a donkey, not a warhorse. His companions are carrying palm branches, not swords.[143] And the monument to his victory will be not a stone monument but a wooden cross.

THE ROYAL ENTRY INTO JERUSALEM

Where has the crowd come from? Both Luke and Mark describe a multitude of disciples accompanying Jesus into the city (Luke 19:37; Mark 10:46). John says that other people coming to the city for the feast hear that Jesus has come and throng to catch a glimpse of him (John 12:12-13). John also mentions that people from Jerusalem who know about the raising of Lazarus have come out of the city to meet

Blessed Is He Who Comes in the Name of the Lord

We have seen how we need to understand the Feast of Booths to understand Peter's response to the Transfiguration (see boxed text on page 179). Now, as Jesus enters Jerusalem for the last time, the upcoming feast is Passover, but we need to turn our attention to the Feast of Booths again to understand what the people were thinking.

During the Feast of Booths in the fall, the Jews thanked the Lord for the year's harvest. But they also implored God for autumn rain to ensure the next year's harvest. On each of the seven days of the feast, a priest bearing a golden pitcher would leave the Temple, followed by crowds of worshippers, and go down to fill the pitcher at the pool of Siloam. All would then process behind the priest with the pitcher back to the Temple courts, each person holding a bundle of branches. Called a *lulav*, the bundle consisted of a long palm branch with willow and myrtle branches bound to it in accord with a command in Leviticus.[146] The people made their booths for the feast of these same branches.

Following the priest, the people would go to the Temple and circle the altar waving the palms, and the water from the pool of Siloam would be poured out there as both an offering and a prayer for rain. On the seventh day, the procession would circle the altar seven times. As they processed, they would chant Psalm 118, the last psalm of the Hallel,[147] singing the last verses repeatedly: "Save us, we beg you, O LORD! [In Aramaic, "*Hosanna*, O Lord!"] O LORD, we beg you, give us success! Blessed be he who him (John 12:17-18). They are all swept up in the excitement of the moment and begin joyfully to acclaim Jesus as the King of Israel, the Son of David.[144] They wave palm branches, shout "Hosanna," and cast their cloaks on the road, a sign of a royal welcome.[145]

In John's Gospel, Jesus decides to enter the city on a donkey after the acclamations and palm waving begin (John 12:14-15). This act is intended to correct the crowd's mistaken idea of who he is. They are right to recognize him as King. But Jesus wants them

---

enters in the name of the LORD! We bless you from the house of the LORD. The LORD is God, and he has given us light. Bind the festal procession with branches, up to the horns of the altar!" (Psalm 118:25-27).

The Feast of Booths had become increasingly messianic and nationalistic in tone over the two hundred years before Jesus. Judas Maccabeus had defeated the Greeks, retaken Jerusalem, cleansed the Temple of its pagan abominations, and rededicated it in December of 164 BC. To commemorate the occasion, he had proclaimed another feast, in December—the Feast of Dedication, or Hanukkah—which was celebrated like the Feast of Booths, replete with palms and hosannas (2 Maccabees 10:6-7). Later, when Judas' brother drove the pagans out of the citadel (in 142 BC), the Jews took possession of the fortress waving palm branches (1 Maccabees 13:51).

Originally, "Blessed is he who comes in the name of the Lord" was most likely intended as a greeting to pilgrims coming to Jerusalem for the feast. But by Jesus' day, it had come to be understood as the greeting for a future messiah, who would do what Judas and his brother had done, and more. "Hosanna" was transformed from a plea for rain to a plea to God also for the messiah. This is what people were thinking of on that Palm Sunday when they cried, "Blessed is he who comes in the name of the Lord!"[148] "Hosanna" had become, in their minds, the joyous acclamation of praise with which they would greet the messiah.[149]

to know that he comes not as a political liberator but as a peaceful ruler, seated on a humble donkey. He has come not to accomplish their national dream of smashing the Gentiles but to carry out God's plan of saving all people. In fulfilling this passage from Zechariah, he illustrates for them and for us the beatitude "Blessed are the meek" (Matthew 5:5):

> Rejoice greatly, O daughter of Zion! Shout aloud, O daughter of Jerusalem! Behold, your king comes to you; triumphant and victorious is he, humble and riding on a donkey, on a colt the foal of a donkey. I will cut off the chariot from Ephraim and the war horse from Jerusalem; and the battle bow shall be cut off, and he shall command peace to the nations; his dominion shall be from sea to sea, and from the River to the ends of the earth. (Zechariah 9:9-10)[150]

Jesus is not fooled by the acclamations and fanfare. He has no ambition for worldly glory. In fact, as Paul tells us, he has willingly emptied himself of heavenly glory (Philippians 2:5-7) to accomplish, in his Passion, his Father's will and our salvation.

DOMINUS FLEVIT, THE LORD WEPT

The Mount of Olives is about three hundred feet higher than the Temple Mount. Its western slope affords spectacular views across the Kidron Valley down into the Temple complex. Herod had spared no expense in the Temple's reconstruction. Josephus describes the sight of it from the Mount of Olives in this way:

> The exterior of the structure lacked nothing that could astound either mind or eye. For, being covered on all sides with massive plates of gold, the sun was no sooner upon it than it radiated so fiery a flash that people straining to look at it were compelled to avert their eyes, as from the rays of the sun. To approaching strangers, it appeared from afar like a snow-clad mountain; for all that was not overlaid with gold was of purest white.[151]

It must have been a breathtaking sight. No wonder one of the disciples is moved to exclaim, "Look, Teacher, what wonderful stones and what wonderful buildings!" Jesus' response must have been deflating: "Do you see these great buildings? There will not be left here one stone upon another, that will not be thrown down" (Mark 13:1-2).

Jesus knows that Jerusalem, though its name means "city of peace," sadly prefers the warhorse to the donkey. He has given the people the opportunity to choose peace; their fate is in their own hands. Knowing what they will choose and what the horrible consequences will be, he breaks down and weeps. If only they knew what made for peace! But they have failed to recognize their savior (Luke 19:41-44).[152]

In the traditional place on the slope of the Mount of Olives where Jesus stopped to weep over the city, there stands a small but beautiful chapel called Dominus Flevit, meaning "the Lord wept." It is built in the shape of a tear drop. Antonio Barluzzi, the architect of the chapel, placed tear jars at the corners of the dome, since it was here that Jesus, the Divine Bridegroom, wept over the impending destruction of his beloved, the daughter of Jerusalem. The chapel is surrounded by the trees called spina-christi, or thorn of Christ, to help us remember the crown not of gold but of thorns that was presented to the King by the city he loved.

JUDGMENT

All the Gospels tell us that, during the last week of Jesus' life, he continues his ministry of teaching. All the Gospels also note that a prominent theme during these days is judgment. The judgment coming upon Jerusalem is part of it, but Jesus also addresses the inevitable judgment each individual must face when the Son of Man returns in glory on the last day.

To go back and forth between the Mount of Olives and Jerusalem, one must pass through the Kidron Valley. The valley is a vast graveyard, its cemeteries dating back as far as the ninth century BC. The landscape of this valley provides an ominous backdrop for Jesus' teaching on judgment. During the last week of his life, Jesus and the disciples would leave Bethany early in the morning and then return each evening, twice a day passing through this reminder of death.

Many people struggle to reconcile the image of God as a loving Father and Jesus as the gentle shepherd, on the one hand, with the idea of Judgment Day and the possibility of eternal punishment on the other. There are parables and images about judgment that use the image of an angry king who hurls people into prison or worse (for example, Matthew 18:23-35 and 25:31-46). These are, it should be remembered, parables. The point is not to describe the character of the king but to underline the horrible and eternal consequences of resentment and indifference to suffering.

Jerusalem's impending fate helps us interpret these parables. Jesus offers the palm of peace. Jerusalem stubbornly insists instead on the sword. It is not an angry God or a vengeful Jesus who will send Roman legions to destroy Jerusalem. It is the foolishness of the nation that will bring this fate upon itself. Watching it, God weeps. That is what the tears of Jesus mean.

In several places in John's Gospel, Jesus clearly rejects the role of condemning judge and explains that condemnation is self-imposed. Here he speaks to Nicodemus:

> For God sent the Son into the world, not to condemn the world, but that the world might be saved through him. He who believes in him is not condemned; he who does not believe is condemned already, because he has not believed in the name of the only-begotten Son of God. And this is the judgment, that the light has come into the world, and men loved darkness rather than light, because their deeds were evil. (John 3:17-19)

In John's Gospel, the final words Jesus speaks before the Last Supper bring us back to the words to Nicodemus:

> If any one hears my sayings and does not keep them, I do not judge him; for I did not come to judge the world but to save the world. He who rejects me and does not receive my sayings has a judge; the word that I have spoken will be his judge on the last day. ... [The Father's] commandment is eternal life. (John 12:46-50)

There is no better contemporary summary of Jesus' final teaching on judgment than the words of C. S. Lewis: "There are only two kinds of people in the end: those who say to God, 'Thy will be done,' and those to whom God says, in the end, '*Thy* will be done.' All that are in Hell, choose it. Without that self-choice there could be no Hell. No soul that seriously and constantly desires joy will ever miss it. Those who seek find. To those who knock it is opened."[153]

THE SEED AND THE FRUIT

Attempts were made on Jesus' life several times in the course of the public ministry—at the synagogue in Nazareth according to Luke (4:28-30) and during the Feast of Booths in John (7:30). Jesus slipped through their hands again and again because, as John notes, "his hour had not yet come." But the hour has finally arrived. And instead of walking away from danger, Jesus walks right into its midst.

Jesus has said that he came to give his life as a ransom for "the many" (see Matthew 20:28), which in the Old Testament is an expression meaning the entire covenant people. In his ironic prophecy, Caiaphas says it is better for one man to die than for the entire nation to perish. But in commenting on this, John expands what Caiaphas says: "Jesus should die for the nation, and not for the nation only, but to gather into one the children of God who are scattered abroad" (John 11:51-52). This editorial comment from the evangelist is directly linked to the visit of some Greeks, described in the next chapter of John, who come to the disciples asking to see Jesus. "The children of God who are scattered abroad" refers not only to the dispersed Jews of the Diaspora but to all the children of Adam, the nations of the world (the Gentiles) represented by these Greeks. What Jesus is about to do will finally, once and for all, open the way to a people of God that is truly universal, fulfilling the promise to Abraham that all the nations of the world will find blessing through his descendants (Genesis 18:18; 22:18).

This is the way Jesus himself sees his death: "And I, when I am lifted up from the earth, will draw *all men* to myself" (John 12:32, emphasis added). We have seen that during the public ministry, Jesus' main mission has been to the lost sheep of the house of Israel. Bringing the twelve tribes back together, gathering into one flock the lost sheep, is even symbolized by the number of his core leadership team, the Twelve. Now, however, it is time to graft onto this remnant all who are willing to become sons of Abraham by faith. In many places in the Old Testament, Gentiles are pictured as streaming toward the holy hill of the Jerusalem Temple.[154] The Temple is to be "a house of prayer for all peoples" (Isaiah 56:7). All the prophetic dreams of the gathering of the nations will be fulfilled.

Throughout his preaching, Jesus has indicated that he and his Father desire fruit—the parable of the sower and the seed where some bear thirty, sixty, or a hundredfold is one example (Matthew 13:8). A negative example of the failure to bear fruit is given in the parable of the wicked tenants.[155] In the last week of Jesus' life, he and the disciples pass a fig tree on which he finds lots of leaves but no fruit, and he curses the tree. This is a prophetic sign of the fate of the shepherds of Israel who are all religious show with no fruit befitting repentance, as John the Baptist put it (Matthew 3:8).

As powerful as his ministry of preaching and healing has been, it is now time to bring things to a head. Fruit has been borne, but only the firstfruits; the plenteous harvest will begin through what Jesus is about to do:

> Truly, truly I say to you, unless a grain of wheat falls into the earth and dies, it remains alone; but if it dies, it bears much fruit. He who loves his life loses it, and he who hates his life in this world will keep it for eternal life. (John 12:24-25)

Jesus is the leader in laying his life down. By giving himself away, he will win the world. But this principle, announced here to explain the meaning of what is about to take place for the redemption of the world, has implications for his followers. In all four Gospels,

Jesus makes it clear that discipleship means embracing this wisdom, which is so contrary to the wisdom of the world. Living this principle in day-to-day life is what Jesus means by carrying your cross daily (Luke 9:23). "If anyone serves me, he must follow me; and where I am, there shall my servant be" (John 12:26).

UPROAR IN THE TEMPLE

When Judas Maccabeus triumphantly entered Jerusalem in 164 BC, it was because the pagans had desecrated the sanctuary and had to be driven out. After Jesus' triumphal entry into the city, he too has to cleanse the Temple, but this time it is God's own people who are polluting his Father's house. Merchants and their wares are the immediate target of the cleansing, but they are there by the power of the chief priests.

Under Caiaphas, the selling of sacrificial animals and the changing of currency seems to have been moved from the area outside the Temple courts into the Court of the Gentiles itself. This was a violation of the very purpose of that court, which was to give pagans a place where they might worship the God of Israel.

In Jesus' time, the Temple was in the wrong hands and had come to symbolize the wrong things. Annas, who had been high priest for nine years, had managed to get a sort of dynasty going. It was his son-in-law Caiaphas who held the office that fateful year, but Annas was still high priest emeritus.[156] Before the Temple was eventually destroyed in AD 70, Annas would succeed in getting five of his sons plus a grandson to serve additional terms as high priest. Every notable Christian to be martyred in the Holy City—from Jesus to Stephen, James the son of Zebedee, and James the brother of the Lord—would be executed under a high priest of Annas' family.

Tithes, Temple taxes, the sale of animals for sacrifice—the Temple was big business, and it was all controlled by the high priest, his assistant chief priests, and their families. None of the high priestly families during the Roman era were much loved by the people, but the family of Annas and Caiaphas was particularly disdained for its greed and skill at repression.[157]

Moreover, the Temple was the center of the banking system. It contained the records of everyone's debts. When the anti-Roman Jewish rebels took over Jerusalem in AD 66, the first thing they did was to burn the records of the Temple treasury, so much did that treasury symbolize debt bondage.

So there is quite a bit behind Jesus' reference to Jeremiah: "Has this house, which is called by my name, become a den of robbers in your eyes?" (Jeremiah 7:11). In one sense, Jesus is cleansing the Temple of moral corruption and restoring it to its rightful use as a house of prayer for the "little ones" of Israel and all peoples. It is telling that after clearing out the Temple, Jesus uses the restored space to heal the blind and the lame and to enjoy the company of children. It is the little ones who cry out, "Hosanna to the Son of David!" (Matthew 21:14-17).

But there is much more to his action than this.

We need to understand that the whole Temple system required money changers so people could pay the Temple tax. Roman coins bore the idolatrous image of the divine Caesar dressed as a pagan high priest. The use of such coins would defile the Temple, so the Roman coins had to be changed into other currency before the tax could be paid. And Jewish lay people offered sacrifices at the Temple, so they needed to buy doves, sheep, and even oxen.

The elimination of all trade in the Temple area would mean an end to the sacrificial cult. To end it would indeed be a messianic act of the last days, according to the very last verse of the book of the prophet Zechariah: "And there shall no longer be a trader in the house of the Lord of hosts on that day" (Zechariah 14:21).

"That day" has arrived. Jesus is about to replace the sacrifices of old with a new, definitive sacrifice that will never have to be repeated. And he is about to replace the old Temple with the Temple of his risen body (John 2:19), which will truly become a house of prayer for all peoples from every race and tongue and nation.

JUDAS' DEAL

The chief priests understand the threat to their position and their livelihood all too well. Jesus' action in the Temple jolts them into urgent action. One of Jesus' disciples, whom John describes as a thief (John 12:6), can perhaps be bribed.

We don't know for sure where the deal is arranged—it could have been in the Temple courts themselves or at the palace of Caiaphas on the hill overlooking the Temple. But Judas Iscariot is offered money to hand Jesus over privately and quietly, so as not to provoke a riot (Matthew 26:5).

The price? What value do the chief priests and Judas place on the life of the Son of God? It is very little—no more than the Old Testament "book value" for a slave: thirty pieces of silver.[158]

CHAPTER 16

THE SUPPER
AND THE GARDEN

Jesus had friends in Jerusalem as well as in Bethany. The names of two we know: Nicodemus and Joseph of Arimathea. The unnamed man who provided the dining room to Jesus and the disciples may have been another. We know he was not poor; the supper was held not only in an upper room but in the upper part of the city, not too far from Herod's former palace. This room, known traditionally as the Cenacle, was to be the location for more than one momentous happening in the weeks to come. This night, it would be the venue for what Jesus knew would be the Last Supper with his disciples.

DO THIS IN MEMORY OF ME

We think of a day beginning at midnight; for Jews in Jesus' time, the day begins at sundown. So as evening falls and the disciples gather with Jesus for a meal, the final day of Jesus' earthly life begins. It is the day of his exodus, his departure to the Father. And it is the Exodus from Egypt that Jews are about to celebrate in the Passover festival.

At meals, including Passover, the host pronounces a blessing over the bread: "Blessed are you, Lord our God, King of the universe, you who have brought bread forth from the earth."

A similar blessing is spoken over the cup of wine that is shared on the Sabbath, Passover, and other festive occasions. Jesus probably also begins his blessing of the bread and wine with these traditional words of thanksgiving, but he goes on to say some additional things that are surprising and unprecedented.

Our earliest written witness to Jesus' novel words at the supper is actually not in the Gospels but in Paul's first letter to the Corinthians, written about twenty years after the occasion.[159] Paul quotes a very set, traditional narrative that was most likely passed on to him shortly after his conversion. He, in turn, had handed it on to the Corinthians and wanted to remind them of it:

> For I received from the Lord what I also delivered to you, that the Lord Jesus on the night when he was betrayed took bread, and when he had given thanks, he broke it, and said, "This is my body which is for you. Do this in remembrance of me." In the same way also the chalice, after supper, saying, "This chalice is the new covenant in my blood. Do this, as often as you drink it, in remembrance of me." For as often as you eat this bread and drink the chalice, you proclaim the Lord's death until he comes. (1 Corinthians 11:23-26)[160]

Luke's account is very close to Paul's in its wording. He also records Jesus having called this the "new covenant in my blood" (Luke 22:20) and notes the Lord's command to "do this in remembrance of me" (Luke 22:19).

Jesus is here instituting a memorial.

The Passover festival was a memorial of the saving event of the Exodus from Egypt, the greatest act of salvation of the covenant people. It is critical to understand that in ancient Israel, "memorial" did not mean an occasion in which people psychologically and subjectively call to mind an event that occurred in the remote past. It meant celebrating and entering into the experience of an event that was, in the memorial, *re*-presented—in other words, presented again, made present again here and now. To celebrate the Passover for a Jew was to participate in it personally, in the present moment. The Mishnah makes this clear:

In every generation a man is obligated to regard himself as though he personally had gone forth from Egypt, because it is said, "And you shall tell your son on that day, saying: 'It is because of that which the Lord did for me when I came forth out of Egypt.'"[161]

Jesus is making present his sacrificial death and his risen life in an anticipatory way a few hours before his death and resurrection occur. In telling his disciples to do this in remembrance of him, as a memorial of his saving work, he is telling them that each time they do it, they will be making its saving power present again, until he returns in glory. His death and resurrection will be the new and definitive exodus; this meal will be the new and definitive Passover memorial.

SACRIFICE, BLOOD, AND COVENANT

In any animal sacrifice, such as that of the Passover, the blood of the victim represented the life of the animal. Since all life belongs to God, the blood was completely drained and was "poured out" at the foot of the altar. In the case of the Passover offering and the most common sacrifice, the peace offering, the sacrificial victim was subsequently eaten by those who offered it. If you did not eat the victim, you had no part in the sacrifice. Those who partook of the sacrifice shared a common life with one another and with God. Another name for a sacrifice like this was a sacrifice of thanksgiving or a communion sacrifice.[162]

The first covenant, on Mount Sinai, was inaugurated with a unique sacrifice—half of the blood of the sacrifice was poured out at the base of the altar, and half was sprinkled on the people as the "blood of the covenant." This created a community of life between God and his people, making them a family. Moses and the elders then ate the sacrificial meal in the presence of the Lord (Exodus 24:8-11). The Gospels of Mark and Matthew both use the same phrase as the Exodus account—"blood of the covenant" (Matthew 26:28; Mark 14:24).

Jesus is instituting a new covenant through a new and unique sacrifice. Every time this sacrificial meal is repeated, the new covenant and the saving act that inaugurated it will be made present again. Jesus, the Bread of Life, is the sacrificial victim whose body is offered as food under the form of bread. Those who do not partake in the sacrificial meal have no part in the sacrifice.

To offer his blood under the form of wine is even more striking. As we have seen, life, which is from God, resides in the blood, according to the Jewish understanding (Leviticus 17:11). Thus, kosher law forbids blood to be consumed by human beings, for it belongs exclusively to God, from whom it comes. To this day, there are Orthodox Jewish rabbis whose professional work involves supervising the slaughter of animals to guarantee that all the blood is drained from the body after an animal's death. Only then can the label on the meat package say "kosher."

For Jesus' disciples to be given the blood of the Lamb of God for their drink means that his life, the eternal life, will be coursing through their veins. This is *zoe*, the divine life, the real life, that has been one of the key themes of John's Gospel. It means God no longer holds anything back. All is given in the life of his Son. His blood is the new wine, the choice wine (John 2:10), the divine life that now comes to reside within Christ's disciples, which can truly make them new from the inside out. It is no accident that it is on this night, in the context of this gift, that Jesus says, "I am the way, and the truth, and the life" (John 14:6).

Jesus' gift of this new life, this power to become new, is like engraving his teaching not on tablets of stone but on living hearts:

> Behold, the days are coming, says the LORD, when I will make a new covenant with the house of Israel and the house of Judah ... I will put my law within them, and I will write it upon their hearts; and I will be their God, and they shall be my people ... I will forgive their iniquity, and I will remember their sin no more. (Jeremiah 31:31-34)

Purity of heart, which Jesus proclaimed "blessed" in the Beatitudes, now becomes possible. The disciples' hearts will be purified by Jesus' blood, poured out at the altar of the Cross and given in the Eucharist. Blood nourishes every cell of the human body. But it also cleanses by carrying away impurities.

THE LAST SUPPER IN JOHN'S GOSPEL

The longest account of the Last Supper is found in John's Gospel, where five chapters are devoted to what transpired there. Many people wonder why the story of the institution of this new meal, the Eucharist, is missing from John's lengthy account.

Remember that the miracle of the multiplication of the loaves is presented by all four evangelists as pointing forward to this meal. For John, it seems, there is no need to repeat what Jesus so clearly taught in the Bread of Life discourse following the multiplication of the loaves:

> Truly, truly I say to you, unless you eat the flesh of the Son of man and drink his blood, you have no life in you; he who eats my flesh and drinks my blood has eternal life, and I will raise him up at the last day. For my flesh is food indeed and my blood is drink indeed. He who eats my flesh and drinks my blood abides in me, and I in him. (John 6:53-56)

By the time John's Gospel was written, Christians had been celebrating this memorial for decades. The reality of Christ's sacrifice and the gift of his Body and Blood under the forms of bread and wine were well known. The words Jesus used to institute it, as we see from Paul, were also well known.

What was, and still is, in danger of being forgotten is the meaning and purpose of this meal. The entire Last Supper discourse in John should be viewed as a commentary on this extraordinary gift, called the Eucharist, from the Greek word meaning thanksgiving. *Eucharisteo* is the verb used by Paul and Luke in their Last Supper accounts when they note that Jesus "had given thanks" (1 Corinthians 11:24; Luke 22:17).

To emphasize what the Eucharist truly means, John tells us, during the meal Jesus performs an unexpected prophetic action. He suddenly rises, takes off his outer garment, and begins washing the feet of his disciples.

They are aghast. There is nothing in the Passover Seder or in Jewish etiquette that would make sense of such an act. According to Jewish law, a master could not even compel one of his slaves to wash anyone's feet, so degrading was this task considered.[163]

Nonetheless, Jesus washes the feet of every one of them—even the feet of Peter, who he knows will deny him, and of Judas, who will later that night betray him.

We here must recall the words of Paul's letter to the Philippians (2:6-11). Though the Word is divine, dwelling in the serene heights of heavenly glory, he freely plunges to the depths of human misery, joining himself to our frail nature, entering our turbulent world. As if this act of humility were not enough, he humbles himself further, accepting the status of a slave. Now, in stooping down to wash the feet of his disciples, Jesus lowers himself *below* the status of a slave. The love of the Father, as we saw in the story of the Prodigal Son, is extravagant. So is the humility of the Son.

Why does he do this at the beginning of the Last Supper? This act is a parable of his whole human existence, an interpretation of his impending death, and a proclamation of the meaning of the Eucharist. John sums it up this way: "Having loved his own who were in the world, he loved them to the end" (John 13:1). He is washing them with his love—symbolized here by the water, expressed a few hours later in truth by his blood, poured out at the altar of the Cross.

Love to the end means both love to the very conclusion of his life and love to the utmost, to the furthest extremity imaginable. It is love that drives him to lower himself and give his life away. No one will take his life from him. He himself freely lays it down (John 10:18). Others do not humble him; he humbles himself.

This love to the end, this love without limit, is what becomes our food in the Eucharist. All who receive the foot washing and the meal must be ready to provide the same foot washing and meal. We cannot receive Love unless we are willing to become Love.

Judas is washed and receives the blessed food. He desecrates the gift immediately by betraying Love. He thereby brings a curse upon himself—"It would have been better for that man if he had not been born" (Mark 14:21). In contrast, those disciples who have accepted the gift, who will go on to become foot washers in turn, are proclaimed blessed in one of only two beatitudes in John's Gospel: "If you know these things, blessed are you if you do them" (John 13:17).

THE INTENDED FRUIT OF THE EUCHARIST

Jesus, in the last moments before the Supper, proclaims that the goal of his death is the bearing of much fruit (John 12:24). In the Last Supper discourse, he who gives us his blood under the form of the fruit of the vine calls himself the true vine. We are branches who must remain in vital union with him, the vine.

Jesus chooses to emphasize two aspects of this mystery of intimate, vital union. The first is that we cannot hope to bear fruit unless we "abide" in the vine. This is the same word Jesus used in the Bread of Life discourse: "He who eats my flesh and drinks my blood abides in me, and I in him" (John 6:56).

The Eucharist, then, is a primary means by which we maintain and deepen our intimacy with him and are infused with his life. If we fail to nurture this intimacy and receive this gift, we will not have the vitality necessary to bear fruit.

If we draw life from the vine and still fail to bear fruit, we will be removed from the vine as dead branches. If we do bear fruit, we will still be pruned, that we might bear more (John 15:1-2).

What is the fruit to be borne by our attachment to the vine through this sign, this sacrament of the New Covenant in his blood? The most important fruit of the New Covenant is the fruit of the new commandment: "A new commandment I give to you, that you love one another; even as I have loved you, that you also love one another" (John 13:34). He has in mind, of course, the foot-washing sort of love, expressing itself in a thousand acts of humble service and not shrinking even from love unto death: "Greater love has no man than this, that a man lay down his life for his friends" (John 15:13). This love is to be shown to all who need it, of course. But in a special way, it is to characterize the way his disciples relate to one another. John 17, often called the high priestly prayer of Jesus, is a prayer for the loving unity of his disciples, which is to be a sign to the world that Jesus is truly sent by the Father (John 17:21).

From this love flows another fruit—joy, which is a recurrent theme in the Last Supper discourse: "These things I have spoken to you, that my joy may be in you, and that your joy may be full" (John 15:11). Yet another fruit is peace: "Peace I leave with you; my peace I give to you" (John 14:27). Paul describes these things—love, joy, and peace—as key fruits of the Spirit (Galatians 5:22). Elsewhere he describes these fruits as the essence of what the kingdom of God is about (Romans 14:17).

So at the Last Supper, Jesus leaves us not just with final instructions and commandments. He leaves us with new gifts that will empower us to live the new commandment of the New Covenant—his Body and his Blood.

We see that the Eucharist, the gift of the Supper, is inextricably bound up with the call to love as Christ loves. Since it conveys the power to do this, we have no excuse. If in receiving it we refuse to love as Christ loves, we are desecrating the holy gift. This is one of the main points of Paul's teaching on the Eucharist (1 Corinthians 11:27-34).

PETER'S DENIAL AND JUDAS' BETRAYAL

Before the evening is over, Jesus makes two disturbing predictions. The first is that one of the Twelve will betray him: "The hand of him who betrays me is with me on the table," he says (Luke 22:21). And when Simon Peter protests that he would never do such a thing, Jesus shocks him, saying, "I tell you, Peter, the cock will not crow this day, until you three times deny that you know me" (Luke 22:34).

THE GARDEN

The Last Supper takes place in the upper city of Jerusalem. Afterward, Jesus and the disciples depart from there and begin a steep downhill walk into the Kidron Valley and then up the slope of the Mount of Olives to the garden of Gethsemane.

Gethsemane comes from the Aramaic word for "oil press." About a third of the way up the slope of the Mount of Olives is a cave that archaeologists confirm was the site of an olive press in the time of Jesus. The early spring night being chilly, most of the disciples probably shelter in the cave for the night. Jesus, however, takes Peter, James, and John into the adjacent olive grove to accompany him in prayer, under the light of the full moon.

Yet these three, who had slept while Jesus prayed on Tabor, sleep here as well. Jesus is left alone to face his impending ordeal. He knows it is not just death he faces but abandonment, humiliation, and torture. The strain weighs heavily upon him, and his sweat falls to the ground as great drops of blood.

The Fathers of the Church point to Gethsemane as a testimony to how truly human Jesus really is. Healthy human beings naturally have a will to live and to avoid pain and destruction. Over the centuries, many Christians who fully accepted Jesus' divinity have compromised on his humanity, denying that he had a human will. They made him superhuman, without genuine human desires and human needs. In the garden we see him truly tremble before the horror of death. And so he prays, "Father, if you are willing, remove this chalice from me." This petition arises out of his human will, which can only will what is right and good. Yet he submits his human will to his Father's divine will, which is his own divine will as well: "Nevertheless not my will, but yours, be done" (Luke 22:42).

In teaching his disciples the Our Father, Jesus was teaching them his very own prayer. Here he reveals that "Thy will be done" is his own lifelong prayer and program. It will be the key to our salvation.

His "Thy will be done" is not uttered glibly. He makes his prayer as he watches his doom approaching while his closest companions serenely sleep. Through the olive trees, he can see a line of torches winding its way down the slope of the city into the Kidron Valley. It looks like a serpent of fire steadily crawling toward the garden. He can still escape. Fifteen minutes' walk up the Mount of Olives and he could be over the top, able to descend into the Judean wilderness on the other side where they would never find him.

But Jesus has "set [his] face like a flint" toward Jerusalem (Isaiah 50:7; see also Ezekiel 21:1). He has ignored what usually stops us dead in our tracks—fear of suffering, of ridicule, of abandonment by our friends. Now the devil's time has come (Luke 4:13), and Jesus stands his ground. He is ready to endure the sting of sin to blot out sin, ready to face death to overcome it.

This is how it has to be, because the new Adam has to undo the damage caused by the old. Our first parents disobeyed God because they wanted to be like him and exalt themselves over him; they wanted to know "good and evil" on their own terms, not on God's terms (see Genesis 3:5). Charmed by the serpent, they chose pride and so became its slaves.

Once, Adam had lifted his hand against God in disobedience. The new Adam lifts his hands in a prayer of obedience. Thus will the curse be undone by humility. It is the only way. Christ, who washes feet, who rides on a donkey—the new Adam—will crush the head of the serpent by means of loving, humble obedience.

BETRAYAL, TRIAL, DENIAL

Jesus does not flee. It is his disciples who flee. All except one. Judas doesn't flee, because he has brought the soldiers and has shown them which one is Jesus by kissing him. It is the supreme act of false love, made so soon after Judas received the ultimate gift of Love from the Lord himself.

And so Jesus is shackled and dragged, like a captured bandit, back down into the valley with its ancient tombs and back up the slope to the upper city, where Annas and Caiaphas are waiting for him along with a number of hastily assembled members of the Sanhedrin. It is a kangaroo court,[164] where false testimony is given against him and readily believed. He is accused of being a blasphemer and false prophet. They blindfold him and then slap him, taunting him and demanding that he prove he is a prophet by telling them which one has struck him (Luke 22:63-65; Mark 14:65).

THE COURTYARD

Though Peter fled the garden with the others, he follows the arrest party at a distance and waits in the courtyard of the high priest to see what will happen. He hopes to remain incognito, but a servant girl points him out as one of Jesus' followers. Though he denies it, she insists. The more he denies it, the more certain she is; his thick Galilean accent gives him away (Matthew 26:73).

After his third denial, which he utters with violence and cursing, another sound is suddenly heard—a cock crows. Peter can evidently see Jesus, though it seems Jesus' back is turned to him. As soon as the cock crows, Jesus turns and looks at Peter. We imagine that it is a sad, not an angry, look, full of the same love with which Jesus looked on Peter so often in the past when Peter failed. Peter remembers the Lord's words and breaks into bitter weeping (Luke 22:61-62)

THE PIT

In present-day Jerusalem, the Church of St. Peter in Gallicantu ("cock's crow") is built over excavations of what some scholars believe was the palace of Caiaphas. There are prison cells in this complex as well as a cracked cistern that was converted into what appears to have been a secure cell for solitary confinement. The prisoner would have been lowered into this dungeon through a hole in the ground and hoisted out the same way. Jesus may very well have spent the last night of his life in this dark pit, alone. Pilgrims to this place traditionally pray Psalm 88, as Jesus may have done. It is an anguished prayer offered in loneliness and desolation: "I am shut in so that I cannot escape; my eye grows dim through sorrow. ... You have caused loved one and friend to shun me; my companions are in darkness" (Psalm 88:8-9, 88:18).

The pit is a very moving place to pray and to ponder all this. As horrible as physical torture must be, probably the greatest pain of all is rejection and abandonment. It is particularly excruciating when it comes from those you love most and have trusted most. Jesus was betrayed by one, denied by another, and abandoned by all. He bore this suffering and isolation knowingly, willingly, to heal our isolation and loneliness, caused by our own sin and the sins of others. He forgives and empowers us to forgive—even this sort of outrage.

CHAPTER 17

GOOD FRIDAY

It is chief priests who take the initiative to apprehend Jesus. Some of the leading Pharisaic scribes and elders are involved as well. They want Jesus dead for a number of reasons. For three years he has disregarded their Sabbath regulations. Even worse, he is, so they think, a false prophet and a blasphemer who speaks as if he were equal to God. And his dramatic action against the sacrificial and financial system of the Temple threatens the livelihood of the chief priests.

Yet ultimately, they cannot themselves put him to death. For that, they need the support of the Roman governor. And to gain that support, they have to convince the governor not just that Jesus is guilty of violating Jewish religious law but that he is a political threat as well.

JESUS BEFORE PONTIUS PILATE AND HEROD

Judea and Samaria were not very important in the big picture of Roman politics. There were many more prestigious places. But the coast and the trade routes needed to be kept secure, and Palestine was a buffer against the powerful Parthian Empire to the east. So stability was important. A lower-level aristocrat would suffice to serve as its governor, and he would remain in place just as long as he could keep a lid on things.

Pontius Pilate managed to keep his position longer than most governors before and after him—for a full ten years. That means he was uncommonly shrewd. Caiaphas was high priest during those years. The two apparently worked together hand in glove, not necessarily because they were friends but because a good working relationship benefited them both.

A Roman official's work schedule began very early in those days, before dawn. John tells us that a few of Pilate's soldiers were sent with the Temple Guard to Gethsemane the night before (John 18:3). So when the Jewish authorities show up very early at Pilate's doorstep with a prisoner, he is not surprised. He is apparently expecting them.

But the chief priests will not come into the praetorium. They do not want to defile themselves and incur ritual impurity. Ironically, they want to be "clean" to eat the Passover lamb that night, but they do not see that the man they are delivering to the pagans is the true Passover Lamb.

To Pilate, they accuse Jesus of being a rival to Caesar, saying that he claimed to be a king. Perhaps they tell Pilate of the Palm Sunday procession and the shouts of "Hosanna" and "Hail to the King." The emperor Tiberius was a paranoid old recluse by this time, hiding out in his summer palace on the island of Capri. But he took any potential rivals very seriously.

As this cynical politician questions the prisoner before him, Pilate can sense that Jesus is no political enemy. The strange man speaks of a "kingdom not of this world." Pilate is concerned with this world and this world only. And his task is to preserve Caesar's position in it as well as his own. This Jesus, this dreamer, speaks about "truth." What does this mean? The Nazarean is clearly a philosopher or a mystic, not a practical military man.

Pilate hears from the accusers that Jesus is a Galilean, and he sees a potential solution to this troublesome affair. He hands Jesus over to Herod Antipas, the ruler of Galilee and Perea, who happens to be in Jerusalem for the Passover. Herod is pleased, because he has heard about this wonder-worker and hopes to see him perform a miracle. But Jesus remains utterly silent in Herod's presence. So Herod and his men treat him with contempt, mocking him and then dressing him in "gorgeous apparel" fit for a king, and they send him back to Pilate (Luke 23:6-11).

A GUILTY MAN RELEASED AND AN INNOCENT MAN CONDEMNED

Herod's contemptuous treatment of Jesus confirms for Pilate that this man is no political threat. So Pilate goes back to the Jewish leaders outside and declares Jesus to be innocent. From what we know about Pilate, he didn't normally think twice about killing locals if it suited his purposes. But for some reason, his encounter with this man has made him reticent to go along with Caiaphas' murderous scheme, despite their cordial working relationship. He has an idea: There is a Passover custom whereby the Jews can petition the release of a prisoner. Pilate doesn't have the courage to resist Caiaphas directly, so he hopes the crowd will ask for Jesus' release.

Other prisoners are being held, including some who participated in an insurrection and committed murder. One of them, who was probably the rebels' leader, is particularly notorious (Matthew 27:16). His name is Barabbas (another irony), which means "son of the father."[165] To Pilate's surprise, the crowd, stirred up by the chief priests (Mark 15:11), asks for Barabbas' release and demands that Jesus be put to death for rebellion against Caesar (Luke 23:18; John 19:12). The people prefer the bogus "son of the father" to the true Son. As if this hypocrisy were not enough, when Pilate asks if they really want him to crucify their king, they answer, "We have no king but Caesar" (John 19:15). For Jews, this reply is tantamount to apostasy. They are thumbing their nose at God, their ultimate King, and at David's successor, the messiah they claim to hope for.

The last thing Pilate wants is to release a bona fide revolutionary. So he has Jesus scourged, hoping that this will satisfy the blood lust of the crowd.[166] His soldiers brutally beat Jesus and put a mock crown—of thorns—on his head. Pilate leads the bruised and battered figure before the crowd. Declaring Jesus' innocence a second time, he points to him and says, "Here is the man!" He probably means "Look at the poor fellow!" hoping that the pathetic sight will move the crowd to pity. But Pilate has said more than he knows. Another way of translating the phrase "Son of Man" is simply "the Man" (John 19:1-5). Behold the Man. Here stands the Son of Man, the perfect man, the new Adam.

The people in the crowd are not satisfied that he is a humiliated, bruised, and bloody mess. They harden their hearts and refuse all compassion. Instead of asking for his release, they begin to shout, "Crucify him!" Pilate brings Jesus back inside the praetorium and questions him further. Coming out, more desirous than ever to release him, he declares the man's innocence yet a third time.

Knowing Pilate's weakness, the Jewish leaders resort to blackmail. What will Caesar think if he finds out that Pilate, this supposed friend of Caesar (John 19:12), has let off a rival with royal pretensions? There is an implied threat here. If Pilate doesn't give them what they want, they just might send a delegation to Rome to complain. Pilate knows that if this happens, Caesar will open an inquiry, and that will be the end of Pilate's governorship. This is how they had gotten Herod's son Archelaus deposed and exiled.

It is a moment of truth for Pilate. In fact, he has come face-to-face with Truth. He has to decide either for truth and his conscience, on the one hand, or for self-preservation and his career on the other. He who saves his life loses it, Jesus said (Luke 9:24). And this is precisely what Pilate does—he condemns an innocent man to save his own political skin. "Then he handed him over to them to be crucified" (John 19:16).

This is the third betrayal. The first was by Judas, who handed Jesus over to the chief priests. The second was by the chief priests, who handed him over to Pilate. Judas is a representative of the followers of Jesus; the priests are representatives of the Jewish community. Pilate represents the pagan world and all who would compromise truth for the sake of self-preservation.

Who is responsible for Jesus' death? In a very real way, we all are.

Irony abounds. Judas loses his savior, his silver, and his life. Caiaphas wants to keep the Romans from destroying the nation and the Temple, yet his perfidy will soon bring exactly that upon them, the thing he dreads most of all. As for Pilate, a few years after this maneuver to save his career, complaints about him still make their way to Rome. He is recalled and soon vanishes from the annals of history.

CRUCIFIXION

From the beginning to the end of Jesus' life, the details are humiliating. No room in the inn. Born in the stench of a stable. Hunted by Herod's henchmen. Raised in backwater Galilee, the land where the country accent is so thick you can cut it with a knife.

The capital penalty for Roman citizens was beheading, a quick and relatively dignified execution. Jesus' punishments were the ones reserved for slaves and the rebels of subjugated peoples— flagellation and crucifixion.[167]

These punishments were about humiliation as much as pain. The Romans hadn't limited Jesus' scourging to the forty lashes less one of Jewish law (Deuteronomy 25:3). The Roman way was much more brutal and demeaning. Small lead barbells and bits of stone attached to the ends of the lashes left deep bruises and open wounds. The number of blows was limited only by just how close the torturers wanted to bring the victim to the door of death.

Then came the criminal's shameful walk toward crucifixion.[168] Finally, at the place of crucifixion, his last shred of dignity would be taken away. In first-century Judea, men and women typically covered themselves from head to toe, even in the scorching heat. But a crucified man was stripped naked and put on display for all to see,[169] the death squad of soldiers getting the victim's clothing as a gratuity. Sometimes, birds of prey would swoop down to peck at the condemned men, increasing the horror and indignity of the spectacle.

Crucifixion was the slowest, most painful way to die. That was the point of the public display. Risking death to gain freedom might be worthwhile to many. But the pain and humiliation of this torturous death would make potential rebels think long and hard.

Golgotha, the place of the skull, was a small hill just outside a gate of the city.[170] For the Romans, it was important to execute criminals in a place where many people would see the executions and be reminded of the penalty for crimes against the state. The ominous name probably comes from the fact that this place was an abandoned quarry from which all the good stone had been removed. The gouges left in the hill may have resembled the eye and nose sockets of a skull.

Jesus is probably close to death already when Pilate finally sends him to be crucified, which may be why he needed the help of Simon of Cyrene to carry the cross to Golgotha. There he is stripped, nailed to the cross, and hoisted up on it for all the world to see. He is crucified between two others. Once they are nailed to their crosses, an anguished waiting game begins, with crowd and soldiers watching as the three writhe in agony.

FORSAKEN?

During the time Jesus hangs there, suspended between heaven and earth, he utters seven short statements.

One of them, noted in Mark and Matthew, is remembered in the original Aramaic words uttered by Jesus: *Eli, Eli, lama sabach-thani?* "My God, my God, why have you forsaken me?" (Matthew 27:46). Some opponents of Christianity think that, having expected God to deliver him, Jesus cries out here in utter despair. Some Christians also misinterpret his cry, imagining that Jesus, in taking on our punishment for sin, is experiencing its most terrible consequence—namely, separation from the Father and from his grace.

Both interpretations are sorely mistaken. Jesus is neither bewildered nor abandoned. The fact that he bears our sin does not mean he is a sinner. So he cannot ever be truly separated from the Father and the Spirit. The Father and the Spirit were with him at his baptism and at the Transfiguration, and they are with him now.

His words are not an expression of despair or abandonment. They are the first words of a psalm that Jesus would have prayed since childhood. Traditionally, Jews referred to familiar psalms by their first few words, in the same way that we refer to the Lord's Prayer as the Our Father.[171] Jesus' cry from the Cross is the beginning of Psalm 22:

> My God, my God, why have you forsaken me? Why are you so far from helping me, from the words of my groaning? O my God, I cry by day, but you do not answer; and by night, but find no rest.
>
> Yet you are holy, enthroned on the praises of Israel. In you our fathers trusted; they trusted, and you delivered them. To you they cried, and were saved; in you they trusted, and were not disappointed.

The psalm continues to foretell the abandonment, the violence, and the mockery Christ has endured on this fateful day: the beatings, the piercing of his hands and feet, the "dogs" (a derogatory term used in those days to refer to Gentiles) and the evildoers that surround him, even the gambling for his clothing. But it also foretells his deliverance, for God "has not hidden his face from him, but has heard" (Psalm 22:24). So Jesus, even from the Cross, is proclaiming what was manifest in the Transfiguration: that all of Scripture bears witness to him and to what is happening even now on Golgotha (see John 5:39; Acts 10:43). To the very end, Jesus is teaching.

BEHOLD YOUR MOTHER

All the evangelists tell us that some of the women followers of Jesus stand faithfully at the foot of the Cross through the ordeal.

Only John tells us that one of them is his mother and that one of his disciples stands at her side. He is the beloved disciple, the one always seeking intimacy with Jesus. This model disciple may have fled with the others in the garden, but he stands here now by the Cross.

One of Jesus' last statements is addressed to these two figures. "He said to his mother, 'Woman, behold your son!' Then he said to the disciple, 'Behold, your mother!' And from that hour the disciple took her to his own home" (John 19:26-27).

This evangelist, who has told us that he is being very selective in the material he includes in his Gospel (John 20:30; 21:25), does not include this as a random housekeeping detail. This is apparently part of the essential work Jesus was to do, since immediately after describing this final act, the evangelist writes, "After this Jesus, knowing that all was now finished …" (John 19:28).

Jesus had already shared his Father with the disciples in teaching them to call on him as *abba*. Now Jesus shares with them his mother. Discipleship is a personal relationship that makes us part of a new family. And a family must have a mother. Every disciple, represented by the beloved disciple, is entrusted to Jesus' mother and receives her in turn into his heart and his home, so completely does he identify himself with Jesus. And Mary, the mother who is blessed because she was the first to hear the word of God and keep it (Luke 11:28; 1:38), will teach her new children how to surrender and believe even when a sword is piercing one's very soul (Luke 2:35).

HIS GREATEST SERMON

Jesus did indeed have a "well-trained tongue" (Isaiah 50:4 NAB). His words have mesmerized crowds, intrigued Herod, and even made Pilate stop and think.

But for the most part, on this, the last day of his life, he is strangely silent. All the Gospels point out that he says very little during the proceedings before the Sanhedrin, Herod, and Pilate. Nor does he say much during his hours of suffering—just a few words to women mourning him as he makes his way to Golgotha and the seven brief statements from the Cross. As Isaiah had prophesied, "Like a lamb that is led to the slaughter, and like a sheep that before its shearers is silent, so he opened not his mouth" (Isaiah 53:7).

But there is another reason for his silence. Though Jesus is to preach on Good Friday, the message is not to be delivered in words. The language of this sermon will be his body and blood. Keep in mind that Good Friday, according to Jewish reckoning, actually begins at sundown on Holy Thursday. So on the beginning of his final day, Jesus gives us the verbal caption of his last and greatest sermon: "This is my body, given for you; this is my blood, which is poured out for you."

In the final sermon of his Passion, he fulfills and models all his other sermons, particularly the Sermon on the Mount. In emptying himself, he shows us poverty of spirit. In praying "Father, forgive them; for they know not what they do" (Luke 23:34), he manifests love of enemies and unlimited forgiveness, even before people are sorry for what they have done.

So the passion is at once the illustration and the summary of all the words he has ever spoken. "I love you" is not so much something you say as something you do. Diamonds may be a moving testimony to love, but laying down one's life is much more compelling.

WHY DID HE HAVE TO DIE?

Despite all the blood, pain, and torture, violence is not primarily what Good Friday is about. Love is the prevailing theme. There have been many ways of explaining why Jesus had to die and why it saves us. As C. S. Lewis points out, the important thing is to accept the fact that it does save us, and to welcome the gift of salvation that it brings. Explanations of how his death causes redemption are secondary.[172]

The salvation of the world, like all acts of God, is a mystery overflowing with profound meaning that will always exceed our feeble attempts to explain it. But some explanations are unworthy of God and need to be abandoned. God the Father is not an angry sovereign who must vent his rage on someone and impose excruciating punishment before he can calm down and forgive us. Such an explanation would not do justice to the Father's love. And this whole affair must be understood in terms of the Father's gift as well as the gift of Jesus: "For God so loved the world that he gave his only-begotten Son" (John 3:16).

Love fulfills justice and surpasses it. Justice required that humanity repair what it had broken—namely, its relationship with God. A gulf was opened in the Garden of Eden and widened over the centuries. It had to be bridged. A huge debt had been incurred—it had to be paid. It was compensation that was needed. Restitution. The mountain of pride, disobedience, and selfishness had to be obliterated. The unpaid debt of the total love that God deserved had to be paid. It was the duty of each person to love God with *all* one's heart, mind, and soul and one's neighbor *as oneself.* All human beings owed this. Yet not a single human being had ever done this.

But who could ever possibly bear the weight of righting all these wrongs, of counterbalancing the entire history of human evil, of filling in all the gaps? Only a man should. But only God could. So God became man.

Atonement had begun in the womb of Mary. The saving work of obedience, humility, and love continues throughout Jesus' whole life and ministry. But the work has to come to completion, perfection, and fulfillment. Love has to be tested to the breaking point and still endure.

Hell and sinful humanity throws everything it has at him in order to knock him off his path, to induce him to back down. Why doesn't he curse his tormentors and use his divine power to free himself? Because his love for his persecutors and his Father is unstoppable and unsurpassable. Such a relentless love has never before been seen. Obedient and selfless, his is a militant love that will not waver and knows no end. It is love to the utmost (John 13:1). "For love is strong as Death, longing is fierce as Sheol. Its arrows are arrows of fire, flames of the divine. Deep waters cannot quench love, nor rivers sweep it away" (Song of Songs 8:6-7 NAB).

His words "It is finished" mean that he has now done what he meant to do. Finally, a human being has loved God perfectly. Finally, a son of Adam has refused to be mastered by sin. He has loved God to the end. He has resisted evil to the end. The task has been accomplished.

THE STREAM OF BLOOD AND WATER

Depending on his physical condition, a crucified man could take days to die. Given that the next day is the Sabbath, the Jewish authorities want the bodies taken down before evening. The Roman practice in such cases was to use a large mallet to break the legs of the crucified to hasten death. The soldiers realize that this won't be necessary in Jesus' case since it is apparent that he is already dead.[173]

So instead, just to make sure, a soldier opens his side with a lance. Immediately blood and water pours out. In a rather striking way, the evangelist at this point solemnly attests that this information is based on eyewitness testimony and that it is reliable (John 19:31-37). He has not interjected an emphatic statement like this anywhere else in his Gospel. Apparently, he views this as extremely significant.

John himself tells us that this is a fulfillment of Scripture. The line "Not a bone of him shall be broken" (John 19:36)[174] recalls the description of the Passover lamb in the Torah, whose bones could not be broken (Exodus 12:46; Numbers 9:12). According to the chronology of John's Gospel, Jesus is crucified at the same time that the Passover lambs are being sacrificed in the Temple area. John the Baptist had acclaimed Jesus as the Lamb of God at the beginning of Jesus' ministry. That his bones are not broken, against the usual custom, underlines the fact that Christ's death is the sacrifice of the true Passover Lamb (1 Corinthians 5:7).

The Evangelist also sees in the lance wound a fulfillment of Zechariah's mysterious prophecy that "they shall look on him whom they have pierced" (John 19:37; Zechariah 12:10).

But there is even more to this final image of the crucified lamb. Both blood and water stream from the wound in his side. The blood one would expect. But what is the significance of the water?[175]

John has already referred explicitly to one particular verse in Zechariah (12:10), but he has the whole context of the final three chapters of Zechariah in mind. After the text he quotes come these prophecies about the day of the Lord: "On that day there shall be a fountain opened for the house of David and the inhabitants of Jerusalem to cleanse them from sin and uncleanness" (Zechariah 13:1) and, in the next chapter, "On that day living waters shall flow out from Jerusalem, half of them to the eastern sea and half of them to the western sea" (Zechariah 14:8).[176] At the Feast of Booths in Jerusalem, Jesus had told the disciples that for anyone who believes in him, "out of his heart shall flow rivers of living water" (John 7:38). Now we find out that the wellspring of all such streams will be his own pierced heart.

The body of Jesus is the new Temple (John 2:19); from its side flows a stream of living water, which starts as a trickle but as it flows to the sea becomes a mighty, life-giving river that provides nourishment and healing (Ezekiel 47:1-2). "Everything will live where the river goes," says Ezekiel (47:9). A tree in Eden, approached in disobedience, gave rise to death, which inundated all humanity. This tree on Calvary, approached in obedience, has now become the Tree of Life and the source of the living stream destined to cleanse and water the entire world.

CHAPTER 18

THE LORD IS RISEN!

The women set out early to carry out their somber task (Mark 16:1). It is the first day of the week, the day when God said, "Let there be light" (Genesis 1:3). But their mood is black, for the one who had called himself the light of the world lies cold in a dark tomb.

THE WOMEN AND THE EMPTY TOMB

Death's jaws have closed around him, as the whale had swallowed Jonah. But death, like the whale, is in for an unpleasant surprise. It has gone too far. The light of the world has burst out of its dark prison, leaving the cave's gaping mouth open as if in astonishment. The women find an empty tomb. The jaws of death cannot prevail against him.

The women have been traveling with Jesus and his disciples, ministering to their needs. Now a new form of service is asked of them: they are to be the first evangelists. They have courageously come to the tomb out of their intense devotion while the men cower behind locked doors (John 20:19). Their reward is that they are the first to know. Now their task is to announce the good news to the Eleven.[177] All four gospels note that Mary Magdalene takes the lead role in this mission, for which subsequent Christian tradition has given her the title "Apostle to the Apostles."

But the task is not an easy one. The news seems to the disciples too good to be true. Luke puts it this way: "These words seemed to them an idle tale, and they did not believe them" (Luke 24:11). Peter decides to run to the tomb to see for himself. It is just as the women said: empty, with the grave clothes lying there folded. That is puzzling; if grave robbers had taken the body away, they wouldn't have taken the time and trouble to unwrap it and get themselves soiled with the blood. But, despite Jesus' predictions that he would rise again, Peter is still not sure what to make of it all (Luke 24:12; John 20:3-10). Mary Magdalene is left weeping outside the tomb.

The tomb that Joseph of Arimathea made available for Jesus' body is a new tomb, where no one else had been laid. It is only about 125 feet away from Golgotha, and John notes that it is in a garden. Suddenly someone speaks to Mary and asks, "Woman, why are you weeping?" She does not recognize the Risen One immediately. Perhaps, she supposes, this man is the gardener.

By telling us that Mary Magdalene mistakes Jesus for the gardener, John reminds us that the one who speaks to her is exactly that. The old Adam's job was to tend the Garden of Eden, and he spoiled it. Even the natural world was disrupted by his sin, and human sin has been disfiguring creation ever since. The new Adam has risen in a garden and succeeded in restoring humanity to paradise, the new creation.

Mary recognizes Jesus as he tenderly calls her by name. She now has no doubt who it is that stands before her. She believes and responds with loving devotion, "Rabboni!" (John 20:11-16).

The Gospels and the letters of Paul insist on two facts: the tomb is empty, and the risen Lord is seen by many witnesses. What they see is not a vision or a specter. He is changed in appearance, but he is clearly flesh and blood.

Jesus, the new Adam, endured the wrenching apart of body and soul for our sake and rose from the dead endowed with a new, different, glorified humanity. The experiences of those who witness him are all very personal and intimate encounters. Just as in the public ministry, he does not wow and overawe them with a fearsome show of power. Rather, he reassures, encourages, and comforts them. The only overwhelming thing is his mercy. He once again illustrates his own beatitude: "Blessed are the meek, for they shall inherit the earth" (Matthew 5:5).

ENCOUNTER WITH THE ELEVEN

The evening that the empty tomb is discovered, the disciples are gathered together. Despite the locked doors, Jesus suddenly is among them. "Peace be with you," he says.

Not a word about Judas' betrayal or Peter's denial. No recriminations about their cowardly flight in the garden. Only forgiveness and mercy.

After their failure at Gethsemane, they are badly in need of mercy. He gives them mercy plus an awesome privilege: He makes them ministers of his mercy. Though they were not firm in the moment of crisis, he nonetheless reaffirms their calling. The word *apostle* means "one who is sent." And so he says to them, "As the Father has sent me, even so I send you" (John 20:21).

They have been humbled by their failures. They now have no illusions about their ability, on their own, to be faithful. Willpower was not enough. So now he gives them the power of God, the promise of the Father that he had spoken about at the Last Supper. He breathes on them and says, "Receive the Holy Spirit. If you forgive the sins of any, they are forgiven; if you retain the sins of any, they are retained" (John 20:19 23).

Jesus came to deliver us from the power of sin. He continues that work, by the power of the Spirit, through those he sends as apostles.[178]

DOUBTING THOMAS

But one of the Eleven has missed this dramatic meeting on Easter night. We are not told where Thomas went, but when he returns and hears the news, he dismisses it with the same curt skepticism with which the others had greeted the women's first report. Thomas' words are so brash that they have earned him the epithet by which he's been known ever since, for more than two thousand years—Doubting Thomas. "Unless," he says, "I see in his hands the print of the nails, and place my finger in the mark of the nails, and place my hand in his side, I will not believe" (John 20:24).

The following Sunday, they are there again, in the same room, this time with Thomas. Once again, despite the locked doors, Jesus appears among them. He apparently knows what Thomas has said, for after greeting them with the words of peace he had spoken about at the Last Supper, he offers the wounds on his hands and feet and in his side for Thomas to probe. Once again, no recrimination. No condemnation. Just mercy. Thomas' unbelief is a spiritual illness, a cause of suffering. The one who had washed Thomas' feet is willing now to expose to him his wounds in order to heal Thomas' soul. And now Thomas sees; there is no faith really required to acknowledge Jesus risen from the dead as he stands before him. But what Thomas does next is a true act of faith, which goes far beyond what he can see. Though he sees a living man, he recognizes more and exclaims, "My Lord and my God!" (John 20:28).

EMMAUS

The name Cleopas does not appear on the list of the Twelve. But evidently, he and an unnamed friend were disciples who were in Jerusalem on those fateful days. On Easter Sunday afternoon, he and his companion are walking from Jerusalem to a village seven miles away called Emmaus. They are vigorously discussing what transpired when a stranger joins them and starts walking with them. It is Jesus, but they don't recognize him, just as Mary Magdalene didn't recognize him until he called her name. He asks them what they are talking about, and they tell him their sadness and disappointment about what happened to Jesus.

Then Jesus begins to go over the Law and the Prophets, interpreting for them all the things in Scripture that pertain to himself, showing them why the Christ had to suffer and showing them that he ultimately would be glorified.

Was all this easy to find and clearly laid out in the Old Testament? Not in the least. The Scriptures are divine, having been inspired by the Holy Spirit, laden with meaning exceeding the awareness of their human authors. Reading the Scriptures with just human eyes, a person is bound to miss a lot. And obviously many devout Jews did. So on that Easter Sunday afternoon, Jesus explains all the passages that refer to his death and resurrection and opens the two disciples' minds to understanding the Scriptures. He does this by giving them a share in the same Spirit who inspired the Scriptures in the first place.

Ironically, as he does this, they still fail to recognize him. They are about to stop for the evening, and he appears to be going on. They persuade him to stay and dine with them. Unexpectedly, he takes the role of the host or the father of the family at the meal: "When he was at table with them, he took the bread and blessed and broke it, and gave it to them" (Luke 24:30). These words echo what Jesus did in the multiplication of the loaves (Luke 9:16) and at the Last Supper (Luke 22:19).

Finally, at this moment, their eyes are opened, they recognize him, and he vanishes (Luke 24:31). They then rush back in the dark to Jerusalem to tell the disciples what happened "and how he was known to them in the breaking of the bread" (Luke 24:35). This phrase "the breaking of bread" is how Luke will refer to the Eucharist in his second book, the Acts of the Apostles.[179]

We don't know the exact form of the Eucharistic service in the first century. But the earliest witnesses we have from the second and third centuries[180] show that what occurred in the Emmaus story was the general outline of the Eucharist celebrated at that time— the service of the Word of God, with Old Testament Scriptures that point to Jesus, and the service of the Eucharist, where Jesus' words and actions at the Last Supper were repeated over bread and wine. All of the liturgies that come down to us from the early Church have this same format.[181]

Though their hearts were burning within them as Jesus explained the Scriptures, and though they physically saw him, they did not finally recognize him until the moment of the breaking of the bread. The Eucharist becomes, after the Last Supper, a privileged and uniquely powerful way for the disciples to encounter the risen Lord and be infused with his life. Discipleship is about walking on the road, on the way, with Jesus, being drawn ever further and deeper in understanding of the Scriptures. But it is also about stopping and resting with him, being refreshed and empowered in the breaking of the bread. The Eucharist is a nourishing and revelatory reality, the ultimate encounter with the risen Lord.

The Eucharist, then, is not only a memorial of his saving death. It is also a memorial of his resurrection. In every Eucharist, we stand both at the foot of the Cross and outside the empty tomb. It is the risen Body and Blood of the Lord that we receive for our healing and renewal—somehow it imparts to us already, even in this mortal life, some share in his risen life. A generation or two after the Gospels are written, St. Ignatius, bishop of Antioch, will call the Eucharist "the medicine of immortality."[182]

DO YOU LOVE ME?

There is another story about a special meal served by the risen Lord. This time it is breakfast, prepared by Jesus after a miraculous catch of fish on the shore of the Sea of Galilee. The traditional site of this meal is also the traditional site of the multiplication of the loaves and fish at Tabgha.

There are seven disciples in the fishing boat about a hundred yards offshore. They have caught nothing during the night. Now someone speaks to them from the shore and tells them to lower their nets on the other side of the boat. Suddenly, they are struggling with an astonishing catch. Realizing that it is the risen Lord who has spoken to them, the impetuous Peter dives into the water and swims to him. Over their fish breakfast, the Lord asks him three times, "Do you love me?" (John 21:15-17). The charcoal fire brings back the memory of the charcoal fire in the courtyard of the high priest (John 18:18 and 21:9). Peter's triple affirmation of love this morning corresponds to his triple denial that night.

That night in the courtyard, Peter, "the rock," had crumbled. Didn't his denial prove Simon unworthy of the new name Jesus had given him? But Jesus does not reprimand or demote him. As with all the disciples in the room in Jerusalem, he reaffirms Peter and even recasts his role, from fisherman to shepherd. Henceforth, Peter is to profess his love for Jesus by caring for the Lord's sheep. But first this apostle and chief shepherd needs to focus on the task of discipleship. The very last words the risen Lord speaks to Peter are the same as the first words he spoke to him, the ones with which he called him: "Follow me!" (John 21:1-23).

THE MEANING OF EASTER

The story of the empty tomb and the vignettes of Jesus' appearances are important to ponder. But it is equally important to probe the meaning of the Resurrection and its relation to Jesus' death. For all four Evangelists and for Paul as well, it is impossible to understand the Crucifixion without the Resurrection. They are part of one exodus (Luke 9:31), one lifting up and glorification of Jesus, one saving paschal mystery.[183] To understand it, we need to remember the reality of evil and the frightening tangle of problems caused by human sin and recall that the divine plan was to deal with them comprehensively in one saving action.

The serpent's deception in Eden was deadly, for it worked a venomous corruption deep in the heart of humanity. Physical death is not its worst consequence. More fearsome—for our first parents and for all of us—is spiritual death, our separation from God.

Only the perfect love of Jesus could overcome the separation: unstinting, unlimited love to the end. The extravagant sacrifice of his life, poured out for us on the Cross, was the Son's answer to the problem of sin.

The Father's equally extravagant answer to the problem of death came three days later, when Jesus rose from the dead.

Physical death is not beautiful or natural. It is agonizing. Our bodies are not something we put on and take off. They are not like cars that our souls drive around. For us as human beings, the body is intimately intertwined with the immortal soul. Death wrenches them apart, separating what God has joined. We are right to shudder before death, just as Jesus did in Gethsemane.

Jesus does not "come back" from death. He is not resuscitated. His earthly life, his normal mortal life, is not restored like that of Lazarus, who would eventually die again.

Jesus passes through death and comes out on the other side. He confronts death head on, conquers it, and rises, glorified!

The Roman liturgy highlights the drama in the ancient Easter Sequence: "Death and life dueled in a marvelous conflict. The dead Ruler of Life reigns alive!"[184] And the Byzantine liturgy proclaims, "Christ is risen from the dead, trampling down death by death, and on those in the tombs bestowing life!" His resurrection is his victory over our primordial enemies: Satan, sin, and death.

THE NEW HUMANITY

It is almost impossible for us to imagine what the new, glorified body of Jesus is like. Paul calls it a "spiritual body" (1 Corinthians 15:44), but that doesn't really help us. It resembles Jesus' earthly body but not entirely, for Mary and the disciples walking to Emmaus recognize him but not right away. His wounds are evident, and Thomas touches them, so we also know that his body has substance. He cooks and eats food, like the fish breakfast he shares with the disciples by the Sea of Galilee. Yet he can also pass through locked doors.

We simply don't know. So many witnesses saw and spoke to the risen Lord, but the deep mystery of his resurrection remains. In it, we come face-to-face with what is holy. We can only bow before it, giving thanks for the risen life, the new humanity, that he won for us on that first Easter day.

CHAPTER 19

THE ASCENSION AND THE GREAT COMMISSION

The public ministry of Jesus, full of dramatic works of power, was only the prelude to what happened on those three fateful days—during what is often called, in the Western Christian tradition, the Triduum.[185] Jesus' death cannot be viewed apart from his resurrection. The two events can be distinguished, but both are part of the one saving action that Luke calls Jesus' exodus (Luke 9:31).

But Jesus' victory over sin through the Cross and his triumph over death in the Resurrection are still not the whole story. There is a final movement in the symphony of salvation: Jesus' return to the Father when he enters, in his human nature, into the glory the Son had with the Father "before the foundation of the world" (John 17:24). It is the event commonly known in Christian tradition as the Ascension.

GLORY AND KINGSHIP

Just prior to the Last Supper, Jesus says, "The hour has come for the Son of man to be glorified" (John 12:23). Yet immediately thereafter, he speaks of his death. A few verses later, he says, "And I, when I am lifted up from the earth, will draw all men to myself"

(John 12:32). This phrase, "lifted up," says the Evangelist, means "to show by what death he was to die" (John 12:33).

For us, this is paradoxical. Glory and exaltation don't, in our minds, go together with suffering and death. But the entire gospel story is one giant paradox—the call to find oneself by losing oneself, the insistence that life comes only through death, the belief that glory is achieved through humiliation.

John's Gospel highlights this paradoxical quality of the kingdom of God—Jesus' glorification actually begins during the Last Supper, when he washes the disciples' feet. It continues through the entire Passion, as soldiers mock him by plaiting thorns and crowning him as king, as Pilate shows him to the crowds saying "Here is the man!" and once again as a placard[186] is crafted that proclaims "Jesus of Nazareth, the King of the Jews" (John 19:19). John is the only one to tell us that Pilate's sign is an international proclamation, since it is written not only in Hebrew but in Latin and Greek. In a real but ironic way, this placard is an *evangelion*, an announcement of glad tidings that a new King is beginning his reign.

Then Jesus is literally lifted up and suspended in the air, as if to span the chasm between heaven and earth. His arms are spread wide, as if in a gesture of beckoning to himself, from east to west, north to south, the scattered children of God (John 11:52).

All this is intended by the Jewish and Roman authorities as a profound humiliation; ironically, it serves God's purposes by initiating the King's exaltation. One of the first witnesses to recognize the glory amid the degradation is a pagan, the centurion at the foot of the Cross. He is moved, after Jesus breathes his last, to exclaim, "Truly this man was the Son of God!" (Mark 15:39).

This upward movement to glory continues on Easter day. Jesus' body is transformed and "glorified at the moment of his Resurrection" (CCC 659). His glory is veiled lest it overwhelm those chosen witnesses to whom he appears over the following days. Yet each time he does appear, it is from the glory of the

Father's right hand that he comes and to which he returns. He has been exalted (Acts 2:33); he has received full kingship, dominion, and authority (Matthew 28:18). The feast of the Ascension, in a profound sense, is the original feast of Christ the King. The gentle Lamb of God has become the regal Lion of Judah (Revelation 5:5).

Humanity, ennobled by the Incarnation, is now raised above the heavens, sharing in the very glory of God. And now, for the first time in the Gospels, Jesus' glorified humanity is worshipped by his followers (Luke 24:52; Matthew 28:17). Worship, according to the very first of the Ten Commandments, is due to God alone. Jesus' divinity, now shining steadily through his glorified humanity as it did briefly in the Transfiguration, calls for only one response—adoration. The title reserved for God in the Old Testament, Lord, is now applied to Jesus. He is the *pantocrator*, the ruler of everything in both heaven and earth. Every knee shall bow and "every tongue confess that Jesus Christ is Lord, to the glory of God the Father" (Philippians 2:10–11).

MOUNTAIN AND MANDATE

Both Matthew and John tell us that some appearances of the risen, exalted Lord take place in Galilee. Matthew's Gospel concludes with an encounter between Jesus and the Eleven high on a Galilean mountaintop (Matthew 28:16-20). Though no mountain is named, a possible location is Mount Arbel, which towers over what was once the town of Magdala. To the north and west, Arbel provides a spectacular view of all Galilee; to the east lies a majestic vista of the Sea of Galilee and what was, in Jesus' time, the mostly Gentile totrarchy of Philip; to the south one can see the once-pagan Decapolis. The mountain provides a dramatic and fitting setting for the words that Jesus speaks to his disciples on the occasion of this apostolic summit conference.

During the public ministry, Jesus had a great sense of urgency to preach the kingdom of God in as many Jewish towns as possible, for he says, "I was sent for this purpose" (Luke 4:43). When the pagan Syrophoenician (Canaanite) woman came seeking healing for her daughter, his initial response was, "I was sent only to the lost sheep of the house of Israel" (Matthew 15:24). Though he trained and sent out the Twelve to extend his mission, he gave them strict instructions to "go nowhere among the Gentiles, and enter no town of the Samaritans, but go rather to the lost sheep of the house of Israel" (Matthew 10:5-6).

Now that Jesus has been lifted up, it is time to draw all men to himself and gather the children of God who have been scattered abroad. Now that he has received full authority, he announces the full and final mission, which knows no limits. He proclaims the fulfillment of the promise made to Abraham—that in his descendants all the nations of the world would now be blessed (Genesis 12:3; 22:18) and that Abraham would finally become "the father of a multitude of nations" (Genesis 17:5). Overlooking the whole world, Jesus says, "Go therefore and make disciples of *all* nations" (Matthew 28:19, emphasis added).

John's Gospel emphasizes that Jesus' "lifting up" begins a universal, world-wide mission to Gentiles as well as Jews. Mark too records this new, universal missionary mandate: "Go into *all* the world and preach the gospel to the *whole* creation" (Mark 16:15, emphasis added). Luke, in his Gospel, notes that Jesus sends the disciples to "*all* nations" (24:47, emphasis added); in Acts, he records Jesus as telling them that they are to be his witnesses "in Jerusalem and in all Judea and Samaria and *to the end of the earth*" (Acts 1:8, emphasis added).

The mandate is not simply to announce the gospel of Christ's kingship but to make disciples of those who accept the good news, to teach them how to come under the discipline of this master whose "yoke is easy" (Matthew 11:30) and to learn to walk in his ways.

Those who accept the gospel are to be baptized "in the name of the Father and of the Son and of the Holy Spirit" (Matthew 28:19). Often this is thought to be no more than a formula. It is indeed the formula of Christian baptism and has remained so for two thousand years. But it is no mere ceremonial formula. First, three distinct Persons are noted here, whose unity is so profound that we are to baptize not in their *names* but in the *one name* of the Father, the Son, and the Holy Spirit. This is the Trinity of distinct Persons that was manifested in the baptism of Jesus and the Transfiguration.

We have seen that following Jesus as a disciple during his public ministry involved more than adherence to his teaching; before everything else, it meant a personal allegiance to Jesus himself, an attachment to his very person. A disciple must "believe in" Jesus, which is actually expressed by John and Paul through the unusual Greek construction "believing *into*" Jesus.[187] The Trinitarian Baptism mandated in Matthew 28:19 uses the same unusual construction of being baptized "into" the name of the Father, and the Son, and the Holy Spirit. This means to be plunged into the vital interpersonal, divine life of God the Father, Son, and Holy Spirit. Baptism, immersion in water, is a sign of being immersed in the death and resurrection of Jesus and, through that experience, entering into a living relationship not only with Jesus but also with his Father and his Spirit.

So Jesus' disciples are to plunge others into this profoundly relational experience of becoming a disciple of Jesus, a son or daughter of the Father, and a temple of the Holy Spirit (1 Corinthians 6:19). The mandate involves teaching the new disciples to observe *all* that Jesus has commanded (Matthew 28:20), which is nothing other than the will of God. Those who do the will of God are Jesus' family (Matthew 12:50). Those who call God Father discover one another as brothers and sisters, and they recognize Jesus' mother as their mother as well. The missionary mandate, then, involves a great deal of doctrine, which is just another word for "teaching." But it can never be reduced to indoctrination—it is a mission based on a relationship. Both baptizing others and teaching all that Jesus taught involve welcoming people into a new family relationship with Father, Spirit, Son, and all the sons and daughters of God.

The mountain where this mandate, the Great Commission, is given recalls another mountain. Once before, Jesus was taken up a high mountain from whose summit he could see the kingdoms of the world. The price for the world sovereignty he was offered there would have been adoration of Satan. Jesus, however, resisted the temptation to idolatry, the cheap path to cosmic dominion (Matthew 4:8-11). Instead, he paid the costly price of the Cross, so that now the whole world is his to give to his followers as their missionary field, and it is to him that they bow in homage and devotion.

PRESENCE, POWER, AND PROMISE

Even moments before the Ascension, the disciples still show themselves to be stuck in their preconceived notions of Jesus' kingship. Forty days after Easter, Jesus returns to Jerusalem and leads his disciples to the summit of the Mount of Olives. During this final encounter with the risen Lord, the Eleven ask him, "Lord, will you at this time restore the kingdom to Israel?" (Acts 1:6). Their vision is so small. They want him to sit on David's throne and restore his earthly kingdom in Palestine even as he takes his seat on God's throne to rule all of heaven and earth!

But he had predicted their incomprehension at the Last Supper: "I have yet many things to say to you, but you cannot bear them now. When the Spirit of truth comes, he will guide you into all the truth" (John 16:12-13).

He had breathed a measure of the Spirit on them already when he gave them the power to forgive sins (John 20:22-23). But that breath was like a gentle breeze; the gale-force wind of the Spirit is yet to come. This full measure of the holy wind will be given not just to the Eleven but to all the disciples and through them offered to the whole world. It will do more than help them understand the true plan of the kingdom; this coming of the Spirit *is* the kingdom.

It was by the power of the Holy Spirit that the kingdom had broken into people's lives through Jesus' miracles and teaching.

Now this Spirit will come upon the disciples as it came upon Jesus in his own baptism. From his seat at God's right hand, Jesus will now baptize them, which means totally immersing them, in the Holy Spirit, as John the Baptist had predicted (John 1:33). The Holy Spirit will fill them from within, enlightening their minds and transforming their hearts. This heavenly power, not some earthly kingdom, is the true promise of the Father, the ultimate hope of Israel and all humanity. To enter into life in the Spirit, to enter the new realm of God's kingdom, will be to enter the land promised to Abraham and his descendants, of which the land of Canaan was just a sign and a foreshadowing.

The Spirit is so intimately associated with Jesus that Jesus refers to it as "his" Spirit, much as he refers to the Father as "his" Father. Yet oddly the coming of the Spirit can only happen through his departure. In another paradox, Jesus' absence will make possible a new mode of his presence. His going precedes a new coming. Pentecost will be a coming of the Spirit that will never cease. And each Eucharist will be a coming that will continue until that final advent which is anticipated every time the congregation says, "Blessed is he who comes in the name of the Lord. Hosanna in the highest!"

The appearances of the risen Lord have to come to an end. They have lasted, according to the book of Acts, for forty days.[188] During this time, the risen Lord has reaffirmed the disciples, forgiven them, instructed them, and commissioned them. As he leaves them and makes the irreversible and permanent transition to his eternal dwelling at the right hand of the Father,[189] he prepares to empower them. That empowerment will inaugurate the Church. Pentecost will be the Church's birthday.

Jesus tells them to return to the city and wait until they are clothed with power from on high. For the Church is not to be a matter of mere ideas and noble sentiments but of power to transform lives and make all things new. Though his ascension is in some sense a departure, he is not an absentee landlord or a clockmaker God. He who from the beginning of the gospel story has been known as

Immanuel, God-with-us, issues this promise: "Behold, I am with you always, to the close of the age" (Matthew 28:20).[190]

FINAL COMING

The clouds that accompany his final departure remind us of the cloud of the Transfiguration, which is a sign of both presence and concealment. In biblical history, the cloud that led the people by day through the desert had the same double meaning, as did the cloud of glory in the Temple. But those clouds also make us think of the glorious Son of Man in Daniel 7:13 who, accompanied by the clouds of heaven, is presented before the Ancient of Days. This Jesus, this Son of Man to whom all dominion has been given, will return in the same way. "Behold, he is coming with the clouds" (Revelation 1:7).[191]

His final coming will be a time of judgment. Between now and then people will deliberate and make fateful choices that determine their destiny. God respects the freedom he gave us enough to insist that we abide by the decisions we make. The direction in which a person is headed when the Lord returns will be the direction in which he or she is headed for all eternity.

For those who love him, his coming will mean that the messianic blessing tasted in this life as firstfruits will be given in full measure. He came that we might have life and have it more abundantly (John 10:10). His own victory over even bodily death will reach out and transform bodily all those who love him.

When will this take place? The Lord tells the disciples, "It is not for you to know times or seasons" (Acts 1:7). Clearly these words rule out speculation about when and where he will return as well as preoccupation with interpreting end-times prophecies. Such concerns are a distraction and a waste of precious time. We are told instead to be always prepared, awake, and alert (Matthew 25:1-13).

WITNESS AND MESSAGE

We are not to wait passively for Jesus' coming, for there is work to be done. The angels remind the disciples of this on the Mount of Olives when they ask his followers why they just stand there, staring into space (Acts 1:11).

Jesus keeps nothing for himself. All he has he shares with us: his Father, his mother, his Spirit, his Body and Blood, his righteousness, and even his risen life. And we can begin to share in this risen life now, experiencing its regenerating power in our souls and even in our bodies.

When we meet him, our lives immediately begin to change— sometimes in obvious ways, sometimes imperceptibly at first. Our hearts, frozen by fear and selfishness, begin to thaw. Our spirits discover a new life, his life, within.

For now, our responsibility is clear. We must allow his light to penetrate the dark, dead corners of our hearts and souls. And with Mary and Joseph, with the women and the disciples and all those who have ever known him, we must invite the world to join him.

The command "Go therefore and make disciples of all nations" was given not just to the apostles. The mission is vast, and all of us are called to take part. Each of us, as disciples, must be ready to tell others what Jesus has done for us, what he means to us, and why he is the answer to our problems and the world's problems (1 Peter 3:15). Before his final departure, he said, "You shall be my witnesses" (Acts 1:8). This is our commission. It is what we are meant to do and to be.

Witnesses do not need to be perfect. They do not need to be schooled in theology. They simply need to tell honestly what they have experienced. Remember the Samaritan woman at the well? She encountered him. He saw into her soul and offered her a new kind of life, which he called living water. She immediately ran to her neighbors to invite them to meet the one who had told her everything she had ever done. She did not wait until she had years of moral formation and theological education. She just shared what she experienced.

Jesus *is* the Way, the Truth, and the Life (John 14:6). Personalize this message. Think about how Jesus has opened a *way* for you, perhaps a way out of loneliness, perhaps a way out of some kind of bondage. To speak of Jesus as *the truth* could be to share how he has set your life on a firm foundation, provided meaning and stability, how he has helped you to see yourself, others, and all of life in a new light. Proclaiming him as *the life* could be as simple as letting someone know how his love has made you come alive in ways you never could have imagined. However, before sharing anything, first ask questions and listen, understanding a person's story, needs, and desires. This is how Jesus himself approached his encounter with the Samaritan woman. In the story of the encounter at Jacob's well in John 4, both Jesus and the Samaritan woman model for us what it means to share the Good News.

Listening and then sharing our own experience with sincerity and enthusiasm—this is something we all can and must do with the same urgency that drove Jesus to press on to yet another town, reach out to yet another person. People are dying of hunger and thirsting for love. Those who are lonely need to know that they are infinitely loved. Those who are imprisoned and in bondage need to be visited and introduced to the liberating power of the Spirit. The Jubilee of the risen Lord is still in effect, but we don't know how much longer it will endure. There is no time to waste.

He has shared everything with us. As we wait for his final and glorious coming, we dare not keep it all to ourselves. "Go home to your friends, and tell them how much the Lord has done for you" (Mark 5:19)!

ACKNOWLEDGMENTS

When it comes to writing a book, there is a lot of preparation to be done—some proximate, some remote. This book on Jesus flows from a lifetime of following him as well as studying about him. My mother, Patricia Carey D'Ambrosio, taught me my first prayers. My uncle, John Carey, was the first one to tell me to read the Gospels. My parish priest, Fr. Paul Charland, was the first one to put a Bible in my hands. Sr. Fran Conway helped me put Jesus at the center of my life. Fr. John Randall introduced me to the joy and power of the Holy Spirit. How can I ever repay these pivotal players in my life in Christ?

Yet once I had my decisive encounter with Jesus, someone had to do the hard work of helping the teenage rock musician that I was to become a disciplined disciple. Fr. Jim Henderson and Fr. Gerry Dye, along with Don and Pat Turbitt, put hours into that endeavor. Fr. Giles Dimock was my first theology professor and has had a lasting impact. Fr. Avery (later Cardinal) Dulles was my last professor and proved to be an amazing doctoral mentor. To these and all who invested so much in me, I am profoundly grateful. This book would have been impossible without you.

The proximate preparation for this work took the better part of a very intense and challenging year. Many people sacrificed to cover for me while I was holed up in my study, reading and writing away. Special thanks are due to my wife, Susan, who picked up so many of the family responsibilities in my absence and was also my first proofreader. The staff, board, benefactors, and volunteers of the Crossroads Initiative also covered for me in so many ways! Thanks are in order especially to Maribel Ruiz, Emy Cervantes, Mindy Elgahill, Rowena Ignacio, and Cyni Lucky. I am grateful as well to my five children and their spouses, who were patient with me and kept telling me, "Dad, you got this!"

Of course, the team at Ascension was fabulous to work with—special shout-out to Matt Pinto, Jeff Cavins, Edward Sri, John Harden, Jen Eckenrode, Rebecca Robinson, and Rosemary Strohm. And I can't forget the intercessory prayer team whose constant support called down protection and blessings on the project, especially my ninety-year-old mother and my dear spiritual mothers of Regina Laudis Abbey, most notably Mothers Dolores Hart, Margaret Georgina Patton, Noella Marcellino, and Maria Evangelista Fernandez, all OSB.

Following Jesus has been a journey. This book has been the latest chapter in this journey. But a journey is so much more delightful when you have such wonderful traveling companions as these.

FOR FURTHER
READING

Hans Urs von Balthasar, *The Threefold Garland*, trans.
Erasmo Leiva-Merikakis (San Francisco: Ignatius, 1982).
A moving meditation on the mysteries of Jesus' life, death,
and resurrection as pondered in the Rosary.

Hans Urs von Balthasar, *Heart of the World*, trans. Erasmo S.
Leiva (San Francisco: Ignatius, 1979). Exploration of the love
of Jesus according to devotion to his Sacred Heart.

Romano Guardini, *The Lord*, trans. Elinor Castendyk Briefs
(Chicago: Regnery, 1954). The most influential Catholic book
on Jesus in Europe in the twentieth century.

Peter Kreeft, *Jesus Shock* (Singer Island, FL: Beacon, 2008).
A short work that highlights the startling newness of Jesus in
his day and ours.

Joseph Ratzinger (Pope Benedict XVI), *Jesus of Nazareth*, part 1,
From the Baptism in the Jordan to the Transfiguration, trans.
Adrian J. Walker (New York: Doubleday, 2007). The first of his
three books on Jesus' life.

Joseph Ratzinger (Pope Benedict XVI), *Jesus of Nazareth*, part 2,
Holy Week, Vatican translation (San Francisco: Ignatius, 2011). An
attempt to bridge the gap between scholarship and the life of faith.

Joseph Ratzinger (Pope Benedict XVI), *Jesus of Nazareth: The Infancy Narratives*, trans. Philip J. Whitmore (New York: Image, 2012). The conclusion of his series on Jesus.

Frank Sheed, *To Know Christ Jesus* (1962; reprint, San Francisco: Ignatius, 1992). A life of Christ by a prominent lay Catholic apologist.

Fulton J. Sheen, *Life of Christ* (New York: Doubleday, 1958). The most influential Catholic book on Jesus in America in the twentieth century.

Edward Sri, *No Greater Love: A Biblical Walk Through Christ's Passion* (West Chester, PA: Ascension, 2019). An in-depth study of the last day of Jesus' life, from the agony in the garden to his death on the Cross.

N. T. Wright, *Simply Jesus: Who He Was, What He Did, and Why He Matters* (New York: HarperCollins, 2011). An excellent popular work by the most widely respected Anglican scholar today.

NOTES

1   This passage is known as the *Testimonium Flavianum* (Josephus, *Jewish Antiquities* 18.3.3.63–64), reconstructed and translated by John P. Meier, *A Marginal Jew: Rethinking the Historical Jesus*, vol. 1, *The Roots of the Problem and the Person* (New York: Doubleday, 1991), 59–61.

2   Tacitus, *Annals* 15.44, trans. A. J. Church and W. J. Brodribb (1876). Tacitus wrote this about AD 115.

3   In most cases, the distance between the time the authors wrote and the date of the earliest surviving copy of their work is considerable. In the case of ancient historians like Herodotus and Thucydides, the gulf is vast. They both wrote around 450 BC, but the earliest copy we have of the work of either historian dates to AD 900. That's a gap of more than a thousand years! So what about the Gospels? The scholarly consensus is that all four Gospels were composed between AD 60 and 95. We have surviving fragments of some of them from as early as AD 125, full texts of some letters and Gospels from just before AD 200, and full compilations of the entire New Testament from about AD 325. The gaps between the dates of composition and the earliest surviving copies are negligible in comparison with other ancient works. And then there are the sheer numbers of Greek manuscripts of the New Testament that survive from ancient times—about 5,600. The ancient document with the next highest number of surviving manuscripts is Homer's *Iliad*, which has over six hundred. How many manuscripts of other ancient authors survive? For both Thucydides and Herodotus, the answer is eight!

4   Still, there was a gap of several decades between the time of Jesus' public ministry and the writing of the Gospels. How does that compare to the distance between the lives of famous ancient figures and the accounts of their lives which have come down to us? Let's take Alexander the Great for example. He died in 323 BC. The earliest surviving biography of him was written two hundred

years after his death! The better known and more widely read accounts of his life, by Arrian and Plutarch, were written over four hundred years after his death. Nonetheless, they are still regarded by historians as valuable historical sources.

5   For an extensive discussion of these principles, see "Criteria" (chapter 6) in Meier, *Marginal Jew*, vol. 1, 167–184.

6   I am here summarizing and paraphrasing the Second Vatican Council's Dogmatic Constitution on Divine Revelation, *Dei Verbum*, chapter 3 on Sacred Scripture, paragraphs 11–13. See also the *Catechism of the Catholic Church* (CCC), paragraphs 105–108.

7   On this dating for the gospel of Thomas, see Meier, *Marginal Jew*, vol. 1, 135–138, especially the footnotes. See also N. T. Wright, *The New Testament and the People of God*, vol. 1, *Christian Origins and the Question of God* (Minneapolis: Fortress, 1992), 443.

8   "The Gospel of Thomas," 114, trans. Thomas O. Lambdin, *Early Christian Writings*, earlychristianwritings.com/.

9   "The Infancy Gospel of Thomas," trans. M. R. James, in *The Apocryphal New Testament* (Oxford: Clarendon, 1924), available at gnosis.org/.

10   Notable among them were the followers of Marcion, who was excommunicated in Rome in AD 144.

11   Irenaeus, "Against Heresies," III.1.1 on authorship of the Gospels and III.11.8 on why we have four. This was originally written around AD 185. For a good modern translation of these passages, see Cyril Richardson, ed., *Early Christian Fathers* (New York: Macmillan, 1970).

12   Herodotus, who died around 425 BC, referred to the region as Palestine, as did Aristotle a hundred years later in his book on meteorology.

13   Caesar was originally the family name of Julius and his adopted son, Octavian (or Augustus). After Octavian, it continued to be applied as a title of the Roman emperors, even those who were not related to Julius or Octavian by blood.

14   The proclamation of the emperor's birthday as the basis of a new calendar was issued as an *evangelion*. And there is an *evangelion* inscribed in stone in a town in what is now Turkey that dates back to 9 BC, just a few years before the birth of Jesus. It says, "Since Providence, which has ordered all things and is deeply interested in our life, has set in most perfect order by giving us Augustus, whom she filled with virtue that he might benefit humankind, sending him as a savior, both for us and for our descendants, that

he might end war and arrange all things, and since he, Caesar, by his appearance (excelled even our anticipations), surpassing all previous benefactors, and not even leaving to posterity any hope of surpassing what he has done, and since the birthday of the god Augustus was the beginning of the good tidings [*evangelion*, or gospel] for the world that came by reason of him."

15 Two famous triumphal arches that can be seen in Rome, near the Colosseum, are the Arch of Constantine and the Arch of Titus, conqueror of Jerusalem in AD 70.

16 *Tabernaculum* is the Latin word for *tent*.

17 Also called the Feast of Booths.

18 Herod's father, Antipater, was of an Idumaean (Edomite) family that was forced to convert to Judaism around the year 110 BC. Herod's mother was a Gentile, an Arabian princess.

19 The letter of Paul to the Colossians speaks in much the same way about Christ: "He is the image of the invisible God, the first-born of all creation; for in him all things were created, in heaven and on earth … all things were created through him and for him. He is before all things, and in him all things hold together" (Colossians 1:15-17).

20 For more on Mary's role in the gospel story, see *Mary: A Biblical Walk with the Blessed Mother* by Edward Sri (West Chester, PA: Ascension, 2014).

21 Shepherds are on a list of proscribed professions, along with tax collectors, which appears in the Mishnah (ca. AD 200), a compilation of oral tradition preserved by the rabbis and sages that most probably reflects culture at the time of Jesus. Living in the open field, shepherds would have a hard time keeping purity laws. It was also thought that it was inevitable that they would graze their flocks in fields belonging to someone else, thereby stealing their forage.

22 Compare with Psalm 72:10-15.

23 Elias J. Bickerman, "The Warning Inscriptions of Herod's Temple," *The Jewish Quarterly Review* 37, no. 4 (1947): 307–405.

24 Mileage here is approximate, based on most likely route traveled. To travel to Bethlehem from Nazareth, Galilean Jews of the first century most often traveled to the Jordan Valley near what is now Beth-Shean and crossed over to Perea on the east bank of the Jordan to avoid passing through Samaritan territory. They would cross back to the western bank near Jericho, then to Bethlehem via Jerusalem. This total journey was about 113 miles.

25   In Jesus' baptism, he was not literally anointed with chrism. But
     his baptism was interpreted as a spiritual anointing both by Jesus
     himself (Luke 4:18) and by Peter (Acts 10:38). In a similar way, Jesus
     was spiritually consecrated at his presentation. Taking the Nazirite
     vow would have meant never drinking wine or cutting his hair.

26   The genealogies of Jesus in Matthew and Luke mention
     Joseph's father; a second-century apocryphal document called
     the Protoevangelium of James tells us that Mary's parents
     were named Joachim and Anne and that their house, at least
     during Mary's childhood, was in Jerusalem. The document is
     not considered highly reliable historically, but the Orthodox
     and Catholic churches have always honored Jesus' maternal
     grandparents as St. Joachim and St. Anne.

27   This James is not to be confused with either of the two numbered
     among the Twelve: James the son of Zebedee and James the son
     of Alphaeus. James "the brother of the Lord" later became the
     head of the Jerusalem Church once Peter had left for Antioch
     and ultimately Rome.

28   The Feast of Booths is also called Tabernacles, from the Latin
     word for tents or booths.

29   The Psalms of Ascents, Psalms 120–134, appeared to have been
     sung by pilgrims traveling to Jerusalem and ascending the
     southern steps of the Temple leading to the Huldah gates. Other
     psalms also were sung on the way to the Temple, such as Psalm
     84, and others were sung during the feasts, especially the Hallel,
     Psalms 113–118.

30   See Mishnah Sukkah 5:1-4. According to the estimates of Joachim
     Jeremias in *Jerusalem in the Time of Jesus: An Investigation into
     Economic and Social Conditions During the New Testament Period*,
     trans. F. H. and C. H. Cave (Philadelphia: Fortress, 1969), 84, there
     would be approximately 100,000–150,00 people, residents and
     pilgrims combined, in Jerusalem for the great pilgrimage feasts.
     Many if not most of these would likely have attended the great
     nighttime festivities in the Temple Courts on the first night of the
     Feast of Booths or Tabernacles. Herod expanded the courts of his
     reconstructed Temple to accommodate such vast crowds. The
     Mishnah does not tell us how many of these would have participated
     in the torch dance, but the number must have been considerable.

31   The Gospels do not tell us of the tribal affiliation of Mary;
     whatever it might have been, it would not determine her son's
     status according to Judaism of the time of Jesus. That would be
     determined by the tribe of the child's legal father.

32 Joseph died between the time Jesus was thirteen and thirty years old. The critical time for a father to teach his son to be an Israelite man was in the son's twelfth year, since at his thirteenth birthday, the son was legally a man and bound to know and observe the entire Law. The twelfth year was the most intense time of spiritual mentoring between father and son, and we know Joseph was alive at this time and undertook this traditional task.

33 Women were obligated to observe only the negative prescriptions of the law, not the positive ones like attending the three great pilgrimage feasts in Jerusalem.

34 Most of this is still the case for Orthodox Jews today. Only a boy is a *bar mitzvah* (son of the commandments); the term refers not to the ceremony but to the boy, who is being celebrated as an adult male Israelite who assumes all the duties of the law—to keep all 613 commandments of the written Torah plus the oral traditions of the elders. At the ceremony he publicly reads a passage from the Torah in Hebrew since this will be his privilege from this time forward. In the past century, Reformed and Conservative Jews have developed a similar ritual for girls, but Orthodox Jews maintain the ancient tradition.

35 Palestine was trilingual at this time. Aramaic had been the everyday language of most of the Jewish community ever since the Babylonian exile (sixth century BC). Hebrew was the formal language of liturgical prayer but was not used in daily conversation by many except, perhaps, at Qumran. Greek had been the international language of learning and commerce for three hundred years and so was widely known, at least well enough for buying and selling in the marketplace. Latin, however, was virtually never used by anyone other than Roman soldiers and officials, many of whom knew Greek better than Latin.

36 Lucien Deiss, ed., *Springtime of the Liturgy: Liturgical Texts of the First Four Centuries*, trans. Matthew J. O'Connell (Collegeville, MN: Liturgical Press, 1979), 15, books.google.com/.

37 For the text of the beautiful *Birkat Yotser* as it might have been prayed by Jesus and Joseph, see the boxed text "Jewish Prayers" in Session Two of *Jesus: The Way, the Truth, and the Life* Workbook (West Chester, PA: Ascension, 2020).

38 This prayer, also known as the *Amidah*, is still prayed at these three hours by Orthodox Jews today. Near the end of the first centuries, the rabbis determined that this prayer was obligatory for Jews and in some way substituted for the sacrificial worship that had ceased with the destruction of the Temple. For more, see Joachim Jeremias, *The Prayers of Jesus* (Philadelphia: Fortress, 1978).

39   For the text of the *Tefillah* as it was likely prayed in the time
     of Jesus, see the boxed text "Jewish Prayers" in Sesson Two of
     Jesus: The Way, the Truth, and the Life Workbook.

40   Lucien Deiss, *The Mass*, trans. Lucien Deiss and Michael S. Driscoll
     (Collegeville, MN: Liturgical Press, 1992), 52–53, books.google.com/.

41   The most intense year of spiritual formation for a boy would
     have been the year before his thirteenth birthday when the boy
     would become responsible for carrying out all the prescriptions
     of the law as a *bar mitzvah*, a "son of the commandments." Luke
     is careful to note that the episode of Jesus' finding in the Temple
     occurred during this crucial year of his life.

42   *Gaudium et Spes* (December 7, 1965), 22, vatican.va/.

43   Though the majority of scholars identify the Yahad as belonging
     to a wider Jewish sect that Josephus calls the Essenes, the writings
     of this community never identify them this way, and a minority of
     scholars think they are distinct from the Essenes. So we will call
     this Qumran community what they called themselves, Yahad.

44   This text was part of their mission statement in their *Manual of
     Discipline* or *Rule of the Community* 1QS 8:12–16. See Joseph
     A. Fitzmyer, *Responses to 101 Questions on the Dead Sea Scrolls*
     (New York: Paulist, 1992), 107. Fitzmyer's book is perhaps the clearest
     and best introduction to the scrolls and their importance. The author
     was a member of the team that examined and published the scrolls.

45   Qumran means "two moons." At the time of Jesus, the shore of
     the Dead Sea came right up to the edge of the settlement. When
     the full moon rose in the east, it reflected on the surface of the sea,
     and the community members saw a double moon, one in the sky,
     one shimmering on the water.

46   For an overview of the caves searched, the documents found, and
     who discovered them, see Fitzmyer, *Responses*, 1–40.

47   1QS 9:21–22 in Fitzmyer, *Responses*, 119. In fact, as part of the
     entrance ceremony to Yahad, initiates had to participate in a
     solemn cursing: "Then the levites shall curse all the men of Belial's
     lot, taking up the word and saying, 'Cursed be you with all your
     wicked, guilty deeds! May God make you tremble at the hands of all
     vengeful avengers! May He visit you with destruction at the hands
     of who recompense (evil) deeds! Accursed be you without mercy
     according to the darkness of your deeds, and may you be damned in
     the deep darkness of everlasting fire! May God not be gracious to you
     when you call upon Him and not pardon you by wiping away your
     iniquities! May He turn an angry face to take vengeance on you! May
     there be no "Peace" for you!' ... All those who enter the Covenant
     shall say, 'Amen, amen!' (1QS 2:1–10)" (Fitzmyer, *Responses*, 71).

48 Josephus, *The Jewish War* 2.8.2.120.

49 See Matthew 3:5; Mark 1:5; Luke 3:7; and *Jewish Antiquities* 18.116–118.

50 This is referred to as "Judea beyond the Jordan" in the Gospels (see Matthew 19:1). It was "Judea" only in the sense that it was primarily Jews who lived there. In the time of Jesus, it was ruled, along with Galilee, by Herod Antipas while Judea proper was ruled directly by the Roman governor Pontius Pilate.

51 Josephus, *Jewish Antiquities* 13.293.

52 For more information on priests and Levites in the first century, see Jeremias, *Jerusalem in the Time of Jesus*, 147–221.

53 The Mishnah (ca. AD 200) and Gemara (ca. AD 400) preserve such oral traditions, which go as far back as the second century BC. For more on the reliance on the merits of the forefathers, see Jeremias, *Jerusalem in the Time of Jesus and New Testament Theology: The Proclamation of Jesus*, trans. John Bowden (New York: Charles Scribner's Sons, 1971).

54 Contrary to traditional art, which often shows John pouring water over Jesus' head, Jewish ritual washing and baptism were by full immersion. John probably presided while many individuals went into the water at once and submerged themselves.

55 *Manual of Discipline* 1QS 9:11. See Fitzmyer, *Responses*, 53–54.

56 The first three Gospels use the term "kingdom of God" ninety-nine times, and the entire New Testament uses the term 122 times. Jesus uses this term ninety times in the first three Gospels. Clearly, the kingdom of God was the center of his message.

57 Josephus, *Jewish Antiquities* 8.42–49. Compare to the putting to flight of a demon in Tobit 8:2-3.

58 Josephus, *Jewish Antiquities* 18.3.3.63.

59 For the main lines of this typology, I am indebted to John P. Meier, *A Marginal Jew: Rethinking the Historical Jesus*, vol. 2, *Mentor, Message, and Miracles* (New York: Doubleday, 1994), 12. For an extensive review of all the supposed parallels to Jesus' miracles in the Jewish and Greco-Roman world, with bibliography and primary source citations, see chapter 18, titled "Miracles and Ancient Minds," 535–616.

60 Jesus' recorded miracles are far more numerous than the recorded miracles of these two prophets combined. There is another key difference: Elijah's and Elisha's miracles were sometimes punitive and lethal in nature, as in 1 Kings 1:10 when Elijah calls down fire from heaven to consume soldiers sent by the evil Israelite

king Ahaziah. No recorded miracle of Jesus ever directly harmed
a person. When his disciples suggest that Jesus call down fire
from heaven to punish the Samaritan town that refused them
hospitality, Jesus rebukes them (Luke 9:51-55).

61   It is the second part of Isaiah 61:2, which speaks of "the day of
vengeance of our God." Jesus came "not to condemn the world,
but that the world might be saved through him" (John 3:17). But
Isaiah's prophecy will be fulfilled at the Second Coming, on "the
day of wrath" when God "will render to every man according to
his works" (Romans 2:5-6).

62   Stories and teachings from Hillel and Shammai were recorded
only two hundred to two hundred fifty years after their time, in
the collection of oral tradition known as the Mishnah. A couple
of hundred years later, more oral tradition of the sages, known
by this time as the rabbis, was written down in the Gemara.
These two works make up the Talmud.

63   Although Paul and other New Testament writers do not tell
parables in the same way that Jesus does, they do use metaphors
and similes in a similar way. See J. Ellsworth Kalas, *The Parables of
Paul: The Master of the Metaphor* (Nashville: Abingdon, 2015).

64   Perea comes from the word "across." It is the term for the region
the Gospels typically refer to as "across the Jordan." In Jesus' time,
it was a strip of land on the east side of the Jordan River and the
Dead Sea. It was a mainly Jewish region ruled by Herod Antipas.

65   *Rab* is Aramaic for "master" or "lord." *Rabbi* means "my master";
rabbouni is more emphatic. In the time of Jesus, these were
respectful forms of address for a scribe or any honorable figure,
much like "sir." *Rabbi* was not yet a title and was not yet restricted
in meaning, as it is today, to an ordained Jewish teacher.

66   The same is true of the Hebrew word for disciple, *talmid.*

67   The distinctiveness and significance of the Twelve are explained
in chapter 11.

68   At the time Peter was martyred in Rome or shortly after, one room
of Andrew and Peter's home in Capernaum (Mark 1:29) was made
into a Christian place of prayer and eventually a church, whose
ruins we can still see today. One theory is that it was the room
where Jesus stayed when he and the disciples were in Capernaum.
It was a multi-family courtyard home with multiple dwellings for
related nuclear families. To see an illustration of a reconstruction
of this dwelling based on excavations, see Session Four of *Jesus:
The Way, the Truth, and the Life* Workbook.

69   Peter's time in Antioch is attested by Paul's letter to the Galatians.
     His death in Rome is attested by several sources from the late first
     and second centuries. Later tradition has it that Andrew went to
     preach in the town of Byzantium, later renamed Constantinople
     and, still later, Istanbul.

70   The immersion of Baptism is an image of Christian discipleship as
     total immersion in Jesus.

71   This construction, *pisteuen eis*, occurs nearly forty times in John's
     Gospel alone. John 6:35, for example, could be translated "Jesus
     said to them, 'I am the bread of life; he who comes to me shall not
     hunger, and he who believes *into* me shall never thirst'" (emphasis
     added). Most English Bibles translate the phrase as "believing in."

72   Benedict XVI, *Deus Caritas Est* (December 25, 2005), 1. Notice that
     Pope Benedict thinks this is so important that he puts it in the first
     section of his very first encyclical.

73   John Paul II, *Redemptoris Missio* (December 7, 1990), 46.

74   See John 2:13–3:21, 5:1-47, 7:1-13, 10:22. Depending on the route
     taken, the round-trip mileage from Capernaum to Jerusalem
     and back was 160 to 220 miles. It is impossible from the Gospels
     to know exactly how many trips Jesus and the disciples made to
     Jerusalem during the public ministry. Most likely it was between
     five and ten.

75   The long valley that contains the Sea of Galilee (700 feet below
     sea level), the Jordan valley including Jericho (850 feet below sea
     level), and the Dead Sea (1,300 feet below sea level) is delightful
     in winter and early spring. In summer it is miserable—the lowest
     place on earth and very hot. By contrast, Death Valley (in the
     United States) is less than 300 feet below sea level.

76   *Hodos* can also be translated as "road" or "path." Acts 24:5 shows
     us that outsiders called the Christian community the "sect of the
     Nazarenes." Paul instead calls it "the Way" (Acts 24:14). It was in
     Antioch that they were first called Christians (Acts 11:26), and the
     term "Christianity" appears in St. Ignatius of Antioch's letter to the
     Magnesians (section 10).

77   For more on the original Hebrew meaning of *amen* and its roots,
     see Xavier Leon-Dufour, ed., *Dictionary of Biblical Theology*, 2nd
     ed. (New York: Seabury, 1973), 13–14.

78   Customarily, it is assumed that a prophet is one who predicts the
     future. But in Scripture, this is only secondarily the case. When
     God, who knows the future, wants either to warn or encourage his
     people, he often has his spokesman speak about future judgment
     or consolation.

79   This is discussed at length by Pope Benedict XVI in the
     introduction to his book *Jesus of Nazareth*, vol. 1, *From the
     Baptism in the Jordan to the Transfiguration* (New York:
     Doubleday, 2007), 1–8.

80   Pew Research Center, "U.S. Religious Landscape Survey: Religious
     Beliefs and Practices," June 1, 2008, pewforum.org/, as analyzed
     in Sherry A. Weddell, *Forming Intentional Disciples: The Path to
     Knowing and Following Jesus* (Huntington, IN: Our Sunday Visitor,
     2012), 42–47.

81   The Greek word here for "delivered" is *paradothe*, which means
     "handed over, handed down, or passed down," as from one
     generation to another, from father to son. The noun for this in
     English would be "tradition."

82   "Now Moses was faithful in all God's house as a servant, to testify
     to the things that were to be spoken later, but Christ was faithful
     over God's house as a son" (Hebrews 3:5).

83   A prominent hill overlooking the Sea of Galilee, traditionally
     known as the Mount of the Beatitudes, is about a mile and a half
     from Capernaum.

84   In Acts 3:1, we see Peter and John keeping the evening hour of
     prayer. In Acts 10:30, Cornelius tells us that he was observing that
     hour when he had his vision telling him to seek out Simon Peter.
     The early Church never stopped observing these fixed hours of
     prayer; they developed into what we now call the Divine Office or
     the Liturgy of the Hours.

85   Deuteronomy 32:6; 2 Samuel 7:14 (parallel 1 Chronicles 17:13,
     22:10, 28:6, 29:10); Psalm 68:5, 89:26; Isaiah 63:16, 64:8; Jeremiah
     3:4, 3:19, 31:9; Malachi 1:6, 2:10; Wisdom 2:16, 14:3; Tobit
     13:4. God is compared to a father in several more passages:
     Deuteronomy 1:31, 8:5; Psalm 103:13; Proverbs 3:12; Wisdom
     11:10. Israel is called his son in Hosea 11:1 and his firstborn in
     Exodus 4:22.

86   The classic study on this topic is Jeremias, "Abba," in *The Prayers
     of Jesus*, 11–65, which is based on an exhaustive survey of the Old
     Testament, intertestamental literature, the Dead Sea Scrolls, and
     rabbinic literature.

87   Mark is the only evangelist to tell us this in the otherwise Greek
     text of his Gospel, and he only does so once, in his account of
     the agony in the garden of Gethsemane (Mark 14:36). Paul also
     preserves the Aramaic *abba* in Romans 8:15 and Galatians 4:6. To
     address God in this way was so striking and characteristic of Jesus
     that Greek-speaking Christians evidently continued to use and
     teach this word for at least thirty years after the Resurrection.

88 Preserved in Babylonian Talmud tractate *Qiddushim*, translated and cited in Jeremias, "Abba," 19. Another anonymous rabbinic saying is also cited: "Although all things are the work of my hands, I will reveal myself as father and maker only to him who does my will."

89 Pope Francis, in his proclamation of the Holy Year of Mercy, *Misericordiae Vultus*, writes, "God's mercy, rather than a sign of weakness, is the mark of his omnipotence" (6). To support this, he cites Thomas Aquinas: "It is proper to God to exercise mercy, and he manifests his omnipotence particularly in this way" (*Summa Theologiae* II-II q.30 a.4).

90 This was the response of 29 percent of Catholics in the Pew Research Center's 2008 U.S. Religious Landscape Survey.

91 Francis, *Misericordiae Vultus* (April 11, 2015), 6, vatican.va/.

92 "The expression God the Father had never been revealed to anyone. When Moses himself asked God who he was, he heard another name [Exodus 3:14, 'I AM WHO I AM']. The Father's name has been revealed to us in the Son." Tertullian (writing about AD 200), *On Prayer*, cited in CCC 2779.

93 Jesus "is the image of the invisible God" (Colossians 1:15). The Greek word for "image" here is *eikon*, which we render in English as *icon*.

94 John Paul II, *Dives in Misericordia* (November 30, 1980), 13; Benedict XVI, "Regina Caeli" (March 30, 2008), vatican.va/; Pope Francis, *The Name of God Is Mercy*, trans. Oonagh Stransky (New York: Random House, 2016), 9.

95 This expression, used by Jesus in Luke 13:16, shows his high regard for the dignity of women. Though men were often referred to as sons of Abraham in Jewish Scriptures and tradition, we have no woman called "daughter of Abraham" in the canonical Jewish writings, though the expression is found once in 4 Maccabees 15:28, an apocryphal work.

96 This was the famous opinion of Hillel in Mishnah tractate Gittin (90.a-b), which was the prevalent opinion in the first century according to Josephus and Philo.

97 Mishnah Pirkei Avot 1:5, sefaria.org/. Pirke Avot is a tractate of the Mishnah (ca. AD 200); the name can be translated as "chapters of the fathers." The saying, attributed to Rabbi Yose ben Yochanan, is believed to date from ca. 150 BC).

98 Beginning in the era of Gregory the Great (ca. AD 600), the idea that the unnamed woman of Luke 7 was Mary Magdalene and that Mary Magdalene was Mary, the sister of Lazarus, made its way into the preaching tradition of the Western or Latin Church.

Interestingly, such an identification is not found in the Eastern or Greek tradition. Today, it is largely seen that, on the basis of the actual text of Scripture, there is no evidence for viewing these three women as the same individual. This awareness is reflected in the 2016 letter from Archbishop Arthur Roche, Secretary of the Congregation for Divine Worship and the Discipline of the Sacraments, explaining why the memorial of St. Mary Magdalene was elevated by Pope Francis to the status of a feast. The text of the letter can be found online at vatican.va/.

99   Galatians 4:6; Romans 8:15. As we have seen, the fact that this Aramaic word *abba* was preserved as an address for God in the Greek-speaking churches of Rome and Galatia is a testimony to how precious, central, and important the early Christians considered the privilege of using it.

100 The implication is that the man in question is allowed by this tradition to retain the property and benefit from it himself but put it off-limits to any claim his parents might have on it. It was a pious ruse to evade charity. Since this was an oral tradition, not a written tradition, what we know about it is limited to Jesus' reference to it.

101 See Deuteronomy 12:10; Joshua 21:44, 22:4, 23:1; 2 Samuel 7:1; 1 Kings 5:4; Psalm 95:11; Hebrews 4:8-11. For more on the prophetic meaning of the Sabbath, see N. T. Wright, *Simply Jesus: A New Vision of Who He Was, What He Did, and Why He Matters* (New York: HarperOne, 2011), 136–139.

102 See chapter 3 for more on the *Shema* in the prayer life of Joseph, Jesus, and Israelite men.

103 Francis, *Lumen Fidei* (June 29, 2013), 26.

104 Talmud Shabbat 31a, sefaria.org/. The same negative formulation of the Golden Rule can be found in Tobit 4:15.

105 Compare with the story of the rich man and Lazarus in Luke 16:19-31.

106 Mishnah Gittin 90a-b.

107 Benedict XVI, "Midnight Mass: Solemnity of the Nativity of the Lord; Homily of His Holiness Benedict XVI" (December 24, 2011), vatican.va/.

108 A sampling of texts on the theme of gathering: Isaiah 11:11-16, 49:5, 60:1-5; Tobit 13:5, 13:13; Sirach 36:11; Micah 2:12, 4:6; Jeremiah 30:3-9, 31:10; Baruch 4:21–5:9; Ezekiel 20:34, 34:11-16, 37:15-27; 2 Maccabees 1:27.

109 See also Luke 22:30 and Revelation 21:12-14.

110 The RSV-2CE translation of Matthew 10:4 and Mark 3:18 renders his name as "Simon the Cananaean," but this translation is misleading. The word sounds like "Canaanite" or pagan. In actuality it comes from the word "zealot" in Aramaic, and so Luke has done a service to his readers by translating it for his readers as "zealot."

111 Numbers 25:1-15. Both RSV-2CE and NAB translate "zealous" as "jealous." The zeal of Phinehas became proverbial (see Psalm 106:30; Sirach 45:23; 1 Maccabees 2:26, 2:54). Phinehas is the model for the zeal of Mattathias, father of Judas Maccabeus, when he kills an apostate Jew in 1 Maccabees 2:23-26.

112 One clear example is how indignant the other ten disciples are after James and John ask to sit at Jesus' right and left in the kingdom. See Mark 10:41.

113 Mark seems to suggest that the feeding of the four thousand also took place in pagan territory, on the east side of the Sea of Galilee (Mark 8:1-10). This is possible but not clear.

114 Translated traditionally in English as "our daily bread," this phrase does not do justice to the very strange Greek expression that is used *arton ... epiousion*. The best rendering of this, going back to St. Jerome, is "give us today the *bread of tomorrow*," meaning the bread of heaven, the bread of the age to come. This "children's bread" would include healing, deliverance, sonship, forgiveness, all the goods of the kingdom of God. All these are contained in and conveyed by Jesus himself, who is the Bread of Life, to be given at the Last Supper as the Eucharist.

115 Mishnah Shabbat 7:2.

116 For a more extensive explanation of the background of the incident along with commentary, see Raymond E. Brown, trans., *The Gospel According to John I–XII* (New York: Doubleday, 1966), 217.

117 Matthew 14:13-21; Mark 6:32-44; Luke 9:10-17; John 6:1-15. Here we look at this critical event and the Bread of Life discourse in John 6:16-59 only from the perspective of its significance for Jesus' identity. They also have Eucharistic meaning.

118 John 6:3 NAB. *To oros* is singular and means "the mountain." It is the same word used by Matthew in 5:1 for the site of the Sermon on the Mount. The RSV-2CE renders it plural as "the hills," obscuring a point the Evangelist is making here about Jesus' similarity to Moses, who also taught on "the mountain," Sinai.

119 The Greek verb is "to recline, to dine," though the RSV-2CE renders this "sit down." Matthew, Mark, and John all mention the grass. Mark emphasizes the "green" grass; John emphasizes "much" grass.

120 "Sheep without a shepherd": see Numbers 27:17 and 1 Kings 22:17.

121 Grain is grown in the winter in Palestine, when there is rain. The Feast of Unleavened Bread celebrates the harvest of barley, the first grain to mature. Pentecost celebrates the wheat harvest, which takes place in late spring.

122 Exodus 16; Psalm 78:19-20; Psalm 81:16: "I would feed you with the finest of the wheat."

123 A few examples: Hosea 2:2, 2:14-16; Isaiah 50:1, 54:5-8; Ezekiel 16:8-14.

124 Matthew 13:57; Mark 6:4; Luke 4:24; John 4:44. See also his saying, referring to his impending death, "It cannot be that a prophet should perish away from Jerusalem" (Luke 13:33).

125 Psalms of Solomon 17:21-25, trans. G. Buchanan Gray (1913).

126 Matthew 16:13-19. Parallels are Mark 8:27-30 and Luke 9:18-21. The Caesarea Philippi incident is not recounted in John, but there is an important confession of faith by Peter at the end of the Bread of Life discourse (John 6:68-69).

127 As we are focused here on what this episode tells us about Jesus, we cannot develop further what this rich passage teaches us about the role of Peter and his successors in the future time of the Church.

128 See John Paul II, General Audience, December 18, 1996, 1–2, vatican.va/.

129 White garments as indicating heavenly beings are also noted in Daniel 7:9; Acts 1:10; Mark 16:5; Revelation 3:4. Also compare "dazzling apparel" in Luke 24:4.

130 On the road to Emmaus, the risen Christ "beginning with Moses and all the prophets … interpreted to them in all the Scriptures the things concerning himself" (Luke 24:27).

131 Mishnah Sukkah 5:2–4.

132 Josephus tells us it was "a most holy and most eminent feast" (*Jewish Antiquities* 8.4.1). The pagan Plutarch describes the Jewish Feast of Booths in almost the same words (*Quaestiones Convivales* 4.6).

133 Jesus, in Luke 16:9, tells us to use earthly wealth in such a way that when it fails us, "they may receive you into the eternal habitations." The actual Greek expression is "eternal booths."

134 The apocryphal book of 1 Enoch applies the designation "chosen" or "elect one" to the Son of Man of Daniel 7. (See 1 Enoch 39:6, 40:5, 45:3-5, 49:2-4, 51:3-5, 52:6, 55:4, 61:6-10, 62:1.) For the author of this work, the messiah, the Son of Man, and the chosen one are all the same person. A hundred years after Jesus, some Jews saw the would-be messiah Bar Kochba as the fulfillment of Daniel 7:13-14.

135 The customary assumption that Jesus' public ministry lasted three years comes from the three Passovers mentioned in John's Gospel. John says, however, that he is only telling us of a small portion of what Jesus did and said, which probably includes how many feasts he attended. None of the evangelists is concerned to tell us exactly how long the public ministry lasted or how much time elapsed between the Transfiguration and Jesus' final Passover.

136 The phrase "set his face" (Luke 9:51) is an allusion to Isaiah 50:7 where the servant of the Lord has "set [his] face like a flint" in the face of suffering, refusing to be intimidated or deterred by it.

137 Talmud Sanhedrin 85a. Though this was not written down until several centuries after Christ, it was oral tradition of the scribes long before it was written down.

138 Matthew 20:20-21 relates that it is the mother of James and John who approaches Jesus about this. My own mother prefers that version of the story!

139 The cup or chalice as a symbol of suffering can be found in the Old Testament in Psalm 75:8; Isaiah 51:17-22; Jeremiah 25:15; and Ezekiel 23:31-34. We see it in Gethsemane in Matthew 26:39; Mark 14:36; and Luke 22:42.

140 For the three pilgrimage feasts that adult Jewish men were obliged to attend in Jerusalem annually: Passover in early spring, Pentecost about fifty days later in late spring, and Sukkot (the Feast of Booths or Tabernacles) in the fall. The Maccabean Feast of the Dedication would have also seen Jerusalem swell in population, but probably less so since it was not an obligatory feast. For an explanation of the estimated numbers who came to Jerusalem for the three obligatory feasts, see Jeremias, *Jerusalem in the Time of Jesus*. For the actual night of the Passover meal, however, one had to stay within the limits of Jerusalem which included the Mount of Olives but not Bethany, according to Jeremias.

141 The RSV-2CE translates John 11:33 as "he was deeply moved in spirit and troubled" and 11:38 as "deeply moved again." The Greek verb here connotes anger rather than empathy. Jesus is perturbed by this greatest weapon of his enemy, the power of death.

142 From the *Amidah*, in Deiss, *Springtime of the Liturgy*, 11. The earliest surviving text of the *Tefillah* dates from around AD 200. Though we know there were additions to this prayer between Jesus' time and AD 200, this part of the prayer is considered by most scholars to come from before the time of Jesus. For the text of this prayer as it was most likely prayed in Jesus' time, see the boxed text "Jewish Prayers" in Session Two of *Jesus: The Way, the Truth, and the Life* Workbook.

143 Matthew and Mark mention branches. Only John specifies
     palms (John 12:13). Compare Revelation 7:9 where the crowd
     in heaven holds palms.

144 In Matthew 21:9 the crowd uses this specific title, "Son of David."
     In Mark 11:10 they mention the "kingdom of our father David."
     In both Luke (19:38) and John (12:13), they call Jesus the King.

145 Clothing laid down before the king was part of Israelite royal
     custom. See 2 Kings 9:13 for an example.

146 "You shall take ... the fruit of goodly trees, branches of palm trees,
     and boughs of leafy trees, and willows of the brook; and you shall
     rejoice before the Lord your God seven days" (Leviticus 23:40; see
     also Nehemiah 8:13-18).

147 The Hallel (from the word "praise," as in "hallelujah") was a
     collection of festive psalms (Psalms 113–118), which were recited
     at the Feast of Booths, Passover, and the Feast of Dedication
     (Hanukkah).

148 We refer to Jesus' entry into Jerusalem as Palm Sunday on the
     basis of John's account, which mentions the palm branches, as
     noted earlier. And according to its chronology, the anointing at
     Bethany would have occurred at a Saturday night meal, with the
     royal entry taking place "the next day," Sunday (John 12:12).

149 For more on the Feast of Booths through the time of the
     Maccabees, see Roland de Vaux, *Ancient Israel*, vol. 2, *Religious
     Institutions* (New York: McGraw-Hill, 1965), 495–502. For more
     on the Feast of Booths as understood in the time of Jesus, see
     Raymond E. Brown, *The Gospel According to John I–XII* (New York:
     Doubleday, 1966), 326–330, 455–464.

150 John quotes part of this passage in his account of Jesus' entry
     into Jerusalem (John 12:15). But in the first line of his quote
     ("Fear not, daughter of Zion"), the Evangelist seems to reference
     Zephaniah 3:16 ("Do not fear, O Zion") in order to let us know that
     Jesus is fulfilling both passages at once. See the whole context at
     Zephaniah 3:9-20.

151 Josephus, *Jewish Wars* 5.5.6, in Joseph Fitzmyer, *The Gospel
     According to Luke* X-XXIV (New York: Doubleday, 1985), 1330–1331.

152 Caiaphas plotted Jesus' death because he was afraid Jesus would
     provoke the Romans to destroy the Temple and the nation
     (John 11:48). Ironically, the people's rejection and execution
     of Jesus caused the very thing he wished to avoid.

153 C. S. Lewis, *The Great Divorce* (San Francisco: HarperCollins, 2001), 75.

154 This is especially so in the Prophets and Psalms; for example, Isaiah 2:3, 56:7, 60:6; Zechariah 14:16; Psalms 87, 117.

155 Notice that in the parable of the wicked tenants (Mark 12:7-10), the killing of the son is what causes the vineyard to be given to "others," representing the Gentiles.

156 See Jeremias, *Jerusalem in the Time of Jesus*, 147–221, for the ongoing power of a high priest even after he was replaced.

157 See Raymond E. Brown, *The Death of the Messiah: From Gethsemane to the Grave; A Commentary on the Passion Narratives in the Four Gospels*, vol. 1 (New York: Doubleday, 1994), 404–414.

158 Matthew is the only one to mention the thirty pieces of silver (in 26:15 and 27:3-10). The Old Testament background is found in Exodus 21:32 and in Zechariah 11:12-13, where thirty shekels of silver are cast into the treasury. In all the Gospels, especially Matthew and John, the entire background of Zechariah 9:9–14:21 is extremely important.

159 First Corinthians was written about AD 54. According to scholarly consensus (which includes the witness of the early Church Fathers), the four Gospels were written between AD 65 and 95; most think Mark's Gospel is the earliest and John's the latest.

160 The only other time Paul, in a similar fashion, passes on a solemn, traditional statement that he received is the statement of faith in the death and resurrection of the Lord in 1 Corinthians 15:3-8. Obviously, the tradition of what happened at the Last Supper is of supreme importance.

161 Mishnah Pesachim 10:5, quoting Exodus 13:8. For more on the Jewish understanding of "remembrance" or "memorial," see the landmark study by Brevard S. Childs, *Memory and Tradition in Israel*, Studies in Biblical Theology 37 (Naperville: Allenson, 1962).

162 For more on communion sacrifice, see Roland de Vaux, *Ancient Israel*, vol. 2, *Religious Institutions* (New York: McGraw-Hill, 1965), 417–418. For an overview of sacrifices, see chapters 10–13.

163 Midrash Melkita of Rabbi Ishmael 21:2. See Brown, *Gospel According to John*, 564.

164 At a number of points, the proceedings against Jesus that night as described in the four Gospels violate the rules of normal judicial procedure laid out in the Mishnah.

165 In some ancient manuscripts of Matthew 27:16-17 (some Syriac, Armenian, and Georgian), the man's name is given as Jesus Barabbas. Though it is unlikely that this is how it appeared in the original Greek text of Matthew, it testifies to how the early Christians saw this figure as a false messiah, savior, and "son of the father," a counterfeit of the actual Son of the Father.

166 This is the way John presents it, but Luke's Gospel also hints at this intention of Pilate's (Luke 23:16).

167 Cicero calls crucifixion "the worst extreme of the tortures inflicted on slaves" (*Against Verres* 2.5.169). Josephus calls crucifixion "the most pitiable of deaths" (*Jewish Wars* 7.203). In Acts, Luke shows how the magistrates were fearful when they found out that Paul and Silas, whom they had beaten without even a trial or conviction, were Roman citizens to whom it was forbidden to administer such a punishment (Acts 16:37-39).

168 Plutarch tells us that according to normal Roman practice, "each of the criminals carries forth his own cross" (*De sera numinis vindicta* 9.554B).

169 Modesty has traditionally dictated that in Christian art, Jesus is depicted on the Cross with a loincloth. While it is possible that the Romans made an exception to their normal practice out of respect for Jewish modesty, there is no evidence for this, and many consider it unlikely.

170 What remains of the hill is covered by the Church of the Holy Sepulchre. Exactly how high the hill stood from general ground level (the base of the nearby Jerusalem wall) in the time of Jesus is hard to say. In the lowest level of the Church, the St. Helena chapel, one can see the base of the hill and the marks where quarrymen once cut away blocks of limestone. To the current top of the hill where the Cross was most likely planted is about three flights of stairs, perhaps twenty-five to thirty feet.

171 Catholics still do this with papal and conciliar documents as well as prayers. For example, Vatican II's Dogmatic Constitution on the Church is known by the title *Lumen Gentium*, the first two Latin words of the text.

172 C. S. Lewis, *Mere Christianity* (New York: Macmillan, 1960), 57-59.

173 The fact that Jesus expired after only a few hours is a testimony to the extraordinary brutality of the scourging he received.

174 This also refers to the righteous man in the Psalm: "Many are the afflictions of the righteous; but the LORD delivers him out of them all. He keeps all his bones; not one of them is broken" (Psalm 34:19-20).

175 There are several possible medical explanations for this in terms
of the trauma Jesus had undergone and why serum and blood,
distinguishable from each other, should flow from his body.
See Brown, *Gospel According to John*, 946–947.

176 These verses lead to the magnificent conclusion of Zechariah,
which speaks of all the pagan nations streaming to the Temple
in Jerusalem to keep the end-times Feast of Booths (Zechariah
14:16), of which Jesus himself is the fulfillment.

177 Judas abandons the group on Thursday evening and, in remorse,
has taken his own life (Matthew 27:3-10). "The Eleven" is how
Luke refers to the group now (Luke 24:9).

178 In this act of empowering and commissioning the apostles,
the Catholic Church sees the institution of the sacrament of
Penance and Reconciliation, otherwise known as confession.

179 Acts 2:42; also Acts 2:46, 20:7, 20:11, 27:35.

180 We find the first witnesses in the Didache (ca. AD 125), Justin
Martyr's First Apology (ca. AD 165), and the Apostolic Tradition
of Hippolytus (ca. AD 215). For a synopsis of what we learn from
them about the Eucharist in the early Church, see Marcellino
D'Ambrosio, *When the Church Was Young: Voices of the Early
Fathers* (Cincinnati, OH: Servant Books, 2014).

181 Catholic, Orthodox, and other liturgies have maintained this
format for Eucharistic services.

182 Ignatius of Antioch, *Letter to the Ephesians 20.2*, written shortly
after AD 100.

183 Luke speaks of Jesus' "exodus" (9:31); John uses the phrase
"lifted up" (John 3:14, 8:28, 12:32-34).

184 "Mors et vitae duello, conflixere mirando. Dux vitae mortuus
regnat vivus." Roman Missal, Sequence for Easter Sunday; English
translation by the author.

185 *Triduum* is Latin for "the three," or "the three days." Since Jews
begin a day at sundown, the first day of the Triduum is Thursday
sundown to Friday sundown, the second runs till Saturday
sundown, and the third is from sundown Saturday through
sundown on the first Easter Sunday.

186 A placard called a *titulus* was often hung around the neck of a
condemned criminal as he was marched through the streets. This
was probably the case for Jesus as well. We do know that it was
fastened to the Cross above his head. It is notable that all four
Evangelists mention the *titulus* ordered by Pilate.

187 For an explanation of this construction, see chapter 7 under the heading "Believing into Him."

188 See Acts 1:3. Paul gives no time frame but speaks of a succession of appearances that comes to an end and a special appearance to Paul that happens as a unique exception after the last of Jesus' appearances to the original eyewitnesses. See also 1 Corinthians 15:3-8.

189 CCC 659.

190 Matthew 1:23, quoting Isaiah 7:14.

191 See also Matthew 24:30; Acts 1:9-11; 1 Thessalonians 4:17.

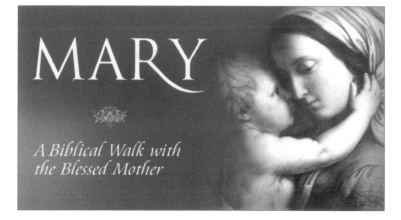

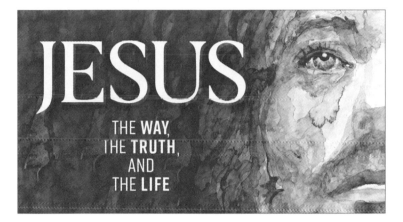